A Banker's Learning Odyssey

At State Bank of India

Rajiv Ranjan

INDIA · SINGAPORE · MALAYSIA

Copyright © Rajiv Ranjan 2024
All Rights Reserved.

TABLE OF CONTENTS

INTRODUCTION

This is the tale of a banker's journey over thirty four years at SBI and, thereafter, five years in an asset reconstruction company.

State Bank of India, formed in 1955, has been a trailblazer in implementing government schemes. The pace at which it has extended its network of branches to the remotest corners of the country would have few parallels in the world.

In the 1970s, SBI launched the Entrepreneurial Development Programme (EDP) for promoting first-generation entrepreneurs, through a specialist wing, Consultancy Services Cell, which yielded good results.

Late in the 1980s, the Bank focused on creating a new Personal Banking Centre structure in the metros and large cities. but also set up a separate process. I made the following suggestions for the proposed PB Centre: strive to build a team and promote a *team spirit* at the designated branches; help the team in evolving suitable supporting procedures at the module level and create a linkage between PB (Personal Banking) deposits and PB loans by allowing sanction of overdrafts to PB customers; start an aggressive campaign for weaning away a certain class of people from postal money order to demand drafts.

Essentially, factoring is purchase of trade receivables, either with or without recourse. Against assignment of the accounts receivable in its favour, a Factor funds it so as to generate instant liquidity for the seller without disruption. It is a receivables management and financing service designed to accelerate the seller's cash flow.

It covers both Domestic as well as Export Receivables, either with or without recourse. The Factor provides finance and bears the risk of default in case of non-payment by the buyers.

It is a specialized and evolved product that caters specifically to the needs of SMEs (Small Scale Enterprises), and differs from bank finance as the *receivables are purchased, not financed*.

It is very different from bank finance because: one, *receivables are purchased, not financed*; and two, it can be either *with or without* recourse whereas bank finance is always with recourse.

Asset reconstruction was evolved as an answer to the distressed debt management problem faced by banks and financial institutions in this country. With enactment of SARFAESI Act as a foreclosure law and spawning of a new institution called Asset Reconstruction Company, or ARC, banks could sell their bad loans to ARCs on Security Receipts (SR)-basis, which was a transformational change.

SARFAESI Act gave the right to the lender to take possession of the secured assets of the borrower in case of default and also spawned asset reconstruction as a new framework under which an Asset Reconstruction Company (ARC) can acquire bad loans from banks.

Internationally, ARCs were set up as centralized government agencies for tackling the bad-debt problem in a banking crisis. Funded by the government, they generally enjoyed special powers to cut short legal procedures and engaged in wholesale purchase of banks' bad loans.

As against this, ARCs in India are private sector entities that operate under a tightly controlled regulatory regime and enjoy *no special powers*. They acquire NPAs through a transparent bidding process by paying only 5 to 15% of the acquisition price in cash, with the balance unpaid amount getting converted into the seller bank's investment in Security Receipts (SRs) issued by the ARC to its asset holders. Under this model, they can neither achieve debt aggregation so as to be able to put pressure on the borrower, nor get funding from co- investors for making acquisitions in cash.

The stressed debts were heavily concentrated in large companies, many of them unviable and difficult to resolve. Under these circumstances, what India needed was a new PARA (Public Sector Asset Rehabilitation) Agency charged with the responsibility of resolving the large bad debts cases.

On 7th July 2021, the National Asset Reconstruction Company Limited (NARCL) was incorporated as a 'bad bank' for handling the stressed assets of Indian banks, and its associate IDRCL (India Debt Resolution Company Limited) given the responsibility to aggregate and resolve the Non- Performing Assets (NPAs) of the banking Industry.

Once NARCL acquires the assets from a bank, IDRCL shall prepare and suggest the proposed restructuring / resolution plan, strategies, etc. for each Underlying Trust Assets. Post the approval of resolution from NARCL, IDRCL shall also assist in implementing it within the RBI framework for ARCs. On the lines of bad banks set up with Government participation in the form of equity in Malaysia and UK, the Indian government has provided a guarantee of up to Rs 30,600 crore to back the Security Receipts (SRs) issued by NARCL.

NARCL is a strategic initiative to clean up the legacy stressed assets, with an exposure of Rs 500 crore and above each. Public Sector Banks hold a majority stake in NARCL and private banks hold the balance. In phase I, fully provisioned assets of about Rs. 90,000 crore are expected to be transferred to NARCL, while the remaining assets with lower provisions would be transferred in phase II.

The strategy focuses on aggregating the stressed assets under one roof so as to ensure efficient resolution of such assets. Since the security receipts issued by NARCL to an investor, who wants to acquire a part or whole of a company's stressed loan assets held by NARCL, will be backed by a Government of India guarantee, it will be another unique strategic advantage for preserving their value and driving the resolution process.

The NARCL-IDRCL structure is the initiative for tackling the large stock of legacy corporate NPAs that banks in India have been grappling with. Under it, cases which have the potential for insolvency resolution under IBC can get resolved quickly and more effectively. *As the holders of these stressed assets and SRs, banks will receive the gains.* This will bring about improvement in banks' valuation and enhance their ability to raise market capital.

SBI: THE LEGACY

State Bank of India (SBI), a multinational Indian public sector bank, is the 53rd largest bank in the world and ranked 298th in the *Fortune Global 500 List* of the world's biggest corporations of 2022. The oldest commercial bank in the Indian sub-continent, SBI's lineage can be traced back to the Bank of Calcutta – the first bank of India, set up in 1806 under the patronage of the Government of Bengal and the East India Company, in the aftermath of four Anglo-Mysore wars fought by the British East India Company with the Kingdoms of Mysore, Travancore and Hyderabad and the Maratha Empire over the last three decades of the 18th century. The Government of Bengal needed the help of a bank to prevent the depreciation of its bills which were the primary means of raising money for financing wars.

Renamed Bank of Bengal on 2 January 1809 as a Presidency Bank, the Bank's operations and structure were severely restricted. Two other Presidency banks – the Bank of Bombay and the Bank of Madras – were incorporated on 15 April 1840 and 1 July 1843, respectively. All three Presidency banks were incorporated as joint stock companies under royal charters and enjoyed the exclusive right to issue paper currency till 1861.

The primary concern of the government being their imperialist interests, the chief functions of the three presidency banks were reduced to: (i) maintaining a stable ratio of rupee in terms of silver or sterling; and (ii) facilitating remittance of "home charges" to England. Their commercial transactions were limited to financing the agency houses of Europeans engaged in trading with England.

Trade financing was allowed in 1866, for the first time, but only to a limited extent.

In 1921, all three Presidency banks were merged into one new bank named the Imperial Bank of India. This was prompted by the government's concern in the wake of the numerous bank failures during 1913-17. The Imperial Bank of India remained a joint-stock company but without Government participation.

Even after establishment of the Reserve Bank of India as the central bank of the country in 1935, the Imperial Bank of India continued to accept deposits and make payments on behalf of the State and Central Governments and operate currency chests on behalf of RBI.

State Bank of India was formed on 1 July 1955 – by transfer of the undertaking of the Imperial Bank of India, after India's central bank (Reserve Bank of India) had acquired a controlling interest in it –, with the avowed objectives of: one, rapid branch expansion, country-wide; two, mobilizing rural savings for national objectives; and three, extending agricultural credit in rural areas to support the programmes of agrarian reforms launched by the various state governments.

Gradually, State Bank came to be drawn into the vortex of government's policies for national reconstruction and development. Thus when the political authority demanded measures to counter concentration of advances in certain industrial sectors, State Bank's pilot scheme for financing small-scale industries was launched. When the Intensive Agricultural District Programme (IADP) and the High-Yielding Varieties Programme (HYVP) were launched by the government, State Bank was chosen as one of the main instruments of social banking. After nationalization of 14 major banks in 1969, State Bank became the pace-setter in implementing the Lead Bank Scheme, Integrated Rural Development Programme (IRDP), Differential Interest Rates scheme for the weaker sections etc., and in deploying credit to the priority sectors as defined by the government.

The Bank extended its network of branches to the remotest corners of the country at a pace that would have few parallels anywhere in the world. Its espousal of direct as well as indirect agricultural financing and financing of small-scale industries has been pioneering. By 1975, the State Bank Group's share in the total number of small-scale industries financed by All Scheduled Commercial Banks (ASCB) had gone up to 45.8% and, in the outstanding credit to them, to 35.3% of ASCB credit to them. (328 words)

In 1960, SBI acquired eight regional banks operating in the then princely states and converted them into subsidiaries of SBI – State Bank of Bikaner (SBB), State Bank of Jaipur (SBJ), State Bank of Hyderabad (SBH), State Bank of Indore (SBN), State Bank of Mysore (SBM), State Bank of Patiala (SBP), State Bank of Saurashtra (SBS) and State Bank of Travancore (SBT). This was prioritized for the sake of development of rural India. The government integrated these banks into the State Bank of India system to expand its rural outreach.

SBI also acquired some of the local banks that had fallen into deep trouble in order to rescue them. These included Bank of Bihar, National Bank of Lahore and Krishnaram Baldeo Bank.

In 2008, the Government of India acquired the Reserve Bank of India's stake in SBI in order to avoid any conflict of interest between the bank and the country's banking regulatory authority.

State Bank of Saurashtra was merged with SBI in 2008 and State Bank of Indore (SBN) in 2009. The historic merger of SBI and its five left-over Associate Banks took place on 1st April, 2017; the whole process went through remarkably well, with no hiccups either on the technology front or the HR front, and smooth customer onboarding.

Since its inception, SBI has been the largest bank in India. Today, SBI has 22,266 branches and 65,030 ATMs (Automated Teller Machines), including 12,872 Automated Deposit & Withdrawal Machines (ADWMs). On an average, over 1.32 crore transactions are carried out every day through these ATMs / ADWMs. With its presence in 227 locations in 30 countries across all time zones, among Indian banks SBI is a front-runner in the International Banking space. Figures in the following 3 tables present the full picture.

TABLE 1: NUMBER OF BANK BRANCHES IN INDIA (*March 2021*)

PUBLIC SECTOR BANKS	%	PRIVATE SECTOR BANKS	%	FOREIGN BANKS	%	TOTAL	SBI	%
86,311	70.2	35,791	29.1	874	0.71	1,22,976	22,221	18.1

(*Appendix Table IV.7, RBI Report on Trend and Progress of Banking in India 2020-21*)

Public Sector Banks (PSB) account for 70.2% of ASCB (All Scheduled Commercial Banks) branches in India, and Private Sector Banks (PVB) for 29.1% of ASCB branches. As against that, SBI branches form 18.1% of ASCB branches, 25.7% of PSB branches and 62.1% of PVB branches.

Performance in 2020–21

Table 2 below gives the SBI figure as a percentage of the PSB figure, the PVB figure and the ASCB figure for all the Profit & Loss Statement items, as well as for some of the important Balance Sheet items, both for FY 2019-20 and FY 2020-21. It also furnishes the growth percentage over FY 2019-20 to FY 2020-21 – for SBI as well as for all the three bank groups (PSB, PVB and ASCB) – for all the items.

TABLE 2: FINANCIAL PERFORMANCE, 2020–21

(Rs in cr)

	SBI	PSB	PVB	ASCB	SBI % PSB	SBI % PVB	SBI % ASCB
Income	308647	831882	545833	1483301	37.1	56.5	20.8
a) Interest Income	265151	707092	451617	1242222	37.5	58.7	21.3
b) Other Income	43496	124790	94216	241079	34.9	46.2	18.0
Expenditure	288237	800064	476357	1361303	36.0	60.5	21.2
a) Interest Expended	154441	431627	232555	695128	35.8	66.4	22.2
b) Operating Expenses	82652	202879	130456	364453	40.7	63.4	22.7
Of which: Wage Bill	50936	123378	50274	186239	41.3	101.3	27.3
c) Provision & Contingencies	51144	165558	113346	301722	30.9	45.1	17.0
Operating Profit	71554	197376	182823	423720	36.3	39.1	16.9
Net Profit	20410	31818	69,477	121998	64.1	29.4	16.7
Net Interest Income	110710	275465	275465	547094	40.2	40.2	20.2

(Contd.)

Advances	2449498	6348758	3939292	10820208	38.6	62.2	22.6
Gross NPAs	126389	616616	205335	837771	20.5	61.6	15.1
Gross NPA %	4.98%	9.1%	4.9%	7.30%	0.5%	1.0%	68.2
Net NPAs	36810	196451	55809	258228	18.7	66.0	14.3
Net NPA %	1.50%	3.1	1.4	2.40%	0.5	1.1	62.5
Fresh Slippage + Increase in O/S	29332	278711	103625	400646	10.5	28.3	7.3
Cash Recoveries/ Upgradations	17632	74685	38824	118584	23.6	45.4	14.9
Write-Offs	34403	134000	69995	208134	25.7	49.2	16.5
Deposits	3681277	9048420	4800646	15590600	40.7	76.7	23.6
Advances	2449498	6158112	3939292	10820208	39.8	62.2	22.6
Investments	1351705	2940636	1512480	4689842	46.0	89.4	28.8
Total Assets	4534430	10782831	6431048	19594617	42.1	70.5	23.1

(RBI Report on Trend and Progress of Banking in India & SBI Annual Report, 2020-21)

SBI Figures as % of ASCB Figures

The number of SBI branches is 18.1% of the number of ASCB branches. As against that, the SBI figures as a percentage of the ASCB figures for important Profit & Loss and Balance Sheet Statement items are:

For FY 2019–20:

Income: 20.4%; Interest Income: 20.6%; Other Income: 19.3%; Expenditure: 19.6%; Interest Expended: 20.9%; Operating Expenses: 21.6%; Wage Bill: 26.1%; Provision & Contingencies: 14.9%; Operating Profit: 18.3%; Net Profit for the Year: 132.8%; Net Interest Income: 20.2%; Gross NPAs: 16.6%; Gross NPA%: 75.0%; Net NPAs: 18.7%; Net NPA%: 79.6%; Fresh Slippage + Increase in Outstanding of NPAs: 109.4%; Cash Recoveries/ Upgradations: 35.1%; Write-Offs: 111.8%; Deposits: 23.2%; Advances: 22.6%; Investments: 22.3%;

Total Assets: 21.9%

For FY 2020–21:

Income: 20.8%; Interest Income: 21.3%; Other Income: 18.0%; Expenditure: 21.2%; Interest Expended: 22.2%; Operating Expenses: 22.7%; Wage Bill: 27.3%; Provisions & Contingencies: 17.0%; Operating Profit: 16.9%; Net Profit for the Year: 16.7%; *(Adjusted Net Profit: 8.1%)*; Net Interest income: 20.2%; Gross NPAs: 15.1%; Gross NPA%: 68.2%; Net NPAs: 14.3%; Net NPA%: 62.5%;

Fresh Slippage + Increase in Outstanding of NPAs: 7.3%; Cash Recoveries/ Upgradations: 14.9%; Write-Offs: 16.5%; Deposits:23.6%; Advances: 22.6%; Investments: 28.8%; Total Assets: 23.1%

As compared to the percentage of number of SBI branches to number of ASCB branches (18.1%, as shown in Table 1), these figures clearly show that SBI has performed well. In FY 2019-20, despite the SBI figure as a percentage of ASCB figure for Gross NPA%, Net NPA%, Fresh Slippage and Write-Offs being high, its Net Profit figure (as a percentage of ASCB figure) surged by 132.8%. Both for FY 2019-20 and FY 2020-21, the SBI figures as a percentage of ASCB figures for Income, Interest Income, Operating Income, Wage Bill and Advances are higher than 18.1%.

SBI Figures as % of PSB Figures

For FY 2019-20, *SBI earned a Net Profit of Rs 14,488 cr, as against a net loss of Rs 26,015 cr incurred by all PSB branches put together.* The percentage figure for number of SBI branches to number of PSB branches works out to 25.7%. As against that, for important Profit & Loss and Balance Sheet Statement items, the SBI figures as a percentage of the PSB figures for the last two years are:

For FY 2019–20:

Income: 36.3%; Interest Income: 35.9%; Other Income: 38.3%; Expenditure: 33.5%; Interest Expended: 34.0%; Operating Expenses: 39.0%; Wage Bill: 39.5%; Provisions & Contingencies: 26.9%; Operating Profit: 39.3%; Net Profit: -55.7% *(Adjusted Net Profit: 2.8%)*; Net Interest Income: 39.5%; Advances: 37.8%; Gross NPAs: 22.0%; Gross NPA%: 0.6%; Net NPAs: 23.4%; Net NPA%: 0.6%; Fresh Slippage + Increase in Outstanding: 22.9%; Cash Recoveries: 25.9%; Write-Offs: 33.0%; Deposits: 35.8%; Advances: 37.76%; Investments: 35.6%; Total Assets: 36.7%

For FY 2020–21:

Income: 37.1%; Interest Income: 37.5%; Other Income: 34.9%; Expenditure: 36.0%; Interest Expended: 35.8%; Operating Expenses: 40.7%; Wage Bill: 41.3%; Provisions & Contingencies: 30.9%; Operating Profit: 36.3%; Net Profit: 64.1%; *(Adjusted Net Profit: 31.2%)*; Net Interest Income: 40.2%; Advances: 38.6%; Gross NPAs: 20.5%; Gross NPA%: 0.5%; Net NPAs: 18.7%; Net NPA%: 0.5%; Fresh Slippage + Increase in Outstanding: 10.5%; Cash Recoveries: 23.6%; Write-Offs: 25.7%; Deposits: 37.2%; Advances: 38.6%; Investments: 39.7%; Total Assets: 38.7%

As compared to the percentage figure of 25.7% for the number of SBI branches to number of PSB branches, for most of the important Profit & Loss and Balance Sheet Statement items the SBI figures as a percentage of PSB figures show better performance.

SBI Figures as % of PVB Figures

The percentage figure for number of SBI branches to PVB branches works out to 62.1%. As against that, for the important Profit & Loss and Balance Sheet Statement items, the SBI figures as a percentage of the PVB figures are:

For FY 2019–20:

Income: 55.4%; Interest Income: 57.3%; Other Income: 46.5%; Expenditure: 54.6%; Interest Expended: 61.7%; Operating Expenses: 59.3%; Wage Bill: 96.5%; Provisions & Contingencies: 37.6%; Operating Profit: 42.1%; Net Profit: 75.8%; (*Adjusted Net Profit: - 3.9%*); Net Interest Income: 39.5%; Advances: 64.1%; Gross NPAs: 71.1%; Gross NPA%: 1.1%; Net NPAs: 97.0%; Net NPA%: 1.5%; Fresh Slippage + Increase in Outstanding: 41.5%; Cash Recoveries: 50.2%; Write-Offs: 109.2%; Deposits: 77.9%; Advances: 64.1%; Investments: 81.0%; Total Assets: 67.8%

For FY 2020-21:

Income: 56.5%; Interest Income: 58.7%; Other Income: 46.2%; Expenditure: 60.5%; Interest Expended: 66.4%; Operating Expenses: 63.4%; Wage Bill: 101.3%; Provisions & Contingencies: 45.1%; Operating Profit: 39.1%; Net Profit: 29.4%; (*Adjusted Net Profit: 14.3%*); Net Interest Income: 40.2%; Advances: 62.2%; Gross NPAs: 61.6%; Gross NPA%: 1%; Net NPAs: 66.0%; Net NPA%: 1.1%; Fresh Slippage + Increase in Outstanding: 28.3%; Cash Recoveries: 45.4%; Write-Offs: 49.2%; Deposits: 76.7%; Advances: 62.2%; Investments: 89.4%; Total Assets: 70.5%.

As against the percentage figure of 62.1% for the number of SBI branches to number of PVB branches, for most of the important Profit & Loss and Balance Sheet Statement items the SBI figures as a percentage of PVB figures are slightly lower. While the percentage figures for Gross NPAs are either at par with or a little higher, those for Net NPAs, Deposits, Advances and Investments are much higher. Overall, the performance of SBI against PVBs is also positive.

Let us look at the performance of all banks from another perspective, now – from the perspective of growth rates for important items achieved by SBI versus PSBs, PVBs and ASCBs as portrayed in Table 3 below.

TABLE 3: SBI GROWTH FIGURES AS % OF PSB, PVB & ASCB GROWTH FIGURES

(RBI Report on Trend & Progress of Banking in India & SBI Annual Report, 2020221)

	SBI FIG AS % OF PSB FIG		SBI FIG AS % OF PVB FIG		SBI FIG AS % OF ASCB FIG		GROWTH % OVER 2019-20 TO 2020-21			
	2019-20	2020-21	2019-20	2020-21	2019-20	2020-21	SBI	PSB	PVB	ASCB
Income	36.26	37.10	55.38	56.55	20.40	20.80	2.02	-0.29	-0.09	0.01
Interest Income	35.93	37.50	57.31	58.71	20.60	21.30	3.04	-1.27	0.58	-0.53
Other Income	38.29	34.86	46.46	46.71	19.3	18.00	3.97	5.65	-3.21	2.90
Expenditure	33.48	36.03	54.64	60.51	19.57	21.20	0.06	-7.01	-9.65	-7.54
Interest Expended	34.03	35.78	61.71	66.41	20.88	22.20	-3.01	-7.77	-10.96	-8.87

Operating Expenses	39.01	40.74	59.35	63.36	21.56	22.70	9.95	5.27	2.99	4.55
Of which, Wage Bill	39.46	41.28	96.53	39.04	26.1	27.30	11.42	6.51	6.16	6.33
Provision & Contingencies	26.88	30.89	37.64	45.12	14.87	17.00	-4.66	-17.06	-20.48	-16.39
Operating Profit	39.25	36.25	42.15	39.14	18.33	16.90	5.02	13.70	13.10	13.98
Net Profit	-55.69	64.15	75.81	-2.32	132.78	16.70	40.88	-	222.31	1018.12
Net Interest Income	39.52	40.19	51.36	56.07	20.18	20.20	-3.01	120.43	10.99	12.55
Adjusted Net Profit	2.84	31.15	-3.86	14.27	-6.76	8.12	1443.09	222.31	263.54	1018.12
Advances	37.76	38.58	64.14	62.18	22.6	22.64	5.34	3.10	67	5.03
Gross NPAs	21.98	20.50	71.14	61.55	16.57	15.09	-15.23	-9.10	-2.02	-6.89
Gross NPA %	0.60	0.55	1.12	1.02	75.00	68.22	-19.02	-11.65	-10.91	-10.98
Net NPAs	23.41	18.74	96.98	65.96	18.68	14.25	-21.28	-14.93	0.11	-10.76
Net NPA %	0.60	0.48	1.49	1.07	79.64	62.50	-32.74	-16.22	-6.67	-14.29
Fresh Slippage + Increase in O/S	22.86	10.52	41.53	28.31	109.40	7.32	-46.19	16.88	-21.05	704.09
Cash Recoveries/ Upgradations	25.86	23.61	50.22	45.42	35.08	14.87	-31.61	-25.08	-24.37	61.37
Write-Offs	33.04	25.67	109.19	49.15	111.77	16.53	-34.33	-24.85	29.74	294.93
Deposits	35.8	37.18	77.94	76.68	23.20	23.61	13.56	6.62	15.43	11.56
Advances	37.76	38.58	64.14	62.18	22.57	22.64	5.34	3.10	8.67	5.03
Investments	35.60	39.75	80.97	89.37	22.32	28.82	29.11	15.65	16.97	0.00
Total Assets	36.65	38.65	67.75	70.51	21.93	23.14	14.76	8.80	10.27	8.77

Here are the key takeaways from the table figures.

SBI leads in the growth rates for Income, Interest Income and Other Income, as well as in Operating Expenses and Wage Bill. The growth percent figures for Operating Profit and Net Profit for PSB, PVB and ASCB are higher than the SBI figures. But that happened because, for all 3 banking groups, the profit figures for the previous year (2019-20) were abysmally low. In fact, PSB Group had a Net Loss of Rs 26,015 cr for that year. FY 2020-21 was a landmark year for SBI as it earned the highest ever standalone Net Profit of Rs 20,410 crore.

For both Deposits and Advances, SBI growth figures – 13.56% and 5.34% – are higher than the PSB and ASCB figures and the Gross NPA% has come down from 6.1% to 4.98%.

For FY 2020-21, the PAT (Profit After Tax) figures for SBI subsidiary companies were: SBI Capital Markets Ltd.: Rs 527.10 crore (Rs 334.49 crore in FY 2019-20); SBI Life Insurance Company Ltd.: Rs 1,456 crore (Rs 1,422); SBI Cards and Payment Services Ltd.: Rs 985 crore (Rs 1,245 crore).

Digital Banking & Other New Initiatives

In November 2017, SBI launched YONO (acronym for 'You Only Need One'), India's first comprehensive digital service platform. With this app on his mobile phone, a customer does not need to visit a branch for certain essential services, such as opening a new bank account, doing fund transfer from his account, arranging cashless bill payments, getting a new loan from the Bank, etc. It is leading the digital revolution within the banking industry.

Retail and Digital Banking is the largest business vertical of the Bank, now, with 99.45% of the total SBI branches involved in it. Because of its multi- channel delivery model (digital, mobile, ATM, internet, social media and branches), customers can carry out these transactions, at any time and at any place. No wonder, SBI has become the largest Home Loans, as well as Education Loans, provider in the country. The Bank's Home Loans portfolio has crossed the Rs 5 trillion, i.e. Rs 5 lakh crore, mark.

YONO is the gateway for customers to perform mobile banking, investment banking and insurance-related services, as well as for shopping. As of March 2021, the number of YONO downloads had crossed 79.60 million.

SBI Wealth is another initiative that provides comprehensive Investment & Insurance Solutions to High Net Worth Individuals by leveraging the Bank's tie-ups for Mutual Funds, Portfolio Management Services and Bonds. It has shown exponential growth in terms of Client Acquisition and Assets Under Management (AUM), with the Number of Clients increasing by 93% from 132,354 in March 2020 to 2,55,196 in March, 2021, and the AUM increasing by 90% from Rs 1,09,061 crore to Rs 2,07,167 crore.

With 62,617 ATMs, including 13,237 Automated Deposit Withdrawal Machines (ADWMs), SBI has one of the largest ATM Networks in the world. Over 1.12 crore transactions per day are routed through it, which works out to 34.02% of India's total ATM transactions. It has also installed 18,073 barcode-based Self Passbook Printing kiosks (SWAYAMs) across 15,857 branches, 45% of which are located in ATM rooms/ e-lobbies available outside branch banking halls for extended hours. Green Channel Counters for making transactions through Debit Cards (for promoting Green Banking), Green Remit Card (GRC) for depositing funds in the bank account and the CTS-enabled self-service Cheque Deposit Kiosk (CDK) for depositing CTS cheques in a hassle-free manner are the other digital initiatives implemented by the Bank. *(CTS, i.e. Cheque Truncation System is a process of clearing cheques electronically rather than processing the physical cheque by the presenting bank en-route to the paying bank branch.)*

The CTS enabled self-service Cheque Deposit Kiosks (CDK) have been deployed at 2,500 branches where outward clearing cheques are more than 50 per day. A receipt with a scanned copy of cheques and details such as cheque number and payee account number is generated for the depositor.

SBI Life Insurance Company Limited, SBI General Insurance Company Limited, SBI Mutual Fund, SBI Cards & Payment Services Limited and SBI Cap Securities Limited are all subsidiaries of

SBI with whom the Bank maintains a close relationship. Working as a Corporate Agent, SBI sells their products to its customers in order to earn a commission or fee. In the same way, the Bank also distributes mutual fund products of UTI Mutual Fund, Tata Mutual Fund, Franklin Templeton Mutual Fund, L&T Mutual Fund, ICICI Mutual Fund and HDFC Mutual Fund. All branches of the Bank are also authorised to open NPS accounts under National Pension System.

Among private life insurance companies in India, SBI Life Insurance Company Limited ranks Number 1 and SBI continues to be the Number 1 Mutual Fund Distributor, having crossed the milestone of Rs 1.10 lakh crore in Asset Under Management (AUM) as on 31st March, 2021. SBI Mutual Fund has also crossed the milestone of Rs 5.04 lakh crore in AUM.

By leveraging the technology for customer segmentation, the Bank has been able to source customers and sell over 1.4 million cards, in the current year, through its branches. Card issuance through digital journey has been received very well by customers and is on a rising trend.

During FY2021-22, SBI's gross non-performing assets (GNPA) came down by Rs 14,366 crore to Rs 1,12,023 crore. Recoveries and upgradation during the year increased by 21.58% to Rs 21,437 crore. Consequently, the gross NPA ratio of the Bank improved by 101 bps from 4.98% in March 2021. The net NPA ratio of the Bank also improved to 1.02% and the provisioning coverage ratio (PCR) to 75.04% from 70.88% last year.

Including AUCA, the PCR stood at 90.20% as of March 2022.

Retail Banking: New Initiatives

Two new End-to-End Digital Loan Journeys were introduced, viz., Pre- approved Two-Wheeler Loan (SBI Easyride) and Pre-approved Business Loan (PABL) for PoS (Point of Sale) customers of SBI subsidiary PSPL (SBI Payment Services Pvt Ltd.). Loans aggregating Rs 21,898 crore have been extended digitally through Analytics-based products in FY2022.

SBI's customer base is steadily increasing across the country, making Retail Banking the most prolific segment of the Bank. It continues to be the most prominent Home Loan provider in the country and the largest dispenser of Education Loans. The Home Loan/Home Loan-related portfolio of the Bank has grown from about Rs 1 lakh crores in 2011 to Rs 5.62 lakh crores as on 31.03.2022, and it accounts for 23.87% of the total advances of the Bank. During FY 2022, the Bank has disbursed close to Rs 1.46 lakh crore of Home loans and Home-related loans and Rs 10,291 crore of Education Loans to 76,301 deserving students – of which 40% were extended to girl students.

SBI leads in the Personal Loans market segment as well. It extends loans to the salaried customers of other banks through SBI Quick Personal Loans. As of 31.03.2022, the Personal Loans portfolio of the Bank (Xpress credit and Pension loan) had reached Rs 2,85,448 crore with a YTD growth of 27.81% (Rs 62,119 crore), contributed primarily by the flagship product Xpress credit (Rs 54,934 crore), which had recorded a YTD growth of 28.49%.

During FY2022, SBI Wealth has shown exponential growth, too, with Investment AUM increasing from Rs 8,592 crore to Rs 14,317 crore, and the number of Clients increasing from 2,55,196 to 2,97,246. The AUM of Clients

also increased from Rs 2,07,167 crore to Rs 2,52,061 crore for the same period. SBI Wealth has been chosen as one of the Best Brands of 2021 by *The Economic Times*.

SBI has introduced a Customer Relationship Management (CRM) system as an integrated platform to engage with customers throughout their lifecycle, enhance understanding of customers' requirements and strengthen the customer-centric approach of the Bank. The CRM portal has been designed to generate leads in CRM applications through various channels, better monitoring mechanism of leads at multiple stages, and booking increased business with lower TAT through customer connect.

Trade Financing

The Bank was the first among all PSBs to register as a financier on the Trade Receivables Discounting System (TReDS) platform, set up to provide finance to Micro, Small and Medium Enterprises (MSMEs) and has presence on all the three TReDS platforms in the country, i.e. RXIL, M1 exchange and Invoicemart. It has been actively participating in the online biddings on the platform and offering competitive rates for the benefit of MSMEs. In FY2022, 14,208 Bills aggregating Rs 2,668 crore were discounted.

With its state-of-the-art technologies, vast branch network and momentum to strengthen its relationship with the corporate world across various sectors, SBI continues to be a significant player in Supply Chain finance. It has extended supply chain finance to over 31,000 dealers and over 12,260 vendors with total sanctioned limits of over Rs 38,680 crore (e-DFS) & Rs 5,825 crore (e-VFS). Thirty-seven new tie-ups were established during the financial year, including CG Power & Industrial Solutions Limited, Skoda, Honda India Power Limited, Bajaj Auto Limited, Nestle India Limited, Ambuja Cement Limited, Trident Limited, and Tata Consumer Products Limited, among others. New e-DFS limits of Rs 5643 crore were sanctioned in this financial year up to 31st March 2022.

SBI Global Factors Private Limited (SBIGFL), a leading provider of factoring services for domestic and international trade, registered a turnover of Rs 4,352 crore for FY2021 as compared to a turnover of Rs 4,394 crore in FY2020.

SBIGFL is a leading provider of factoring services for domestic and international trade. SBI holds 86.18% share in the Company. The Company's services are especially suitable for MSME clients for freeing up resources locked in book debts. By virtue of its membership of Factors Chain International (FCI), the Company is able to ameliorate credit risk from export receivables under the 2-factor model.

The Company reported a PBT of Rs 26.72 crore and a PAT of Rs 18.47 crore during 2020-21 as against a PBT of Rs 40.28 crore and a PAT of Rs 16.77 crore in the previous year.

MY 1983–86 MEMOIRS

The following three objectives were set for the State Bank of India formed in 1955 by transfer of the undertaking of the Imperial Bank of India: (i) rapid branch expansion, country-wide; (ii) mobilizing rural savings for national development; and (iii) extending agricultural credit in rural areas to support the programmes of agrarian reforms launched by the various state governments.

Gradually, State Bank came to be drawn into the vortex of government's policies for national reconstruction and development. Thus, when the political authority demanded measures to counter concentration of advances in certain industrial sectors, State Bank's pilot scheme for financing small- scale industries was inaugurated.

When the Intensive Agricultural District Programme (IADP) and the High- Yielding Varieties Programmes (HYVP) of the government were launched, State Bank was chosen as one of the main instruments of social banking.

Even after nationalization of 14 major banks in 1969, State Bank has been the pace-setter in implementing the Lead Bank Scheme, Integrated Rural Development Programme (IRDP), Differential Interest Rates scheme for the weaker sections etc., and in deploying credit to the priority sectors as defined by the government.

At the same time, the Bank has extended its network of branches to the remotest corners of the country at a pace that would have few parallels anywhere in the world. The Bank's espousal of direct as well as indirect agricultural financing and financing of small-scale industries has been pioneering. As of 1975, the State Bank alone had financed 45.8% of the number financed by All Scheduled Commercial Banks (ASCB). As at 1972- end, State Bank Group's share in export finance worked out to 28% of ASCB export credit. The Bank has maintained its pre-eminent position in these spheres all these years.

State Bank has always had an all-India character and enjoyed a special relationship with the government and RBI right from the beginning. As at June-end 1983, State Bank Group had 3095 currency chests, or 72% of the total, which it maintained on behalf of the Reserve Bank of India.

Work Culture

Because of its historical background, safety of funds borrowed and lent has been the prime consideration for the Bank. The work culture that has evolved is one of adhering to a rigid procedural pattern – primarily, for meeting the safety needs. Grasp of procedures, accuracy and stamina to withstand the prolonged drudgery of repetitive work have long constituted the criteria of efficiency.

Loans and advances granted for certain specific purposes, that fell in the category of Priority Sector Advances (for which targets were set by the Government) were:

a. **Financing Agricultural Operations:** Short-term loans for raising crops and medium-term loans for purchasing pump-sets, tractors, etc. and installing tube-wells; indirect finance of agricultural marketing yards, cooperative banks; financing of allied agricultural activities like fisheries, plantations, poultry, bio-gas plants, etc. The Bank's major strategy for direct agricultural advances was the "village adoption" approach of intensive financing in limited areas, rather than frittering resources away over a wide area. The evolution of specialized branches called "Agricultural Development Branches (ADBs)" was a unique feature geared to serve the ends. Interest rates ranging from 9% to 12% were applied.

b. **Financing of Small Scale Industries (SSI):** Largely for their working capital requirements and, to a limited extent, for purchase of machinery and building construction, with legal nexus provided through hypothecation/ pledge of stocks (raw materials, good-in- process and finished goods), book debts and machinery. Terms were liberalized over the years and the package of services offered was also enlarged. A tiered interest rate structure was biased heavily in favour of smaller loan accounts. The Bank launched several pioneering schemes, such as the Entrepreneur Scheme, Equity Fund Scheme and the trail-blazing Entrepreneurial Development Programme, for the benefit of potential SSI entrepreneurs. For creating a robust infrastructure for appraising SSI projects and providing free consultancy to the existing entrepreneurs, Consultancy Services Cells – with the officers posted there getting selected on the basis of their field of study (like engineering, business management, accountancy, etc.) and then trained in making a detailed capacity assessment at the factory site, assessing a company's financial results, etc. and preparing a full-fledged Techno-Economic Viability Report – were launched at the Local Head Office (LHO) level. Indirect financing through loans for infrastructure development like industrial estates, etc. were also put in place.

c. **Financing of retail trade in goods:** Restricted only to firms having an annual turnover of up to Rs 4 lacs, self-employed professionals and transport operators (using self-driven vehicles or intimately connected with transport operations), at the applicable interest rate (from 12% to 15%).

d. **Financing of wholesale trade:** Included retail trade of more than Rs 4 lacs and medium and large industries financed on strict margin and security terms, and at interest rates varying between 16% and 18%.

While (a), (b) and (c) above constitute Priority Sector Advances, for which targets were set by the Government, (d) is the bread-and-butter advance for the Bank. Apart from these, loans were given to weaker sections of society, for productive purposes, at the highly subsidized interest rate of 4% p.a.

The following two tables delineate certain figures for SBI, public sector banks & private sector banks. Table 4 gives SBI figures for 10 years between 1955 – the year of its inception – and 1983; and Table 5 gives certain important ratios – for SBI, PSBs and PVBs – for the year 1982.

TABLE 4: SBI FIGURES, 1955–1983

(Rs in crore)

	1955	1960	1965	1969	1970	1975	1980	1981	1982	1983
CAP+RES	12	13	16	20	21	76	214	246	284	324
DEPOSITS	226	576	735	1227	1441	3598	9636	11934	13928	17113
ADVANCES	106	232	481	841	1115	2501	7213	8984	10894	11759
AGL ADVS	-	-	-	92	123	241	1111	1440	1567	1892
SSI ADVS	-	4	25	104	152	320	853	1075	1194	1438
SM BUS FIN	-	-	-	7	24	52	304	427	500	625
EXP FIN	-	-	-	69	93	200	475	437	411	428
INVSTT	117	300	264	358	448	1100	3024	3882	4135	5798
NO. OFFICS	497	907	1276	1673	2122	3831	5605	6010	6293	6611
NO. OF EMPLOYEES	14682	24664	37996	59916	67221	106493	150450	162853	172906	183483

TABLE 5: FINANCIAL RATIOS OF SBI & OTHER BANKS, 1982

		SBI	PSB	PVB
1.	Interest & Discount as % to Total Income	84.03	89.04	85.35
2.	Commission, Exchange & Brokerage as % to Total Income	15.93	10.39	13.12
3.	Total Income as % to Working Funds	9.13	8.51	9.76
4.	Profits as % to Total Income	1.11	1.46	3.26
5.	Profits as % to Total Deposits	0.12	0.14	0.37
6.	Profits as % to Total Capital & Reserves	5.61	12.93	29.21
7.	Total Capital + Reserves as % to Total Deposits	2.22	1.08	1.25
8.	Total Advances as % to Total Deposits	74.85	61.87	59.43
9.	Investments as % to Total Deposits	31.38	28.90	30.44
10.	Priority Sector Advances as % to Total Deposits	31.43	32.02	22.63

PSB: Public Sector Banks; PVB: Private Sector Banks
(*Source: Business India, April 26 to May 9, 1982*)

Strengths

A hard look at the organization and systems of State Bank vis-à-vis other Indian banks delineates the following as SBI's major strengths:

i. At the Local Head Office (LHO) level, separate responsibility centres – both for Operations and for Planning & Development – were created, based on the principle of unity of command. Business areas were viewed as 5 market segments: institutional & large customers; individual customers; small industry & business people; agriculturists; and customers requiring foreign exchange services. The Bank had adopted a performance budgeting and review system.

ii. A distributive leadership was formalized both at the Central Office level and at the 13 Local Head Offices. The Central Office was involved in corporate planning and critical credit decisions and in delegating powers of decision-making to LHOs. The latter emerged as both, operational control centres and management control centres.

iii. Formation of Regional "Modules" was another reorganization that was carried out in 1978 – in the wake of unrelenting expansion in the network of branches – so as to bring the Regional Manager closer to his branches and limiting the number of branches under him to 40.

iv. The top leadership of the Bank had been receptive to modern ideas. Thus, apart from decentralization and delegation of authority, new systems like Long-Range Planning, new Performance Appraisal System, Human Resources Development and Management Audit had been introduced.

v. The Bank followed a method of relating personnel costs to business growth goals. The cost was first deflated by rate of inflation, then norms of efficiency were superimposed on this. Only the resultant equivalent of additional staff strength was allowed. This resulted in operational control of costs.

vi. The Bank enjoys a special relationship with RBI and the government. By virtue of maintaining most of the currency chests, it ensured that funds were not left idle at a branch. Whatever deposits emerged were almost totally lent out or transferred to credit-hungry areas.

vii. In International Banking operations, a bank's capital-and-reserves to total deposits ratio assumes greatest significance. At 1983-end, this ratio was 2.26% for State Bank as compared to 0.5% to 0.7% for other Indian banks. The size of operations and of the branch network were also sources of strength.

viii. The Bank's selection, recruitment and training methods compared well with national standards.

ix. It had the largest reservoir of banking specialists in the fields of agricultural finance, foreign exchange, etc.

x. The Bank had its own system of Audit and Inspection of branches which was very thorough. In the organizational set-up, Inspection Department had been accorded its due importance. Every branch was inspected by an Inspector at intervals of 2 years, with the report being submitted directly to the Managing Director.

Weaknesses

On the other hand, following were the main weaknesses of the Bank:

i. Close connection with government and RBI bred complacency.

ii. There was a clear dichotomy between the value systems of Central Office top management and LHO top management. The bureaucratic mode of functioning prevailed at the LHO, Regional Office and Branch levels. This stifled entrepreneurial responses to challenges.

iii. Unchecked growth of trade unionism, both amongst workmen staff and officers, had created vested interests and almost a parallel authority structure. It is the workmen's union that used to get an upper hand in all matters, with the officers' association being a poor follower. The creation of more hierarchical tiers in the organization (under the regional 'modules') had accentuated the unions' usurpation of management authority by distancing top management of LHO from operating levels, and giving rise to identical tiers in the unions' own structure. Timid management was at the root of these ills.

iv. Seniority-based promotion system stifled the drive to work and show results. It was always safer to pass the buck, somehow, and bide your time till you moved away from a position.

v. Even though good in absolute terms, the often marginal (and, sometimes, negative) differential between officers' and workmen staff's pay made it a demotivator for officers.

vi. In spite of structural changes, the old procedure-orientation and decision-making, solely on the basis of notes put up by subordinates, continued.

vii. Steeped in the culture of virtually no-accountability for clerks, and all for officers, officers were no almost like clerks sitting in managers' chairs.

viii. In the game of one-upmanship played by the workmen's unions, control aspects were deliberately allowed to be diluted. Because of one- sided accountability, the advantage of power balance had shifted in favour of the workmen.

ix. There was no system of upward communication of problems from the lower rungs. So, instead of a problem-solving approach, one of shutting the eyes to problems had taken root. For the same reason, the delegation of authority and de-centralization of decision-making remained mostly on paper.

Organizational Analysis

Earlier, the superordinate goal of the Bank was procedural accuracy and meticulousness in maintaining the customers' accounts. This was sought to displaced by one of growth in business but the system structure and staff were yet to be geared for it. Emphasis on several disparate aspects had led to goal-multiplicity and confusion.

Here is an attempt to apply the McKinsey 7S criteria for evaluating the Bank's performance at that time vis-à-vis its competitors:

a. **Strategy:** The Bank had recognized government as an important 'customer'. It had wholeheartedly supported developmental and social programmes up to the desired extent, and thence launched itself on new growth areas. In the sixties, it was agricultural segment of the market; in the seventies, it was replaced by international market and merchant banking for corporate customers, with leasing getting identified as the new area for growth.

b. **Systems:** A mechanism for planned obsolescence of systems and procedures was lacking. The top-down approach did not allow developing systems in tune with organization's or customers' needs.

   Systems of performance budgeting, management information and performance appraisal degenerated into paper-filling routines because of absence of a system of free and frank information flow from bottom to the top. So, instead of meaningful reviews taking place and problems getting tackled, they were allowed to fester. Protocol-worship and a note-based decision-making system were the prime culprits.

c. **Structure:** The organization was much better structured than its competitors but there was need to infuse new life into it. In the absence of a driving force to channelize efforts in the chosen direction, the potential benefits that could have been extracted from the established structure did not accrue. For instance, while specialist support to branches for all the 5 market segments was supposed to be provided by the respective functionaries of the Planning wing at the LHO (Local Head Office), actually this got reduced to issuing instructions and liaising with government and corporate bodies at the upper level. No efforts to explore the market's needs or to guide a particular branch in its environs, for meeting the challenges effectively, were made.

d. **Staff:** The quality of the Bank's manpower resources was getting widely acknowledged as amongst the best in the country, but, at the middle and lower rungs, managerial competence was still rare.

   The organization was not yet a good training ground for producing managers. The clerical- and mediocrity-bias in the organizational philosophy was still pronounced. The quality of clerical staff was good, but they needed to be properly oriented.

e. **Skills:** Specialized skills in agricultural and industrial credit, foreign exchange, merchant banking and government business were well recognized.

f. **Styles:** Appropriate for a premier bank of the country and living up to its image of a socially committed one. However, respect for professionals was not demonstrated in full measure by the organization.

Critical Success Factors

a. **Human Resources:** Banking is an industry whose 'products' are manufactured exclusively by its people. The 'production' or output is not easily quantifiable, nor is it visible in concrete terms. Yet the quality of 'production' has an important bearing on the bank's market.

   Therefore, the morale of the people employed, the values inculcated in them and the capacity of the management to take work from them are all important. Fullest utilization of potential by proper development and posting, encouraging entrepreneur-rial risk-taking – rather than risk-avoidance – and keeping vested interest at bay are the key factors.

b. **Control of Clerical Staff:** Managerial control over clerks, cashiers and officers engaged in routine jobs is a critical factor in ensuring safety of funds, prompt and polite services to customers, growth of business and optimization of resources.

   The critical success factors analysis reveals vital gaps in these two areas.

The Bank's employees at all levels had not been so involved as to identify themselves with the corporate mission of growth. The earlier superordinate goal of ensuring safety of funds through meticulous book-keeping had long been abandoned but without 'growth' or any other thing being enshrined in its place.

Thus the systems and procedures, established long time back to serve the earlier goals, were sought to be enforced even in the changed circumstances. An orientation towards 'market' or 'growth' would mean, first, finding out the market needs and, next, to attune the resources to meet these. This was not yet visible in most areas. The entrepreneurial drive was very much held in check by the procedural brakes.

Similarly in the matter of clerical and other staff, too, the colonial hangover continued. In those days, the basis of control was unquestionable authority of the organizational elite and distrust of the 'native' clerks. This vertical control was supplemented by horizontal control – competition among the operatives to meticulous book-keeping. The Accountant was the high priest and procedures and accuracy the reigning deity. Every transaction was entered at a number of places to check and cross-check. The essence of a clerk's duty was making all the entries at the right places, and that of an officer consisted in verifying the correctness of the entries, with his/her initials being proof the same.

This system was obviously meant for a situation of *class banking* rather than mass banking. As against a prolonged drudgery of repetitive work, the focus of effort should have been the customer. For the large volume of daily transactions involved at bigger branches, computerization should have been the logical answer a long time back. The clerk's potential could have been utilized more fully by avoiding duplication of work and giving them more and more responsibility. The accountability trap – officers alone being responsible for lapses in maintenance of accounts without giving them the needed organizational support – was neither fair, nor efficient. Worse still, it didn't have customer at the centre.

In the matter of effecting control, too, the problem should have been tackled at its roots. Because of a timid approach to labour management, coupled with accountability at one end only, the officers' elan had vanished. The differential in pay and perks between clerks and officers was so small and that in responsibility so large that many clerks refused to take promotion. They were not liable to be transferred, so they could spend their entire work- life in one branch. By virtue of their long association with one place, they acquired powers through informally established practices, vested interests, knowledge of things, influence over colleagues, etc. Many of the unpromotable promotees were also back among them as officers. Such officers owed allegiance to the same values as clerks, and were incapable of controlling their former fellowmen.

The bureaucratic mode of functioning ensured that decisions affecting vital interests of the Bank were not taken fast and much less implemented.

Demonstration of the right values by top management was, thus, lacking; persons with doubtful integrity kept ruling the roost and could not be touched because of lack of hard evidence. Contrasted with that, a minor *bona-fide* mistake or a procedural lapse could cause as much mental agony to the employee as a bigger one.

The tying down of responsibility to the individual, as well as to procedures, ensured two things. First, there was no team-responsibility for a given task.

The concern was not with the overall performance in achieving goals but with acquitting oneself well by merely following the procedures. Second, with vested interests galore and the bureaucratic management ensuring no way of throwing out or sidelining the unscrupulous ones, such employees fattened themselves at the expense of the organization. They were scrupulous in observing procedures, so they could not be caught on the wrong foot; whatever else they did was off the record, and so not cognizable. A spate of frauds in banks in the country was a manifestation of this.

Because of management's inability to come to grips with the real problems of the organization, the tendency to sweep all problems under the carpet developed. All managers in the hierarchy, up to the top, had a short-term perspective. If no major problem erupted during their tenure, they would not face any challenge. The emphasis was, thus, not on problem solving but on responsibility shifting.

Recommendations

1. Computerization of branch operations has already freed the hands of Bank officials from routine activities. Their potential should be fully utilized in putting 'customer' at the centre of operations.
2. The future lies in offering new services. Systematic market research into the needs of different market segments and new service possibilities should be taken up.

3. Computerization has already solved the clerical staff versus officers' control problem to a great extent. The nexus between development of vested interests among some of them and their power to sabotage operations can be broken by proper selection of persons who would control the key operations.

4. The elan of officers should be brought back by increasing their perks and giving them more authority and a say in selection of their teams.

5. Specialization in branch operations to take care of large volumes, as well as in rendering services at the macro level should be gradually widened.

6. Clerks as well as junior officers should be given responsibility for their portfolio of customers rather than just for accounting.

7. Bureaucratic functioning should give way to an entrepreneurial style based on innovation rather than mediocrity. The organization must reward managers for their total performance. Appropriate methods must be developed to measure this, removing the many lacunae in the present system.

8. A system for upward communication of problems, etc. and a problem- solving approach in place of the present-day buck-passing should be developed.

THE FOREX RATE CONUNDRUM (1986–1988)

The Bank branches were facing a tough competition from other banks, including foreign banks, in quoting fine exchange rates and had lost certain big business deals because the rate quoted by another bank was even finer than the finest rate we could offer.

Quoting foreign exchange rate to the transacting branch, at a given time, was the responsibility of the Foreign Department Branch (FD) of SBI. And FD's opinion in the matter was: "No other bank has the capability to quote finer rates than ours and yet make a profit on the deal." Hence the conundrum.

In a paper presented at a Conference, held at SBI's Foreign Department in June 1988, the problem was analyzed in detail and suggestions for solving it were made.

Problem Analysis

a. Organizational Constraints

A "close rapport" between the Dealing Room at FD and the branches from where the transactions emanate (including Overseas Branches at Mumbai, Delhi, Chennai, etc.) has not evolved. So, an iterative process of quoting finer & still finer rates – based on feedback from the operating branch about the strategy followed by the competitor bank – is not available. With the setting up of Dealing Rooms (DR) at 3 other places, communication between the DR and the Operating Branches has improved;

i. Because of the large volume of Sales (Imports) transactions at SBI, our currency position is lopsided, and we are not comfortable quoting finer rates for sales transactions;

ii. Foreign Banks remain short of rupee resources, so they quote "loss rates" for Sale transactions.

iii. Because of the large volume of Sales (Imports) transactions at SBI, our currency position is lopsided, and we are not comfortable quoting finer rates for sales transactions;

iv. Foreign Banks remain short of rupee resources, so they quote "loss rates" for Sale transactions;

v. Because of the large volume of Sales (Imports) transactions at SBI, our currency position is lopsided, and we are not comfortable quoting finer rates for sales transactions;

vi. Foreign Banks remain short of rupee resources, so they quote "loss rates" for Sale transactions.

b. Key Decision Variables (KDV)

While quoting exchange rates, we need to count profit not just from the forex rate but also from the commission and interest earned;

c. Process of Decision Making

i. The main parameter for quoting exchange rate is the "market rate" as gleaned either from the Reuter Monitor Terminal (in case of low-value transactions), or obtained from brokers (in case of high-value transactions). Manager (Rates) quotes a "fine rate", and any further refinement is possible only with Chief Dealer's advice; and a "Break- Even" rate can be quoted only at DGM's, or higher, level. In this mental decision-making process, the 'high' or 'low' value of the transaction (i.e., the size of the deal), as also its relative importance for being given 'discounts', are based on macro-level perceptions. Thus, a deal which appears big at the branch, or even at a certain LHO level, may be considered small, and as such ineligible for favourable treatment, at Foreign Department level.

The thumb rules that usually apply to discounts appear to conform to wholesaler's discount in trade – based on size of the deal. Only, in this case, instead of being prescribed, discounts have to be extracted from FD, by a constituent of the Bank, through hard bargaining.

ii. Other parameters may come into the reckoning of FD, if especially fine rates are sought from it, citing reasons like value of connection, size of the deal, competition faced from another bank in retaining/acquiring business, etc., are:

  a. Position, i.e. whether the whole-Bank position in respect of the relevant foreign currency happens to be overbought or oversold at that moment and by how much;

  b. The average overall rate at which position is being carried;

  c. Discount to be given, if any, because of the quantum of business involved;

  d. A further discount allowable at FD's discretion if it is perceived that retaining/acquiring the business is critically important on account of the customer's value of connection for the Bank or in order to counter competition from another bank;

  e. Nature of Decision-Making *Per Se*: Four things need to be taken note of insofar as the nature of decision-making *per se*, is concerned.

Firstly, even though it may be possible to identify the decision-making variables rather easily, the decision in itself is not fully structured. That is to say, it is not as if, given certain values of the decision variables, a precise quantitative value of the final outcome (quotation for the rate) could be predicted as from a formula.

Rather, a large amount of qualitative (human) judgement goes into the process. It must also be appreciated that even if a tight structuring of the decision-making is attempted by laying down precise norms, etc., the process of quoting a rate in a given situation will remain "semi-structured", or dependent on human judgement, to a large extent, because of the element of bargaining in the market-place involved.

Secondly, decision-making is heavily centralized at FD level ensuring neglect of regionally/locally significant factors in favour of a macro- level, even-handed approach. The lack of flexibility resulting from this is sought to be justified on two counts: one, since the market rates are continuously changing, dealers have to take decisions about rates to be quoted in split seconds; and two, if lower tiers were also allowed to participate in decision- making, the present system of transfer pricing between FD and individual branches would go haywire.

Thirdly, even though the market rates are either read from the (computer-ized) Reuter Monitor terminal or obtained over hot lines, the vehicle for decision-making is manual calculation. In this mode, not only is generation and explicit evaluation of alternatives not feasible but even keeping in view the absolute value of exchange profit to be made on the deal is perhaps not possible. The dealer's ingenuity lies entirely in knocking off a minimum number of pips from the market rate of the moment and quoting a rate that will satisfy the consumer. However, the essence of good quality decision-making lies in an explicit evaluation of alternatives which is not done at present.

Fourthly, because of the manual mode of operation, no guidance from the past data is available on tap to the decision maker, except perhaps what is retained at the back of his mind on account of past experience. Even the calculation of 'position' and the average rate at which it is carried is done manually, at regular intervals during the day. The FD computer caters only to the requirements of back-office accounting and generation of MIS reports.

The MIS reports, at best, serve the purpose of making an historical analysis of past decisions. They are hardly the tool for aiding the FD officials' decision-making process.

d. Suggestion : Install a DSS

There is an urgent need to install a computerized Decision Support System (DSS) to aid in generating feasible alternatives, taking into account the relevant factors explicitly. Human judgement should then be applied to decide which alternative is the best.

A DSS is a computer application that supports decision-making of managers by providing them with flexible access to relevant models and data.

The key features of a DSS are: flexibility in use; ability to process models and/or data; focus on a decision problem; and scope for incorporating human judgement in dealing with the decision problem.

DSS is best for 'semi-structured" problems. A structured problem is one which can be modelled and to which very little scope exists for human judgement. For instance, computation of profit for a 's operations, given the values of sales revenue and various expenses, etc.

In such a case, a stand-alone, classical model of computer application is enough. On the other hand, if the problem is too vague or "soft", not lending itself to any structuring whatever, then it is best left to human judgement. An example would be: given a set of job definitions and a group of employees, from amongst whom to select persons for matching them with the job positions.

A "semi-structured" problem is one in solving which it is best to use both a mode/access to data base as well as human judgement. FD's fine rates quotation problem certainly falls in this category. Access to a model (so that the relevant factors could be explicitly considered) and/or a data base on past as well as current deals (so that customer-, as well as competitor banker- specific response could be determined) could substantially enhance the quality of human decision-making. Because of the added facility of flexibility in use, the decision-maker can fashion his own model, define the limits of feasibility or change the parameters for evaluation – and do all this himself interactively. With a DSS in place, pencil pushing and mental processing will be reduced considerably.

A DSS can be set up with the help of a personal computer (PC), using an appropriate software package like Lotus 1-2-3 etc. The interface design can be such that the whole process is "menu-driven", that is to say, every step to be taken is clearly outlined for the user in English language on the screen; the machine asks for, and accepts data at every stage; and, above all, the various parameters, the model to be used and the limits stipulated, etc. can all be decided interactively by the user himself. Thus, he can generate and evaluate the alternatives himself the way he wishes, without having to depend on a computer specialist. The great advantage of having a DSS is that the

decision-maker remains a master of the process; he is not reduced to being a slave – either to the computer specialist or to the latter's use of complicated models which, quite often, prove to be counter-productive insofar as the quality of decision-making is concerned.

In the schematic diagram shown below, two approaches to setting up a computerized DSS for enhancing the quality of decision-making with respect to the rates quotation problem are outlined. The first one is the simpler of the two, and can be easily implemented right-away without disturbing any of the organizational processes. For the large majority of cases, this DSS should suffice. Recourse to the second, more complicated one, would be required to be taken in those handful of cases where a coup de grace must needs be delivered to a tough competitor. Implementing this would, of course, require certain changes in the existing organizational processes. Perhaps that would be the future direction the organization has to take.

DSS I

As shown in the schematic diagram below, all that this basis DSS seeks to achieve are: (i) Replacement of the existing system of periodic manual calculation of average exchange rate at which Foreign Currency Position is carried, by a computerized one so that at the end of every deal which is booked, the average rate is instantly computed and made available to the decision-maker; and (ii) Introduction of a simple model for computing a range of fine rates.

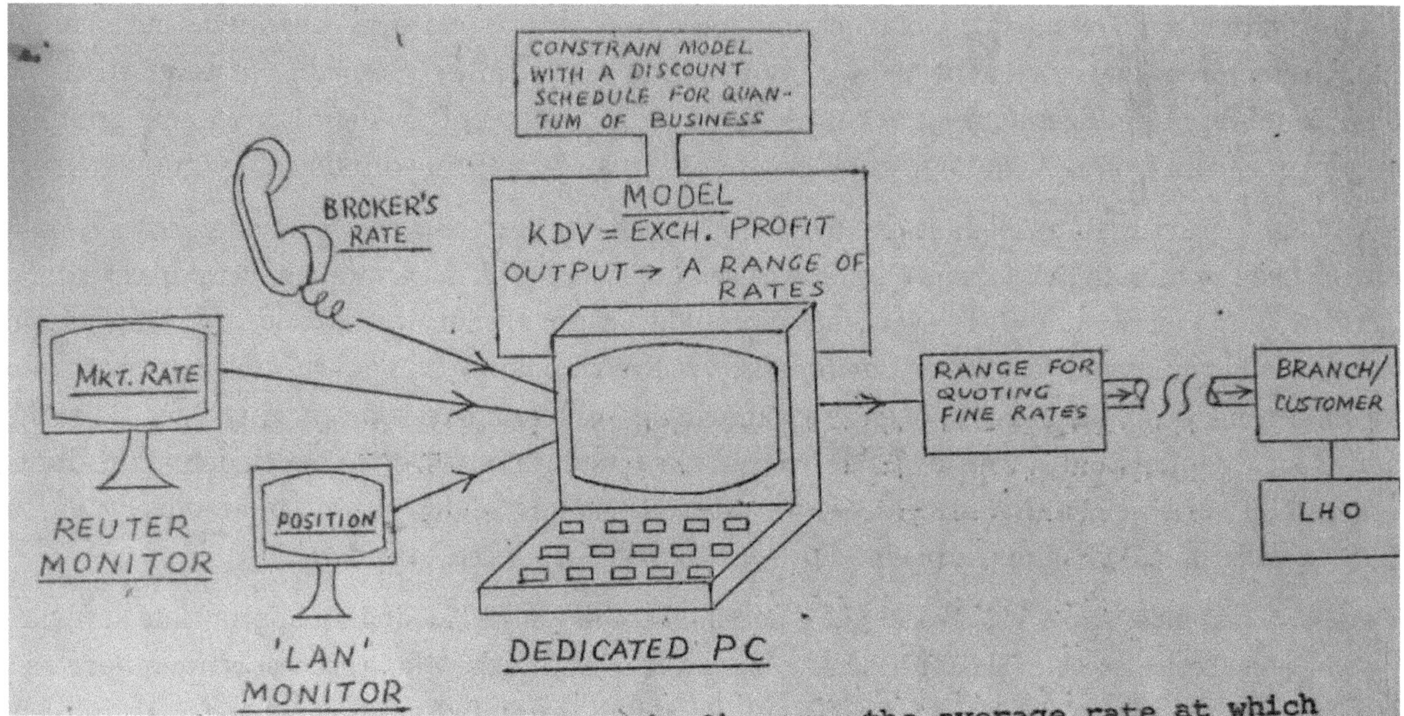

The Key Decision Variable (KDV) remains the amount of exchange profit to be earned, but the model is constrained with a discount schedule linking any further refinement in the rate to the quantum of business. Its chief merit lies in there being available, in front of the decision-maker's eyes, an absolute value of exchange profit to be made on the deal, after all discounts. Under the existing manual system, he has no clear idea of the exact profit amount at the time he is quoting a fine rate – for, at that moment, all that he is concerned with is knocking off a few 'pips'.

In addition to that, the DSS assists in human decision-making by specifying a range of 3 discrete values of fine rate within which the dealer may quote, depending upon his judgement – the rate obtained without constraining the model with discount schedule and the break-even rate. This should result in improvement in the quality of decision-making because 3 clear sign posts are now available for guidance of the decision-maker in his journey leading to the final decision.

In the schematic diagram, the average rate at which position is being carried at the moment is obtained from a separate monitor connected with similar other monitors (PCs) in a Local Area Network (LAN). In computer terminology, these may be referred to as Slave terminals which simply display the results of processing done at the Master terminal. The model is actually implemented at the dedicated PC available with the decision maker. Using an application software package, the model itself is set up on the machine from beforehand; in actual operation, all that the decision maker has to do is to read the market rate and the average rate of position from respective screens before him, and key in the figures in his PC. Within seconds, processed figures (as well as the details of processing) appear on the computer terminal, for him to judge the situation and quote a fine rate. He may, if he so wishes, go in for fresh computations with a changed set of parameters, or choose to defer the decision till such time as more favourable market rate comes to be offered.

DSS II

Here, the model is slightly complicated. First of all, the Key Decision Variable (KDV) itself is not just 'exchange profit' but the algebraic sum of exchange profit, interest and handling commission. While the DSS I model had only one constraining factor, this one has three – Quantum of Business, Value of Connection and Nature of Competition.

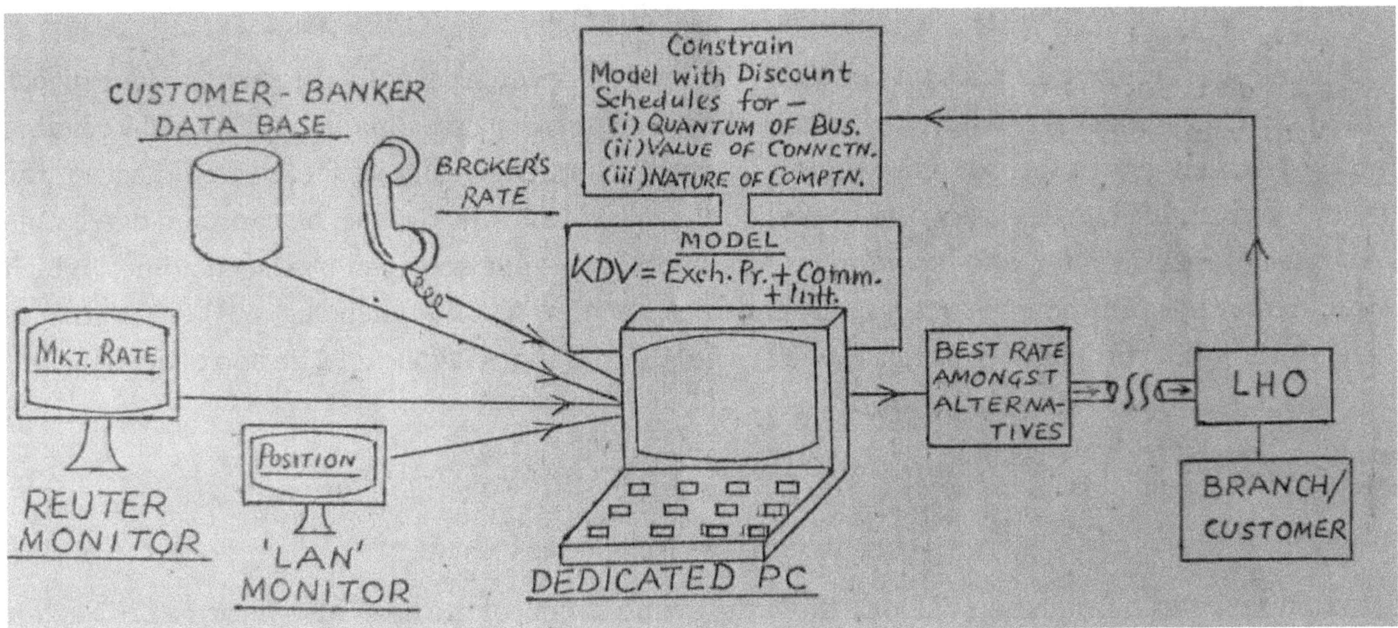

An appropriate discount schedule for the customer's value of connection to the Bank is envisaged on lines similar to the schedule for quantum of business. Classifying the value of connection into A, B and C categories may be the method to be adopted for purposes of applying the discount schedule on a case-to-case basis. The classification decision should approximately rest with the concerned Local Head Office.

A further discount schedule is envisaged for the nature of competition faced – is it moderate or tough? Who are the competitor banks and what sort of competition have they normally provided in the past? What has been their strategy in the past? In order to devise an appropriate discount schedule after taking all these qualitative information into account, it is necessary to draw upon two sources: one, a banker-specific as well as customer-specific historical analysis of past deals; and two, information about the customer and the competitor banker from the field level (LHO/ Branch). The former is envisaged in the form of a Data Base attached to the dedicated PC; the latter is best communicated over telephone. (With the setting up of the SBI Integrated Telecommunication Network, instant communication between the Branch, LHO and FD should not remain a distant dream.)

The DSS, here, is primarily meant for generation and evaluation of alternatives. This takes place in the following manner.

After the Market Rate (obtained either from the Reuter Monitor or from the broker) has been fed into the PC, the DSS picks up 5-6 different values (this can go up to any number depending upon the design) in the neighbourhood of the given rate – say, market rate plus or minus 2 pips, plus or minus 4 pips, plus or minus 5 pips, etc. – and generates values of the KDV for each of them. With such an array of KDV available to him for his guidance, the decision maker can keep a close eye on the market rate movements and know the implications of every shift, in terms of approximate KDV value, by relating it to them. He is, thus, able to explicitly evaluate alternatives.

He remains free to take his own decision – he may either quote a good rate (which, he expects, would satisfy the consumer while, at the same time, earning him a reasonable profit) just by reading it off the screen, or ask the customer himself to specify a range within which he would accept the quotation from his banker. Using the DSS to do the calculations in reverse, he can then determine the range of market rates, corresponding to the quotation range specified by the customer, which would result in minimum, yet acceptable, earnings for him. As and when the market rate comes either within this minimum earnings range or one which is more favourable, he books the deal and informs the customer of having done so.

Scenario

A typical scenario for decision-making under DSS II may be as follows:

12:00 p.m. : Branch contacts FD for a fine rate, giving details of the deal. Also informs LHO about the critical importance of keeping business to ourselves.

12:30 p.m. : FD makes first offer to Branch.

1:00 p.m. : Branch informs LHO of customer's rejection of FD's first rate.

1:15 p.m. : LHO contacts FD; pleads for a finer rate. FD informs LHO that for any rate finer than that, the responsibility for reduction in profit or increase in loss on the deal would rest with LHO. So, the Circle Management must take a decision to compensate FD for the loss.

1:15 – 1:30 P.M. : CMC Members at LHO are informed of the necessity to consider the situation and take a decision.

3:00 – 3:30 P.M. : CMC Members meet and arrive at a decision in favour of compensating FD.

3:45 P.M. : FD is informed of CMC's decision and a still finer rate is requested for.

4:30 P.M. : FD quotes its second fine rate to LHO.

4:45 P.M. : LHO informs Branch of FD's second fine rate.

Lastly, it may be mentioned in passing that although it may be possible to combine the information processing, spread over three computer screens in the schematic diagram above, into only one computer screen, but it may be construed as an infringement of the rights given to the Bank by the Reuter Monitoring Service.

SICKNESS IN SMALL INDUSTRY: SOLVING THE ENREPRENEURIAL TANGLE (1976–1982)

There are four sub-systems that play in industrial sickness – problem of market-place, or production, or finance, or technology. If the unit has to remain clear of the woods, all these four sub-systems must keep adapting themselves to the changing environment. The unit's performance will deteriorate as soon as any of these go out-of-step with the environment. If corrective action is not taken in time to re-align the sub-systems concerned, performance will deteriorate and the unit will become "sick".

It is essential for every unit to possess an inherent capacity to: one, adapt itself to change through innovation; and two, to underwrite the risk associated with the futurity of operations involved. They constitute the entrepreneurial core of the unit and any deficiencies cause the sub-systems to falter. One root cause of this systematic mis-alignment is a relative weakening of the entrepreneurial function.

It will be myopic if we soft-pedal the issue of evaluating the entrepreneurial bona fides of the person behind the project. At the time we consider nursing of a sick unit, examining this aspect, too, is vital.

The rationale for nursing sick units is not just to guard against loss of either production or employment – simply because, with most industries remaining saddled with enough un-utilized capacity, at the macro level and in the long run, production is hardly affected. And subsidizing employment at the cost of efficiency should certainly not be the aim.

In the event of a unit going sick, only the labour of the failed entrepreneur goes waste. Any productive facilities set up by him can always be taken over by another entrepreneur for proper use. Policies of the state must be geared to promoting efficiency, growth and development and a smooth sailing for the entrepreneurs all the way up through the industrial field, while blocking the passage of non-entrepreneurial people.

The current system of promoting industries through supportive measures like provision of infrastructure, physical inputs, technical expertise, cash incentives, subsidies, etc. has this latent weakness – it tries to promote industries without promoting entrepreneurs. The core, around which the supportive measures should have been built, is itself missing. Hence the spectacle of the industrial scene in the small scale industries (SSI) abounding in non-entrepreneurs and pervaded with sickness.

In order to apply the necessary correctives, the main thrust of the official policy must shift to: (i) attracting the right entrepreneurial talent to the industrial field; (ii) fostering development of their potential further through inculcation of the right attitudes and imparting the necessary skills; and (iii) reinforcement of the entrepreneurship attitudes and skills in the developing as well as the existing entrepreneurs through encouragement and positive action.

By any reckoning that is a tall order indeed, with social, political and even cultural implications. However, in spite of the formidable odds, a model worked by the State Bank of India on the above lines has yielded considerable positive results which earlier attempts had failed to do. In the following paragraphs, we endeavour to examine the State Bank model in depth.

The model is called the Entrepreneurial Development Programme (EDP), launched by the Bank for promoting first-generation entrepreneurs in the backward regions of the country. The E. D. Programme's significance lies in the fact that it has been conceived as a total package – from tapping the entrepreneurial potential right up to financing and setting entrepreneurs up in industry. Its one-month long training programme is a unique blend of motivational and technical inputs disseminated in a manner designed to make the participants internalize the knowledge.

Through the services of a specialist wing, called the Consultancy Services Cell, the EDP participants are actively assisted with classified information on industrial projects as also in researching the environment so as to facilitate the choice of a worthwhile project and in actual preparation of the project report. Necessary support from the government agencies is sought to be arranged through the Bank's mediation. Finally, specially formulated schemes for financing EDP projects uniquely provide, *inter alia*, for grant of a long-term loan – even for the units' own equity build-up. Constant follow- up and monitoring of projects already set up or underway, by the Bank's Consultancy Services Cell, too, are envisaged.

Postulates

It would be instructive to examine the theoretical postulates underlying this model of development. The modern view is to treat development not merely as a function of capital or technology but as a burgeoning socio-economic process supported primarily by the emergence of a body of entrepreneurs[2].

Entrepreneurs are persons with personality traits especially suited to business situations. They feel, think and act in a way that sets them apart from others. They are naturally inclined to take up activities involving imagination, skill and decision-making. They feel compelled not only to accomplish things but also to continually measure their performance. And they exhibit a deep emotional attachment for their goal.

Entrepreneurs feel the stresses and strains of a difficult situation but do not recoil from one because of their problem-solving attitude. They enjoy successes achieved through their own efforts. While being subjectively confident of themselves, they yet show a remarkable awareness of the realities around: of their own handicaps, of the risks posed by the environment and of the need to seek others' help. Threats are thus perceived as challenges, but only those challenges are taken up which, in the entrepreneur's reckoning afford him a reasonable chance of succeeding through his own efforts. The entrepreneur's actions are always characterized by moderate risk-taking: to him, too low a risk means no challenge, so no promise of enjoyment of the results of one's labours; on the other hand, too high a risk means little hope of success, so not worth taking. Innovativeness and goal-setting are concomitant traits. Not only does an entrepreneur take initiatives but he actively seeks feedback to know how he is performing, learns from experience and assumes full responsibility for his actions. The satisfaction derived from accomplishments eggs him on to take up bigger challenges; his enterprise thus becomes growth-oriented[3]. Now it is easy to see why some people's enterprises are doomed to fail – they are the ones who merely fulfill an entrepreneurial role without holding the entrepreneurial status.

The State Bank model provides for two-tier screening for selection of EDP participants. The first screening is based upon responses to structured questions in the application form, These are designed to measure the following attributes: specificity of goals; realistic awareness of environment and own resources; locus of internal control (i.e., balance between hope of success and fear of failure); help seeking; leadership qualities; concern for betterment; emotional involvement; motivational strength for starting industry; aspiration for future; attitude to search alternatives; realistic perception of difficulties; activity level shown in the past in starting business; etc.

The second-phase selection consists of the following: class-room tests to re- check on the above attributes in real-life situation; a group exercise to gauge the capacity to take initiatives and withstand shocks; and a personal interview. The most interesting of them all is the story-telling test to measure the "achievement motive", extensively used the world over by David C. McClelland. In this, a person is shown a series of ambiguous pictures for brief seconds. Based upon each picture he writes a five-minute story from his own imagination. It has been empirically established that the story of achievement-motivated persons always contain a significant number of achievement ideas even though the pictures themselves might be perfectly neutral or suggestive of a variety of ideas. A properly trained eye can spot them in the language, thus giving a score for each person's stories. The score then serves as a good measure for selecting potential entrepreneurs. The final tally of scores for selection of EDP participants in the State Bank model is, of course, made up of the scores of all the different tests, group exercises and interview.

Evaluation

The efficacy of the E. D. Programme can be measured only in the long run. If the EDP-trained entrepreneurs consistently turn out better performance than others, year after year, in statistically significant numbers, then only can it be said that the Programme has succeeded in meeting its objectives. Nevertheless, a look at the tangible results generated so far is enough to generate confidence.

The EDP ball was set rolling by the State Bank in the last quarter of 1978. Different Circles conduct their own E. D. Programmes for the backward districts. The run-up to the training programme proper takes about two months' time. By the end of December 1981, a total of 57 EDPs had been conducted all over the country and 1320 persons trained. Assuming a uniform rate per month for conduct of EDPs, there would have been, by then, some 52 programmes of age more than 3 months, involving, on an average, some 1204 persons. This figure denotes the upper limit or the maximum number of EDP entrepreneurs who could have, by 1981-end, either set up their own industries or been in the process of doing so. Out of this, 264 persons, or 22% had already been sanctioned loans another 260, or 21.6% had either submitted their project reports or were on the verge of doing so. Thus, as at December-end 1981, over 43% of the maximum potential were definitely poised to become industrialists. If EDPs of age one year or more only are taken into account, the percentage improves to 64.

Consider that all the EDPs were held in the Planning Commission- designated backward districts having extremely poor infrastructure. A good number of the persons concerned came from backward communities and non- business family environments which was a considerable drag on their steadfastness in pursuing the goal of industry; indeed, some of them finally dropped out only because of family pressure. Yet it was fascinating to see even the persons considered delinquents and not showing much promise during the training, coming back with a vengeance to an entrepreneurial career, after having strayed in other directions, as if drawn to a lodestone.

Similarly, the tenacity with which the bulk of the people clung to their projects, for sometimes as long as two years and in the face of heavy odds, was admirable.

From the banker's credit risk angle, the most significant aspect was that one did not have to check, over and over again, on the entrepreneur's bona fides. The worries, if any, were confined to their being young in age and inexperienced. Of course, that didn't really result in as prompt a clearance of their projects as envisaged, for reasons rooted primarily in organizational inertia. Nor did all the expectations of an intensive follow-up of all the EDP participants, individually, materialize. In spite of that, each one of State Bank's 12 Circles had tangible results to show by December-end, 1981. As on that date, the success rate for different Circles (in terms of the number of EDP participants poised to start their units as a percentage of the total number of persons trained) varied between 24% and 78%. The average amount of loans sanctioned worked out to Rs 1.89 lakhs per EDP unit, with the minimum and maximum for a Circle being Rs 1.31 lakhs and Rs 3.23 lakhs respectively.

The results may be compared with those achieved under the Entrepreneur Scheme, another specially formulated scheme of the Bank launched in 1967 to promote engineering degree and diploma holders and other suitably qualified and/or experienced persons. The unique feature of the scheme is 100% finance of the entrepreneur's project by the Bank, though the total project cost cannot exceed Rs 2 lakhs (earlier, Rs 1 lakh). At the end of the first full year of its operation, 1968, the Bank reported a total of 76 SSI (Small Scale Industries) units financed under the scheme, with an average sanctioned limit per unit of Rs 0.93 lakh and an average utilization of Rs 0.46 lakh. By 1981-end, that is after the scheme had been in operation for 14 years, the number of units financed rose to 7,785 but, significantly, the average sanctioned limit came down to Rs 0.57 lakh per unit.

This happened even as the ceiling for financing units under the scheme was, in the meantime, raised from Rs 1 lakh to Rs 2 lakhs.

Up to 1979, the YOY growth in number of units financed under the Entrepreneur Scheme was modest. Over the last two years after that, there has been a jump. In 1979, Entrepreneur Scheme units formed 1.3% of the total number of SSI units financed by the Bank; in 1980, their share rose to 1.8% and in 1981, to 2.2%. While such increases would have normally been indicative of good progress made under the scheme, this cannot be said to be the case for two reasons. First, the increases have taken place all too suddenly, and inexplicably, after a gap of 11 years from the launch.

Secondly, the same have been accompanied by a thinning out of per unit investment in fixed assets to quite unreal proportions, considering the requirements of modern industry. (*"State Bank Group: A Statistical Profile of the SIB Segment as on December 31, 1981", SI & SB Banking Department, State Bank of India, Central Office, Bombay)*

The conclusion that the post-1979 increases in number do not represent growth in terms of healthy & vigorous SSI units is inescapable. That the Entrepreneur Scheme has been an unmitigated failure is also indirectly acknowledged by the fact that the ceiling on total finance has been retained at the low level of Rs lakhs all these years. The experience of other banks, which also have been operating a similar scheme, has been much the same.

The qualitative difference, in formulation, between Entrepreneur Scheme and EPD is this: while the former is concerned just with an acquired instrumental skill (a professional degree or experience), the latter has a systematic design for examining the entrepreneurial credentials of the aspirants. It would be naïve to imagine that entrepreneurship demands just possessing certain instrumental skills. Entrepreneurship is a much more complex phenomenon encompassing elements of a person's psychological make-up. Even at the level of skills, at least three different kinds are required to be evolved – instrumental, imaginal and system. But it certainly goes deeper than that – linking up, perhaps, with values and even consciousness4.

In the event, it is just as well that pioneering studies by McClelland and his associates point to the close connection which societal ethos has with general level of "achievement motivation" (and so, of entrepreneurship) in the population at a given point of time. In other words, entrepreneurship can be developed, but to facilitate this the right atmosphere must first be created.

APPRAISING A SMALL SCALE INDUSTRIES PROJECT (1976–1982)

Based on the aggregate credit facilities required, Small Scale Industries projects fall in three categories: (1) Category 'C', where the aggregate credit facilities required would be below or up to Rs 25,000; (2) Category 'B', where the aggregate credit facilities required would be between Rs 25,000 & Rs 5 lakh; (3) Category 'A', where the aggregate credit facilities required would be above Rs 5 lakh. Depending upon the category a case belongs to, different forms of application, interview and appraisal will apply.

While application and interview forms have just to be filled in, it is the appraisal of an industrial project that is of crucial importance. Generally, this is taken to mean an evaluation of the project report – including a technical report – that has been submitted on behalf of the unit or even the application itself. If the technical report says, "the project is technically feasible and economically viable", we get satisfied on this count, and then, try to establish the promoter's "integrity", i.e. whether he would be a dependable borrower or not. We also try to find out his means in order to satisfy ourselves how safe our lending would be in the event of the project becoming unsuccessful.

But a mere checking of facts contained in the project report is not project appraisal. Using the cliché-ridden terminology, a project may have been projected on paper as "technically feasible" and "economically viable" and yet, on proper appraisal, may turn out to be not a good bankable proposition at all.

Some of the questions relating to the vital aspects of the project that need to be pondered over are: Can it do with lower investment in fixed assets including plant & machinery? What machinery are the other manufacturers having? What are the advantages and disadvantages of excluding a certain machine – say, one that produces a sub-product that is easily available in the market – or a piece of land? Can a lower- capacity – and cheaper – machine be used in place of the proposed machine?

The next point to focus on is the man behind the project – the entrepreneur. Appraising the entrepreneur is the most important part of the project. Its aim is to determine how well-prepared and how well-equipped he is for establishing his project. One positive factor would be his experience in the relevant field. But just having experience is not enough. The person concerned must have acquired sufficient knowledge and skill to have a competitive edge over other entrepreneurs engaged in manufacturing similar products.

This competitive edge may be in one or more of the following three areas – procurement of raw materials, technical skill in manufacturing the products and in marketing the same.

A competitive advantage in procurement of raw materials would be of importance where the raw materials are scarce. In an industry where manufacturing skills are of critical importance, an entrepreneur may have an edge over others in this area. But in the case of small- scale industries, getting an edge over others in the field of manufacturing skills may not be of great significance simply because the processes are well-known. Even if an entrepreneur does not himself have the know-how, he can easily hire appropriate technical personnel.

It is in the area of marketing and sales that an entrepreneur's capabilities are of greatest relevance to us. If he has knowledge about how to market his products – and the right "feel" of it – then, he has an upper hand over others. For, while in practically all lines of manufacture under SSI, there will be dozens of other people who would know how to manufacture the products but only a few will have marketing acumen.

So, we need to appraise the entrepreneur's marketing acumen by asking him questions like these: What are the assumptions on which sales figures are based? Who will his customers be? How much does he propose to sell to different segments of customers? Why will a customer buy from him rather than from his competitors? What is the normal marketing channel for his products? Does he know how the goods move in the marketing channel and why certain brands move more than others? Does he know what are his strengths, weaknesses, opportunities and threats vis-à-vis his competitors?

Does he take a long-term view of the market and is he aware of the newer products on the horizon (or which are already being marketed) that are going to vie for the purchasing power in the hands of his customer? Does he envisage the direction in which he will diversify in the future? In the immediate present, does he envisage having a product range, i.e. different styles, sizes or qualities of products to satisfy the needs of different categories of customers? Is he thinking of employing any promotion techniques? Is he planning to differentiate his products from those of other manufacturers? Is he pricing the different products on sound basis and is he actually aware of their costs? Does he propose to employ proper pricing strategies?

The answers to these questions would determine whether the entrepreneur has a true sense of his market or not. It is only after he has satisfied us on this count that we should proceed to appraise the project report.

The first step in this would be to make sure that the items of plant and machinery stipulated would be sufficient for the proposed manufacturing plan. Second, examine if there is any scope for reducing investment in plant & machinery or in land & building. Third, put in place a mechanism to ensure that any constraints on production (such as inadequate power supply, scarcity of raw materials, etc.) get spotted in time and remedial measures are taken immediately. Fourth, check that maximum plant capacity for the proposed mix of products has been established and scrutinize every single head of annual expenditure projected for the proposed production plan to make sure that the project report provides adequately for all-power bill, administrative expenses, interest, depreciation, selling overheads, etc.

Fifth, determine the break-even sales level – the level of annual sales at which the unit will attain the position of no-profit-no-loss and compare it with the sales levels projected for the first year. In most cases, units first stipulate a certain sales level in their project report and then go to the market for selling that volume. It should actually be the other way round – how much to produce should be based upon a study of the market. It is better to be realistic, in the first phase, about how much the market is prepared to take and then step up the production level in phases. It does not matter if, in the first phase, the operation level is below the break-even level, so long as the project has the inherent strength to succeed.

Sixth, in case it is a unit which has already been running for the past few years, it affords us an opportunity to compare the operating parameters over the years. For example, the trend in sales would be a pointer to whether the unit is losing ground to its competitors or winning more customers. Certain operating ratios could also be compared to glean out the unit's internal performance over the years; for example, the net profit to sales ratio, or the sundry debtors to sales ratio. The previous year's balance sheet may also be analyzed to bring about the surplus available for investing as margin money.

The seventh step is to assess the working capital requirements of the unit.

The first point to note is that the working capital required is related to the unit's level of operation; so, the operating level for which the working capital requirements are to be assessed must be specified. The second point to note is that working capital is made up of four components: requirement against raw materials, against goods-in-process, against finished goods and against bills receivables. (As an additional cushion, one month's expenses are also included as the fifth component, but usually it is stipulated that the entire requirement under this head would be financed from the entrepreneur's own resources.)

The requirement against raw materials is the landed cost of the raw material stocks required to be kept at the unit for smooth, un-hindered operation.

Depending on how difficult it is to procure the raw materials and how long it will take to procure it etc., the quantum of stocks that is required to be kept is assessed. For ease of assessment, it is estimated as so many months' or weeks' consumption (which, effectively, means linking it with the level of production). Once the quantum of raw material stocks has been determined, its value is easy to compute by multiplying it with the landed rate per unit,

i.e. the rate arrived at after adding transportation costs to the purchasing rate.

The finished goods stocks required to be kept by the unit would depend on several factors like the minimum quantity dispatched to customers, transportation bottlenecks, inspection delays, etc. The easy way to assess is, as in the case of raw materials, to estimate the quantum of stocks as so many weeks' production. The value to be put on finished goods stocks would be based on actual cost of production calculated as per the profitability statement.

The quantum of stocks of goods-in-process depends on the length of the manufacturing cycle. Total raw material cost and half of the overhead cost are taken into account to assign a value to it. However, for the sake of convenience, we may even value it at full cost of production, as in the case of finished goods.

The requirement against bills receivables will depend on the proportion of credit sales in total sales and the average time period for collecting bills receivables. Suppose the sale value of bills (credit sales only) raised in a year is Rs 1 lakh and bills remain outstanding for 3 months. Then, the requirement against bills will be Rs 25,000. Strictly speaking, we should consider only the actual cost of production in respect of goods sold through bills, but for convenience sake taking sale value is permitted.

After computing the working capital requirements individually, appropriate margins against each category are applied and the permissible limits computed.

The last step in appraisal is computation of the repayment capacity of the project in respect of term loan installments (interest on term loan having already been charged in the profitability statement). The repayment capacity is denoted by the size of the difference between net cash accrual (net profit after taxes plus depreciation) and repayment obligations. Cash accruals equal to twice the figure of repayment obligations are considered good enough for SBI.

DECODING FINANCIAL STATEMENTS (1976–1982)

We all know the *nitty-gritty* of 'Financial Statement', or at least its two popular versions – the balance sheet and the profit & loss account. We also know that business companies, including banks, have a statutory obligation to get these statements prepared, and audited, every year.

Let us begin by asking three questions. One, what does 'income' mean?

Two, how is 'income' different from 'funds' or 'working capital'? And three, what does 'liquidity' of a company mean?

A little reflection will show that funds are generated by a company out of its income. (Of course, there are other means of generating funds, too – like bank borrowings, for example.) But, even though income generates funds, you can't pay the company's bills directly from income or profit; for that, the company ought to have 'funds' with it. Funds may either be in the form of cash, including the balance available in the company's bank account, or liquid assets. The latter are also known as 'current assets'. Current or liquid assets means such assets as are readily realizable – cash, stocks and receivables – and may, therefore, be relied upon for meeting the company's liabilities in the short term.

The total resources of the company are represented by assets which are sub- divided in two categories – fixed assets and current assets. We have already covered the characteristic features of current assets. By contrast, fixed assets represent those investments that are not normally realized in the usual course of business – such as land, machinery and equipment, tools and spares, etc.

There are two other categories of assets – miscellaneous assets and intangible assets. Loans and advances given by the company to its members or outsiders and investments in securities fall in the category of 'miscellaneous assets'. 'Intangible assets' represent investments that have gone into the creation of things of value for the company, which are not in the form of any physical goods – for example, patent rights, preliminary expenses and accumulated losses, if any (which have to written off over a period of time), goodwill, etc.

Balance Sheet

The balance sheet of a company as on a particular date is a concise, at-a- glance representation of its own *resources* as they stood on that particular dayand the *sources* of those resources. The two have to be in perfect balance, hence the name 'balance sheet'. This statement, then, is a statement of what the company owns and what it owes. What it owns – or its resources – are called 'assets' and are placed on one side of the balance sheet; what it owes are called 'liabilities' and are placed on the other side.

The counterpart of current assets is 'current liabilities' – debts that must be paid during the current accounting year; for instance, sundry creditors for purchases, interest accrued on loans, various provision accounts, etc. The counterpart of fixed assets is 'long-term liabilities', such as medium term loans from banks or moneys borrowed from friends or relations on a long term basis, debentures, etc.

A peculiar feature of the cash credit system of financing in vogue in our country is that even though, for all practical purposes, our cash credit limits are long-term advances, these are included in current liabilities because they are repayable on demand and granted for a period of one year only.

Where does the company's own 'equity' fit in our scheme of things, then? Equity is best understood as the accounts representing ownership rights in the company. No *resources* are contained in these accounts, nor do they represent bank balances. Rather, they are the financing accounts showing *sources of assets* and, therefore, fall on the liabilities side. But they are neither current liabilities, nor long-term liabilities. They represent liabilities of the company to its own owners – the partners or the shareholders. Equity includes not only the capital actually contributed by the owners but also reserves or the accumulated profits of the company.

Computation of Working Capital

Working capital is the amount of capital available for a company's day-to- day operations. It is the company's investment – or liability in case it gets funded by a cash credit/working capital loan taken from a bank – that keeps on rolling from raw materials, to goods-in-process to finished goods. Net working capital – or the excess of current assets over current liabilities – determines the liquidity of the company, if the cash credit loan taken from a bank is included in the current liabilities. If it is not included, then it has to be added to the net working capital in order to arrive at the company's liquidity.

Income or Profit & Loss Statement

The central idea behind preparing income statement is to summarize the financial results of a company's operations over one accounting period, usually a year, so as to figure out how it has fared in the course of the year in respect of its business. The three most important figures in the statement are: Operating Income or Earnings Before Interest & Taxes (EBIT), Earnings Before Tax (EBT) and Net Profit after tax.

Here is an example of a company's Profit & Loss account for two years:

DYES & CHEMICALS PVT. LTD.

PROFIT & LOSS ACCOUNT STATEMENT

(AMT IN RS)

		PREVIOUS YR	CURRENT YR
TOTAL REVENUE	:	1,64,740	65,900
COST OF GOODS SOLD	:	(91,020)	52,720
GROS PROFIT	:	73,720	13,180
ADMNSTRTIVE & SELLING EXPENSES	:	15,400	6,160
DEPRECIATION	:	30,000	28,000
OPERATING INCOME (EBIT)	:	28,320	(20,980)
INTEREST	:	(20,340)	(21,360)
EARNINGS BEFORE TAXES (EBT)	:	7,980	(42,340)
INCOME TAX PAYABLE	:	(1,600)	(0)
NET PROFIT	:	6,380	(42,340)

Just by making year-to-year comparisons, we will be able to glean some information that may lead us to important conclusions.

By comparing a particular year's for each of the four measures of profit – EBIT (Earnings Before Interest & Tax), EBT (Earnings Before Tax) and NPAT (Net Profit After Tax) – with those of earlier years, we can figure out in what areas the costs have escalated. Whether the direct product costs have to be analyzed for effecting reduction, or the adminstrative expenses need to be curbed, or the borrowings need to be restricted, etc., etc.

Marginal Analysis

The Profit & Loss Statement may be presented in another fashion for the sake of what is called the 'marginal' or 'contribution' analysis. This approach is based upon the assumption that the production cost (or 'cost of goods sold') is composed of two different kinds of costs – one, that is directly proportional to the volume of production and the other that is more or less fixed with respect to the volume of production. A little reflection will show that this reflection is only partly correct – often, a third type is also encountered which may be called the 'semi-variable' type of expenses. These expenses are characterized by the fact that while they do not remain exactly fixed with respect to the volume of production, they are not proportionately variable either; they only go up slightly if the level of production increases.

Examples of such types of expenses are: travelling & conveyance, advertisement & sales, promotion expenses, etc.

For purposes of marginal analysis, we bracket the semi-variable expenses with fixed expenses. But we should not lose sight of the fact that the total of fixed and semi-variable expenses remains more or less fixed at one level only over a certain limited range of production. If there is a quantum jump in production level, the fixed and semi-variable expenses also get raised to a higher level. The situation is depicted graphically here:

An income statement, in the marginal analysis format, for the same company – M/s Dyes & Chemicals Ltd. –is furnished below:

DYES & CHEMICALS PVT. LTD.

PROFIT & LOSS ACCOUNT STATEMENT
(MARGINAL ANALYSIS FORMAT)

(AMT IN RS)

	PREVIOUS YR	CURRENT YR
TOTAL REVENUE:	1,64,740	65,900
VARIABLE COSTS:	(52,670)	(36,300)
MARGINAL CONTRIBUTION:	1,12,070	29,600
FIXED COSTS:	83,750	50,580
OPERATING INCOME (EBIT):	28,320	(20,980)
INTEREST:	(20,340)	(21,360)
EARNINGS BEFORE TAXES (EBT):	7,980	(42,340)
INCOME TAX PAYABLE:	(1,600)	(0)
NET PROFIT:	6,380	(42,340)

Break-Even Sales

Once information is available in this format, we may also calculate the break-even level of sales – the level at which a unit is at the threshold of making profits. If it happens to be operating below the break-even level, then the marginal contribution from the unit's operations is not sufficient to cover the fixed costs. Once the sales level goes above the break-even level, the marginal contribution obtained from sales starts building up profits.

A simple formula for computation of break-even sales is:

B. E. Sales (in Rs) = [(Net Sales) × (Fixed & Semi-Variable Costs)] / Marginal Contribution

If both the variable and the fixed costs remain strictly variable and fixed respectively, then the value of break-even sales given by the formula would always be the same, no matter what value of net sales we start with. Since fixed costs have a tendency to move up a little bit, with jumps in the production level, the break-even point also shifts accordingly.

Funds Flow Statement

In the course of its operations, a company continually generates and uses, both short-term and long-term, funds. For instance, availing of loans from a bank, induction of capital, collection of bills and cash sales of finished products are sources of funds; as against that, purchasing items of fixed assets or raw materials, payment of interest and/or repayment of term loan installments to the bank and meeting day-to-day expenses are application of funds. Over a given period of time, the aggregate of sources of funds must match the aggregate of application of funds.

In order to figure out the flow of funds that took place over the period of the last balance sheet, we have to look at figures, both at the commencement and at the close of the year. Thus, an analysis of the figures for the last two successive years' balance sheets would disclose the movement of funds over the last accounting year.

The figure under each head of assets and liabilities in the last year's balance sheet has to be compared with its counterpart In the previous year's balance sheet for determining whether there has been an increase or decrease in its value over the accounting year period. A decrease in the value of an asset indicates generation of funds and an increase in its value, application of funds. In the case of liabilities, the opposite would apply – a decrease in the value of a liability indicates application of funds and an increase in the value, generation of funds.

There are two other sources of funds: one, net profit (operating income minus interest & income tax) in the Profit & Loss Statement; and two, non- cash charges – a write-down of the value of certain assets which does not involve cash payment but is treated as an accounting expense. Depreciation and amortization are the two most important categories of non-cash charges.

Depreciation is a non-cash charge that is deducted as an expense in the Profit & Loss Account, every year, in order to account for the wear and tear of the plant & machinery, equipment, etc., and build a buffer for their replacement in future. Amortization is very similar to depreciation – the only difference being that it does not apply to any fixed assets but only to intangible assets such as patents, trademarks, licenses, etc.

To sum it up, the sources and uses of funds emanate from:

Sources of Funds: 1) Decrease in Assets; 2) Increase in Liabilities; 3) Funds from Operations: Net Profit After Tax, Non-Cash Charges (such as Depreciation & Amortization)

Uses of Funds: 1) Increase in Assets; 2) Decrease in Liabilities Depending on its objective, a funds flow statement may be prepared in two ways: (i) based on measuring changes in cash; or (ii) based on measuring changes in net working capital.

A Funds Flow Statement under method (i) and another one under method (ii) are presented in the tables below:

CASH FLOW STATEMENT: COMPANY XYZ

Cash Flow From Operations (in Rs)	Current Year	Previous Year
Net earnings	65,900	164,740
Additions to cash		
Depreciations	28,000	30,000
Decrease in Accounts Receivable	21,940	25,300
Increase in Accounts Payable	-	52,500
Increase in Taxes Payable	-	4,500

PARTICULARS	AMT (RS)	AMT (RS)	CHANGES IN WORKING CAPITAL	
	CURRENT YEAR (IN RS)	PREVIOUS YEAR (IN RS)	INCREASE (IN RS)	DECREASE (IN RS)
A. CURRENT ASSETS:				
CASH & BANK BALANCES	20,500	9,200	11,300	0
INVENTORIES	75,000	42,500	32,500	0
TRADE RECEIVABLES	104,500	63,300	41,200	0
PREPAID EXPENSES	3,940	3,998	-	58
TOTAL (A)	**2,03,940**	**1,30,808**	**85,000**	**58**
B. CURRENT LIABILITIES				
ACCOUNT PAYABLE	7,000	4,000	5000	0
OUTSTANDING EXPENSES	10,183	8,333	2,000	0
TOTAL (B)	**17,183**	**12,333**	**7,000**	**0**
NET WORKING CAPITAL (A-B)	**186,757**	**118,475**	**-**	**-**
NET INCREASE IN WORKING CAPITAL	**68,282**			

Subtractions from Cash Increase in Inventory	(-)	60,500
Net Cash from Operations	1,15,840	2,16,540
Cash Flow from Investment in Equipment	-	(1,12,000)
Cash Flow from Financing	-	-
Cash Flow for Current Year	1,15,840	1,04,540

Statement of Changes in Working Capital

Cash Budgeting

While analyzing two successive years' balance sheets in terms of a funds flow statement does reveal the manner in which the movement of funds has taken place in the past one year, a company also needs to know its month-to- month cash requirements in the future. The exercise undertaken for this purpose is called cash budgeting. In case of drawing up a rehabilitation plan, cash budgeting assumes greater significance because release of funds by the financing branch to the unit has to be planned according to the cash budget projections.

The first step in drawing up the cash budget for a unit is to settle its monthly production plan. Next, all stipulations which have a bearing either on requirements of cash for the unit's operations or on receipt of cash by it, at the different stages of time, say at monthly intervals, are formulated and set on paper in quantitative terms. Based upon these, the month-wise cash requirement for the unit is computed, showing the expenses under appropriate heads. In the same fashion, month-wise projections of cash receipts are made under suitable heads. The difference between expected cash disbursal and cash receipt for a month gives the figure for cash deficit or cash surplus for that particular month, depending upon whether disbursal is more than receipt or the receipt is more than disbursal.

It would normally happen that during the initial months, the unit's level of operation being low, the cash deficit figure will go up. Gradually, as surpluses are generated, the cumulative cash deficit figure will start coming down. After it gets completely wiped out, any further accretion of surplus from operations would represent the 'net surplus' generated by the unit. It may be mentioned here that the surplus generation reflected in the cash budget is not the true surplus (which would get reflected as net profit in the unit's profit & loss account for the year) because non-cash charges like depreciation do not come into picture at all as far as the cash budget is concerned. For purposes of arriving at the accounting profit, however, these have to be taken into account.

The drawing up of cash budget is best illustrated through an example.

Example: M/s. Patna Instruments are to start production from 1st January, 1982. The production plan envisaged for the coming six months is as follows: January – 900 units; February – 1200 units; March – 1800 units; April – 2100 units; May – 2100 units; June – 2400 units. The selling price per unit is Rs 40 and the variable costs per unit of production are: Rs 8 for materials, Rs 12 for labour wages and Rs 4 for other expenses. The fixed expenses amount to Rs 15,000 per month. One-third of the aggregate sales in a month are expected to be for cash and the remaining on 1 month's credit. Expenses are payable in the month in which they are incurred, except for raw materials in whose case payment to the suppliers is made 1 month after purchase. The requirement for stocking of raw materials may be ignored.

CASH BUDGET FOR JANUARY TO JUNE, 1982

Production Plan:	Jan	Feb	Mar	Apr	May	Jun
Units	900	1200	1800	2100	2100	2400
Sale Value (Rs)	36000	48000	72000	84000	84000	96000
Requirements (Cash)						
1. Wages	10800	14400	21600	25200	25200	28800
2. Materials	-	7200	9600	14400	16800	16800
3. Expenses:						
a) Fixed	15000	15000	15000	15000	15000	15000
b) Variable	3600	4800	7200	8400	8400	9600
4. Total	29400	41400	53400	63000	65400	70200
Receipts (Cash)						
1. Cash Sales	12000	16000	24000	28000	28000	32000
2. Collection of Bills	-	24000	32000	48000	56000	56000
3. Total	12000	40000	56000	76000	81000	88000
Cash Deficit	17400	1,400	-	-	-	-
Cash Surplus	-	-	2600	13000	18600	17800
Cumulative Requirement	17400	18800	16200	3200	-	-
Surplus	-	-	-	-	15400	33200

PERSONAL BANKING (1988–1990)

This is my Note to the then Head of my Local Head Office (LHO) in response to the SBI Chairman's idea of setting up Personal Banking Centres in the metros and large cities.

A practice, very common in organizations, is to focus on matters relating to 'structure' almost to the exclusion of those relating to the 'process'. Thus, adding a new department or spinning off one from an older one, or 'reorganizing' the organization chart or, lately, defining the role sets and mouthing catchy phrases for 'corporate missions' are some of the most frequently encountered management solutions to problems of sub-optimal performance in organizations. However, rarely does one come across a management decision to look at the 'process' – where it is getting choked, what organizational factors are responsible for this, whether the process has become dysfunctional over the years, etc., etc. Where tinkering with the structure once or twice, or even thrice does not produce results, the remedy usually applied is – 'more of the same'.

In view of the above, it is refreshing indeed to find the Chairman's *DO* (Demi Official) letter mentioning that the Bank needs to not only create a new structure (Personal Banking Centres) but also set up a separate process. In my understanding, maintaining management focus on this would be key to the success of the suggestion.

Paragraph 6 of the DO letter pinpoints the exact tasks cut out for the proposed Personal Banking Centres (PB Centres): improving premises, décor, amenities and work-flow; arranging appropriate technology interventions; sharpening the selection and training processes; sizing up the industrial relations climate; instituting market intelligence and market research practices; and rejuvenating members of the staff so that innovation, product development and public relations come to be regarded as a part and parcel of an employee's offering to the organization in the form of service.

The crucial question is: How would the proposed PB Centres be able to deliver the goods when the same has not happened with the existing structures that have been in place for years?

Let us take an example.

Whenever the reasons for lack of motivation, on the part of some of our people, for making that extra ounce of efforts needed to get more business are discussed, an oft-heard comment is: "What extra are you going to give me if I work extra hard – an increase in pay or an out-of-turn promotion? If no, why should I make extra efforts? On the other hand, what can you take away from the shirker next door?"

The counter to this sort of argument simply is that in spite of the objective situation being as it is pointed out in the comment quoted above, there are some people (in every organization) who have an inner urge to excel. We need to focus on the *process* for spotting them, nurturing them, and positively stroking them whenever they produce results. The 'structure' (including rules and regulations, procedures, decision-making authority etc.) should be made subservient to the *process* rather than the other way round.

I would, therefore, venture to make the following suggestions for the proposed PB Centre:

a. It should strive to build a team and, then, promote a *team spirit* at the designated branch/branches. The first requirement for that would be to choose a leader. The touchstone for that (whether a certain person will be a good leader or not) would be: Does he have followers? The leader should have some say in selecting his team members. And, finally, there should be constant monitoring to separate the odd-man-out who might muddle the *process*.

b. It should also be made explicit that responsibility for the tasks already identified will be that of the team and not of any individual – both for success as well as failure.

c. In line with the concentration strategy, the task should be enunciated in brief – if possible, in just one line. A good example could be: "We'll ensure that no PB business, whatever the value, is driven away by any of us." At least in one urban branch, this is reported to have worked very well.

d. The team at the designated branches should be helped in evolving suitable supporting procedures such as: i) Every employee keeps the monthly performance budgeting figures at his desk; ii) After sending the weekly telegram on Friday, all employees, including the managers, discuss the performance figures, as well as any other matter relating to customer service/business development impinging upon them; iii) Before the branch manager prepares the draft budget or goes to the Regional Manager (RM) for settlement of the final budget, he discusses the figures, again, with everyone and tries to arrive at a consensus.

e. Supporting procedures also need to be evolved at the module level. For instance, generally there is considerable inhibition about permitting overdrafts to PB customers. Time has come for the forward and backward linkages between PB loans and PB deposits to be appreciated by us and such inhibitions are shed.

f. In instituting marketing, the common perception that it has more to do with collection of quantitative rather than qualitative information from the market-place must be disabused.

g. Another good idea is to have a system for investigating unexpected successes in order to understand how to exploit an opportunity. Quite often, a case of unexpected success is a symptom of some structural/systematic changes taking place in the market which might very well present an opportunity to innovate in product development or market segmentation. (A case in point is the unexpected growth in aggregate PB deposits of a Circle contributed mostly by non- divisionalized branches.) Likewise, the significant success stories at branches should be documented for 'organizational learning'.

h. In marketing again, the niche approach may be quite useful. For instance: Identify the pockets of concentration of NRIs in the area; send a letter, along with an account opening form and a pay-in-slip, to the NRIs abroad; arrange for introduction, after receiving the account opening forms, to be done through the NRI's local contact; etc.

i. Another approach could be: Start an aggressive campaign for weaning away a certain class of people from postal money order to demand drafts.

(July 19, 1988)

BANKING IN THE U.S.: A STRATEGIC PERSPECTIVE (1991–1995)

Commercial banking has undergone a fundamental change in the U.S. That the days of bricks-and-mortar banking are over is a truism here these days.

Two things have happened. One, with the process of disintermediation taking hold, the larger corporate customers have all moved away from banks; and two, technology has become the most critical element in the strategic planning process for banks. In fact, technology has become so important that it has become *a* – if not *the* – business of banking.

The future seems to hold the promise of accelerating change – something that may alter commercial banking – as we have known it – in fundamental ways. The Savings & Loan (S&L) debacle has let loose the forces of over- regulation upon commercial banks and the pendulum has swung in the opposite direction – from under-regulation in the eighties (with the number of supervisors slashed and the capital adequacy rules given a go-by), to over- regulation now.

But a regulatory chokehold is not the answer. For, there is a fundamental problem involved here which, once again, is being shoved under the carpet. The problem is the government's guarantee to the depositor that his/her deposit in the bank is *risk-free*. Which it isn't – and cannot be – so long as the businesses that banks indulge in are not risk-free.

While the popular perception is that the S&L Crisis was largely the result of fraud and greedy wrongdoing, studies have shown that no more than ten to fifteen percent of the losses can be attributed to this factor. Public policy directly contributed to the brewing crisis by promising the moon – deposit insurance. It became an instrument that cut both ways. The depositor was tempted to put his money at the bank that offered the highest return, without the fear of ever losing any part of it; and, in turn, the S&L banker had to go out and finance the riskiest of ventures in order to be able to pay that high return to the depositor.

Regulatory oversight can help only up to a certain extent. However, regulators cannot underwrite risk; nor can they manage the beast. Risk is best managed by the entity that takes it – in this case, the banks.

But in order to be induced to do that, their operations must be made subject to discipline. Experience shows that the only discipline that works is the market discipline. Bank regulators cannot perform that job because: one, they neither have the expertise nor can they get too much involved in it; two, as public officials charged with the responsibility of ensuring the safety and soundness of banks, their focus is on pressuring the banks to *minimize*, rather than *manage*, the risk; and three, even if their diagnosis turns out to be right, there is no way to copy the market mechanism's quick response to events as evident in the stock price movements.

If the deposits of the failed S&Ls had not been insured, before putting their money the depositors would have insisted on having accurate financial data on them. They would have known that they needed to measure the risk associated with their investment decision, much as they do when they invest money in stocks or bonds, or in mutual funds.

Future Directions

Therefore, the suggestions for reform that have been made are based upon the premise of extending the market mechanism to the banking industry. One suggestion would have the banks split themselves up into two different entities – one, termed Monetary Services Companies (MNCs), whose deposits (largely checking accounts) would be insured but who would also have the obligation to invest only in safe, liquid assets such as government or quasi-government paper; and the second, a commercial banking institution whose deposits would not be insured.

The latter's assets would be funded out of either uninsured deposits or commercial paper, just as finance companies are funded today, and it would thus remain under the market discipline. The MNCs would be subject to strict regulatory supervision in order to ensure that they are investing only in the permissible safe assets, and not lending to their parents and affiliates. The burden of regulatory supervision would be substantially reduced for the latter class of banks.

Commercial banking may thus be moving close to investment banking.

Even such a momentous transformation of commercial banking looms on the horizon, the business of investment banking is booming. The small-cap, over- the-counter (OTC) stock exchange NASDAQ, for instance, is growing by leaps and bounds. Its daily volume was over 317 million shares at a value of

$6.5 billion in the first quarter of 1994, second only to New York Stock Exchange's (NYSE's) 321 million shares valued at $11.0 billion. It has steadily gained trading volume share from NYSE. Between 1983 and 1993, NYSE's share in the volume of shares traded declined from 54.5% to 48.5% even as NASDAQ's increased from 40.2% to 48.2%.

NASDAQ is all set to acquire new technology at a cost of $180 million – a technology that will give traders the increased functionality, speed, capacity and capability and enable it to meet the future requirements by increasing its capacity five-fold. It will afford traders the freedom to design individualized- screen displays for NASDAQ data while plugging real time data into other analytic programs.

Already, the NASDAQ system has revolutionized trading in the US. Today, a NASDAQ trader can, sitting In his bedroom, participate as actively in the securities market as anyone on Wall Street. The coming marriage between computers and communication, the so-called "information highway", will add more breadth and depth to the operations of the OTC exchange. In combination with the on-rushing globalization wave, experts say, a few years down the line this will result in a virtually global integration of the securities industries.

For commercial banks, of course, that translates into more bumps ahead on the road, more change. For one, it would bring home banking within the realm of possibilities. For another, even those corporates that do not have access to the capital market, and are dependent on loans from a commercial bank today, will gain it tomorrow. Commercial banks would increasingly find themselves losing their traditional markets to the investment banks.

The Bond of Technology

In fact, this is already happening. Today, technology is being used as the engine for spawning strategies in all the different areas of a bank's functioning. More than anything else, it provides the bonds for integrating the same.

A telemarketing strategy, for instance, would be decided upon depending on what technology is available and has been set up. Bank of America (BoA) is currently offering a "Seven-Minute Auto Loan Program" to consumers – it guarantees that within seven minutes of a customer hanging up his telephone after furnishing the required information to a BoA loan processing officer, a decision would be conveyed.

Also, the most successful commercial banks today are those that have been getting into more and more non-traditional areas. Home banking (giving the customer the facility to operate on his bank account without moving out of home – via the much-touted "information superhighway") is still some way off in the future. Some banks have, however, started harvesting technology they had developed for in-house use. Others are leveraging technology for achieving quantum jumps in productivity and/or customer satisfaction. Here are some examples.

Huntington Bankshares' Huntington Treasury Management Company provides image capture technology for services such as cheque clearing, cash management, etc. to more than 4,000 banking clients. Its services are more efficient as well as cost-effective because it has the Sun Microsystems hardware to take advantage of high volumes.

Huntington Bankshares itself has invested over $10 million in the Personal Banker Automation System so as to achieve a "non-negotiable" standard of customer service. Even during non-traditional banking hours (between 5 pm and 6 am, Monday through Friday, and all day long during weekends).

Secrets of Success

The secret of success for banks these days is the "cross-sell ratio" – the average number of products per customer. The higher the ratio, the more advantageous that bank's position becomes. Hence the race to get into more and more products, and generates higher volumes – with the aid of technology.

Firstar Information Services Corp provides an array of services including customer processing, deposit processing, cheque processing, savings and general ledger services as well as consultation. SunTrust Service Corp provides back-office operations, ATMs and cheque processing for its 34 affiliates.

Fifth Third Bancorp's Midwest Payments Systems subsidiary, which is now the third largest provider of electronic funds transfer services in the US, contributes substantially to the former's fee income.

The non-bank banks have also invaded the preserve of banks. Thus, Sears, Roebuck the department store retailing giant, also sells credit cards, insurance, real estate broking, home mortgages and other financial services. Since the non-banks are not subject to the same regulations as the banks, they enjoy an enormous advantage.

As a result, banks are now into all sorts of things as well. Traditional banking is out, *new banking* is in.

Leading banks are already making most of their money from fee-based income. Thus, last year, fee income accounted for 70.6% of the earnings for Bankers Trust, 68.2% for JP Morgan, 62.9% for First Chicago, 50.9% for MBNA Corp, 57.6% for Continental Bank, 51.8% for Citicorp, etc.

The *fee incomes* are coming not only from currency operations, derivatives, cash management, mergers & acquisitions, portfolio management & advising, and custody services but increasingly more from selling technology – providing services to customers, deposit and cheque processing, home banking, imaging, etc. Also from equity research, infrastructure leasing, factoring, venture capital and mezzanine finance.

The trend towards *bank sales of mutual funds* is well established and growing. As of September, 1993, mutual fund assets were at $1.9 trillion and, within a couple of years, are expected to overtake retail bank deposits.

How US Banks Organize Themselves

In the US, retail banking operations are organized truly on the lines of industry. Typically, a bank would have centralized Marketing, Sales, Production, Escrow or Documentation, and Collection departments for, let us say, the residential mortgage business in the Southern California district. The departments are not located in the same place – Marketing may be located in Los Angeles, Production in San Diego, Escrow in Anaheim.

Marketing and Sales would have target for applications aggregating, say, $1 billion in a year. They solicit and procure applications from prospective home buyers on pre-qualification basis, and forward the same by overnight mail to Production.

Production does the processing, including obtaining credit reports and checking other credentials of the applicant, and then either sanctioning or rejecting the loan. If the loan is approved, they also negotiate the terms therefor (a bank may be offering ten different variations of the same basic scheme – adding a "point" here or subtracting one there, based upon combinations of instalment payments, start-up period, concessional – "teaser" – rate of interest during the first six months, etc.) and forward the paper to Escrow or Documentation.

Escrow or Documentation arranges for execution of documents, escrow closing, and disbursement of the loan. It also ensures that all the terms of the sale, as between the buyer and the seller, have been met.

In the midst of all these activities, the role of the bank branch concerned is limited to providing the services to its customers as well as to the various departments involved.

The advantages of having such an organization structure, obviously, are: one, efficiency in operations because of the division of work, consequent specialization, and virtual automation of the work of data collection and decision-making aided, of course, by computerized processing; and two, a separation of the various functions among different individuals located in different departments, which makes for relative impartiality in decision- making. Both are extremely important to ensuring compliance with the various consumer laws and regulatory requirements while maintaining the standards of customer service, and yet remain cost-effective enough to face the competition's challenge.

This is also the best way perhaps to organize a bank for tackling volumes. Which is what retail banking is all about – its chief characteristic is not the products but the process. Retail banking requires a bank to set up processes that would let all the branches know, and replicate, what has succeeded at one or two branches, and shun what has not. The process therefore has to be organized around frequent sharing of experience among different units, and constant evolution of techniques and standardization of systems and procedures.

And Where We Stand

Our strategy in the US, as in other foreign centres, has been niche marketing at best, and a 'muddled', or no, strategy at worst.

Retail Banking

In a market where the banks thrive on designing and introducing ever new products, and expanding into all sorts of markets (the newest concept being "supermarket banks" (a bank counter at the local food and drug superstore offering many retail banking services), we are content with displaying in our windows age-old products – take it or leave it!

Hamstrung by the small size of our operations, we have shied away from true retail banking operations (auto loans, investment management & trust services, residential mortgages, home equity lines, credit cards, etc.). The perceived risk, presumably, being this: what if the systemic risk turns out to be overwhelming in case we are unable to achieve the minimum volumes?

But that precisely is the problem: we can't start reaping the benefits unless we reach a certain minimum size, and play the game by its rules.

First and foremost, we must establish the right systems & procedures for evaluating performance and recognizing merit; and next, for dealing with business risk as a mature corporate citizen.

Second, we must develop a strategy for being the right size in the right market. The 'growth strategy' we have followed all along – start from the scratch, grow at a snail's pace if ever, and all the while rely only upon eighteenth century products and a narrow market niche, with only generalists steeped in Indian banking leading the charge – will always remain a wishful dream.

If we mean business, we will have to grow by acquisition, and be of a certain minimum size – with a local business base.

Probably, it will involve taking some risks, but there is no reason why we cannot learn to set up proper systems and procedures (like the other international banks have done) that will help us make informed product- market decisions through measurement of risks involved and evolve a decision-making structure, and system, that behoves a mature organization. Right now, our methods of risk assessment itself are archaic, and not designed for the marketplace in which we are operating.

That seems to be the only way we can overcome the fundamental problem of 'size' and 'risk'.

The 'Wholesale' Arena

We have been somewhat more comfortable playing the 'wholesale' market game, but have neither the financial muscle nor the risk-taking ability to make a go of it. We have even shied away from developing expertise in the sunrise areas on account of our risk-averseness.

Here we have operated on the fringes, at best. While we have been doing rudimentary money market & currency operations, we have not ventured into securitized assets, mezzanine finance, leasing, factoring, interest rate swaps & other derivatives, treasury investments, venture capital finance, etc.

In the circumstances, we can do no better than offering traditional banking services to the two natural market niches – the ethnic Indian population, and the India-related business segment.

We have thus almost become an island, doing banking Indian-style, in the most competitive, and technologically advanced, market in the world today.

We have on offer the same products (commercial loans to the middle and low markets, letters of credit, collection of non-L/C bills, remittances, etc.) to the identified market niches as we do in India – and upon much the same terms.

The norms that we normally stipulate could be lifted straight out of our Indian textbook. We are so much out of touch with the ways of U.S. banking that that the structuring of our loans has become counter-productive. Rather than granting two separate loans secured by separate collaterals, we have carried to the U.S. the practice of granting loans on a mixed collateral basis (a charge on inventory and receivables, plus a mortgage, say on the guarantor's residential property for the same loan). But under U.S. laws and practice, enforcing such a mixed security is both a cumbersome process and entails far more risk than is realized. It will also presume a certain minimum volume to be handled. Likewise, we do not fully comprehend the risks associated with asset-based lending in a developed market like the U.S. Asset-based lending has to be a much more involved exercise here, with proper organizational gearing-up being pre-requisite to it. Yet we have gone ahead with granting of such loans on the lines which these loans are structured in India.

As a result, while examining our operations, the regulators have of late begun to articulate what amount to an expression of "culture shock" – a wide hiatus between our practices and norms, and those obtaining at American banks.

Our collateral-based approach actually translates into foot-dragging when action is called for, as opposed to the U.S. banker's matter-of-fact, strictly professional, approach. Where a local banker would not hesitate in calling up a loan, we tend to give a much longer rope to the borrower. Where the regulators expect us to be aggressive in quantifying the weaknesses and providing for the risks involved in problem loans, we tend to do the opposite for fear that "accountability-fixing" will have to be done.

And the name of the "accountability-fixing" game is: finding the most convenient peg on which to hang the blame for a failure. While one little procedural lapse may be enough for fixing the blame on some, others get away with murder because "nothing can be proved against them". Hardly ever is an attempt at finding out the "batting average" for people is made.

Our (ethnic Indian) borrowers have mostly carried the practice of poor organization from back home – that is, working without either a well- formulated business plan of action, or technology-driven operations, or an up-to-date accounting and financial management system.

A certain bias against specialization in our organization thwarts formulation and adoption of new products. That perhaps explains our inability even to properly research the small niche market that we have identified for ourselves, and come up with new product or service offerings.

As mentioned earlier, we have yet to think of building up expertise in any sunrise area like trust & investment services, currency operations, interest rate swaps, business advisory services on India, etc.

For a shrewd businessman, an economic downturn is perhaps the best time to buy properties. But we have no expertise in real estate appraisal, in the buying and selling of properties, and in a property's income generating capacity, so we cannot evaluate whether or not a given proposal involves more than an acceptable level of risk.

At a time when world trade is fast changing, and many large, international companies are no longer transacting business with their counter-parties through L/Cs (in order to save the substantial cost involved), we are clinging to the same old products. While other banks straightaway offer "supply bill" type of financing to their corporate customers across national boundaries, what we offer, at best, is a bills discounting facility (which requires an underlying L/C, and its attendant costs).

We do not enter or exit particular industries after appropriate industry-risk evaluation, as banks in the US and other developed countries do very often.

Above all, our system is geared to supporting the philosophy of low volume, low risk, low losses, low profits; theirs is wedded to booking high profits by taking risks, going after volumes, employing right technology, innovating new product offerings and, in the end, making adequate provisions.

What Needs to be Done

First of all, we need to correct some of the organizational and strategic deficiencies alluded to earlier – those relating to minimum size of operations, performance evaluation, procedures for dealing with 'risk', the bias against 'specialization', etc. The "common thread" (between the existing and the new product-market) analysis points up the direction we need to take with regard to the future products and markets. We need to develop capabilities, looking for a pay-off over the long term.

Now may be just the right time to do so, since the opening up of the Indian economy provides us with a great opportunity. It also provides us with a readymade common thread and synergy in our niche markets.

The world over, the trend is towards *disintermediation*. Privatization is in full swing in China, the former Soviet Union, Eastern Europe and Latin America. Western investors are investing directly in the form of equity in these emerging markets. During the 12-month period ended March, 1994, assets in the emerging market mutual funds in the US increased from $918 million to $6.7 billion. Moody's estimate that East Asia alone will need $1 trillion over the next six years.

The balance of power, in the meantime, is shifting in favour of *investment banking*. In the US, the process will be further aided by the regulatory assault on commercial banks, thrifts and savings & loans.

Since developing countries are likely to grow faster, the investors will get higher returns from their investments in those countries than what they will get from investments in US companies. The *flow of capital* is, therefore, likely to be from the US (and other developing countries) to countries like India. In fact, in certain knowledgeable quarters, already an apprehension is being expressed that increasingly it is in the marketplace of these emerging countries that the terms on which investors anywhere in the world would be willing to invest money would be decided.

It is therefore time we geared ourselves up for taking advantage of the emerging situation. Several merchant bankers from Europe and the US have already set up shop in India for doing portfolio investments. With our close contact in the ethnic India community in the US, we could do good business by *channeling their investments into Indian companies*.

At the same time, powerful social forces are at work; as many as 104 of a total of 1300 stockbrokers of a securities firm based in Southern California were found to be ethnic Indians, and another 82, Filipino-Americans.

Such a high representation of ethnic Asians (in particular, Indians), which is out of all proportion to their share in the local population, is indicative of the fact that *ethnic markets* have emerged as an important segment of the stockbrokerage business – because there is enough money sitting with the ethnic Indian (and Filipino) population in the US, waiting to be tapped for financial planning and investment. And, to have advisers who can educate him about the way things happen in the marketplace.

With India opening up to foreign investors, the scope for offering several other *new services in the wholesale domain has vastly improved:* floatation of Floating Rate Notes on behalf of Indian companies (for raising long-term funds) in the US market; reverse tie-ins, such as *teaming up with a merchant banker in the US, to set up a mutual fund programme* for portfolio investment in India; setting up *facilities for US Exim Bank-guaranteed securitized import financing programme* for the bank's own clients (a $116 million such programme, supported by our bank's guarantee at the Indian end, was reportedly set up by the Bank of New York recently for Essar Gujarat); fee- based services like *India Acquaintance Seminars* for US company executives planning to set up ventures in India; *liaison work* between US citizens and companies interested in doing business with India on the one hand, and their Indian counter-parts on the other; *equity research* in India capital market & advising; *custodial services for US companies' portfolio investments* in India; evolving a *uniform authority- and decision-making structure for loans to Indian corporations* having subsidiaries/offices abroad such that a request for, say, clean working capital facilities required by the subsidiary in the US could be quickly decided upon.

Corporate Strategy

Formulating corporate strategy amounts to choosing a pattern of objectives, purposes or goals and major policies and plans for deploying the resources and achieving the goals.

The strategy statement defines what business the company is in, who its customers are and what they value the most. The goal is a long-term development of the enterprise by matching opportunity and corporate capability at an acceptable level of risk. When faced with a strategic problem, seeking solutions in operating and administrative changes is not of much help.

In formulating strategy for a business, it is useful to establish a "common thread" – a relationship between present and future product-markets in order to have a clear grasp of where the company is headed. This common thread may be either in technology or in similarity of needs. Strategic change is nothing but a realignment of a company's product-market scope.

A company may plan for either an expansion or a diversification strategy for growth. There are four different strategies based on a product-market matrix: Market Penetration (existing product, existing mission), Product Development (new product, existing mission), Market Development (existing product, new mission), and Diversification (new product, new mission).

Diversification is more drastic – and riskier, too – because it involves a simultaneous departure from familiar products and familiar markets.

Again, depending upon the related-ness of the customer and the technology, four kinds of diversification are possible: Horizontal Diversification (same type of product, related or unrelated technology); Vertical Diversification (firm as its own customer, related or unrelated technology); Concentric Diversification (similar type of product, related or unrelated technology); and Conglomerate Diversification (new type of product, unrelated technology).

Whether it is the expansion or the diversification strategy that should be pursued will depend on the competitive advantage likely to be conferred on the company in the event of its implementation – such as, a commanding position in the new industry or a "breakthrough" product which obsoletes previously available products.

More importantly, search for the common thread must look inward at the synergy available within the company – its ability to make good on a new product-market entry. The resulting common thread may be aggressive, requiring that new entries make use of an outstanding competence possessed by the company (say, a nationwide network of branches, or leadership in computer applications to banking), or it may be defensive, requiring that the new entries supply some key competence which the company lacks (say, capabilities in sunrise products like forex derivatives, M&A, mezzanine finance, transactions processing, etc.), or it may be a combination of both.

Synergy is particularly useful in charting out growth areas in an industry whose boundaries are ill-defined and changing, which certainly applies to the baking industry.

In today's more dynamic business environment, strategy must also be dynamic. The strategic process in such an environment has been likened to an interactive videogame, as opposed to the earlier metaphor of chess.

The essence of strategy, according to this view, is not the structure of a company's products and markets but the dynamics of its behavior.

Competitive success depends on transforming key processes into strategic capabilities. The capabilities themselves are created by making strategic investments in a support infrastructure that links together traditional Strategic Business Units (SBUs) and functions.

Capability is a set of business processes strategically understood.

Capabilities-based competitors identify their key business processes, manage them centrally, and invest in them heavily, looking for a long-term payback.

Example is given of Walmart's "cross-docking" system in which goods are continuously delivered to the discount retailer's warehouses, where they are selected, repacked, and then dispatched to stores, often without ever sitting in inventory. The inventory and handling costs are t making possible the everyday low prices.

But cross-docking is extremely difficult to manage. To make cross-docking work, Walmart has to make strategic investments in a variety of interlocking support systems far beyond what could be justified by conventional ROI criteria. A private satellite-communication system that daily sends point-of- sale data directly to Walmart's 4,000 vendors is just one of them.

STRESSED ASSETS MANAGEMENT (2004–2006)

UPCCL Story

Originally, a State Government undertaking, UP State Cement Corporation Ltd. (UPCCL) had been closed for 10 years and was under liquidation. The High Court Judge, Mr. Sunil Ambwani, a no-nonsense judge of unimpeach-able integrity, had entrusted the task of carrying out sale of the Company's assets to an Asset Sale Committee comprising of the Official Liquidator and the State Government representative. Bypassing the Official Liquidator and the High Court, however, the State Government had gone ahead and completed the process of inviting bids, opening the offers and declaring the lone qualifying bidder, Grasim's bid as successful. Not only that, it had sugar-coated the deal by offering several concessions, such as waiving licence fee for the captive mines, permitting sales tax dues to be written off, etc., to the successful bidder. According to one estimate, the value of concessions given amounted to Rs 900 cr.

The Judge threw the Government approval out and ordered re-tendering, with the condition that all the concessions offered by the Government earlier will apply. He entrusted the task to a reconstituted Asset Sale Committee (ASC), with representatives of IDBI and SBI being included as members this time.

Members of the reconstituted ASC, however, had no idea about how asset sale should be conducted and had a fixation about two points mentioned in the order of the High Court Judge: one, that the reserve price should be Rs 271 cr (arrived at by adding the price of a subsequently-discovered asset, valued at Rs 30 crore, to the Grasim offer of Rs 241 cr that the State Government had declared as successful earlier); and two, that it was to be "sale as a going concern" and therefore the norms stipulated by the Government of India for disinvestment should be applicable.

In the very first meeting, I disabused the ASC members on this (with my comments appearing in the Minutes of Meeting (MOM)) and also made a representation to the Court, through the Bank's lawyer, on both counts. I argued that the Hon'ble High Court's mandate was for maximizing realization from sale of the Company's assets; so, the minimum reserve price of Rs 271 crore should not be a limiting factor for such realization.

And secondly, the minimum reserve price of Rs 271 crore was based on the Grasim offer of Rs 241 crore which, as the Hon'ble High Court's Order itself had made clear, was based *not on the estimated value of the Company's assets but, primarily, on the liabilities it owed to the financial institutions, banks and its own staff.* The amount offered was just 4.4% more than the total liabilities of Rs 230 crore.

Therefore, the minimum reserve price of Rs 271 crore stipulated by the Hon'ble High Court should be taken more as an indicative number (based on the limited information then available) below which any offer could not be accepted. It did not mean that even if a reserve price higher than this could be realized, it would be precluded on account of the Hon'ble High Court's stipulation of Rs 271 crore as the minimum reserve price.

And, finally, the only valuation report on record was one by a government- approved valuer. I pointed out that this Report valued the land, building, plant & machinery, automobiles, raw materials, etc. of the Company's three units but left out what was perhaps the most valuable asset of the Company – its mining rights.

I therefore argued that a fresh valuation of the Company's assets be carried out and a transparent process of sale of assets, designed to ensure maximum realization, stipulated. This would involve preparation of a Preliminary Information Memorandum, finalization of advertisement inviting expressions of interest, short-listing of interested parties, preparation of a detailed Confidential Information Memorandum, facilitating due diligence on the Company's assets by the bidders, calling for and evaluating final bids, valuation of Company's assets and fixing of a reserve price, selecting the best offer, preparing a draft Sale Agreement (after discussion with the winning bidder), etc.

The High Court Judge, Mr. Ambwani, was very supportive and my exertions resulted in a grand success – as against the earlier offer of Rs 241 crore from Grasim, the Company received the highest bid of Rs 459 crore from Jaypee Associates – reputably, the second highest bid in the history of High Court-supervised liquidation and sale of assets in the country at that time. I also marshaled such arguments and put in place such mechanisms that the High Court approved a total payment of Rs 32 crore, from out of the sale price of Rs 459crore, to SBI even though the SBI Board had approved an OTS (One Time Settlement) for Rs 14 crore some 5 years back.

J K Group Companies Story

The J K Group was – and still is – one of the well-known industrial conglomerates of India. As on April 7, 2005, SBI's total exposure (fund-based and non-fund-based) to the Group was Rs 388.44 crore, excluding investment (Rs 20.51 crore) and leasing (Rs 10.47 crore). At that time, SBI's Stressed Assets Management Branch (SAMB), Lucknow had exposure to 3 companies of the Group: J.K. Synthetics Ltd., J.K. Dairy & Foods Ltd. and J.K. Cotton Ltd. All their loans had turned non-performing assets (NPAs).

At that time, J.K. Dairy & Foods Ltd. had, for the last 10 years, been enjoying a Cash Credit limit of Rs 4.20 crore from SBI, and Rs. 7.80 cr from two other public sector banks without any personal guarantees from promoter- directors. Its Tangible Net Worth (TNW) had turned negative on account of heavy losses incurred over the last two years.

In November 2004, we were able to achieve a milestone in the case of J.K. Synthetics Ltd. – the *highest-ever one-time, single-account recovery in the annals of banks in India* Here is a photograph of the cheque of *Rupees Eight Thirty Million Six Hundred Sixty Thousand Six Hundred Thirty Five* submitted by the Company to SBI, SAMB (Stressed Assets Management Branch), Lucknow Branch through which a recovery of Rs 81.36 crore was made on 6 November, 2004:

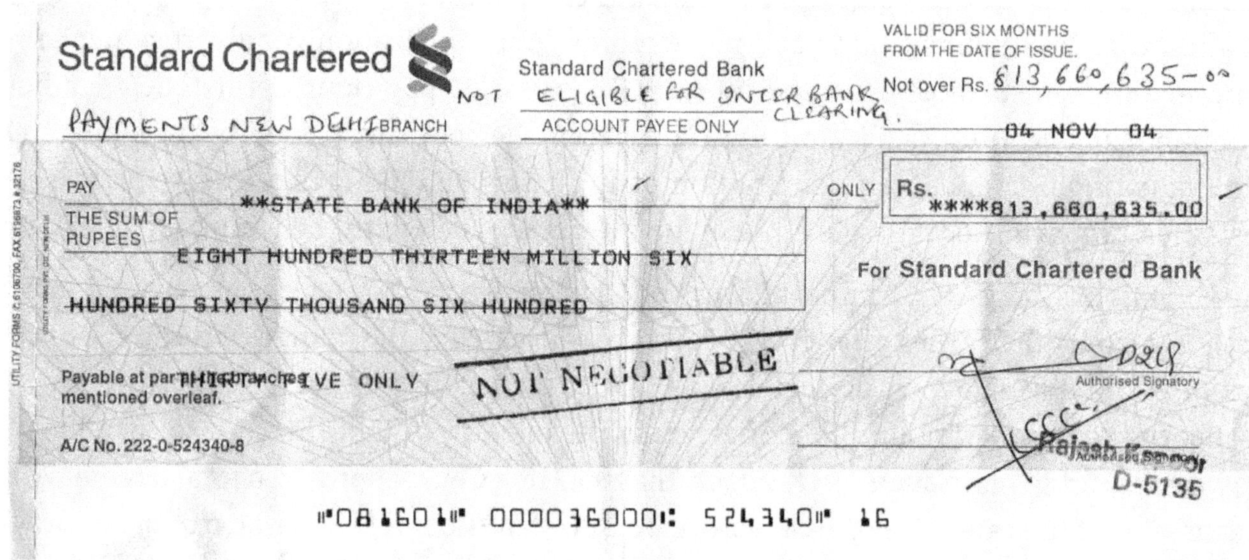

The Company had made a reference to the Board of Industrial & Financial Reconstruction (BIFR) for financial rehabilitation / restructuring, to which we had filed our objections (even though other members of the consortium did not) on the following grounds: (a) Repayment of installments/ interest on unsecured loans taken from associates, while dues of secured creditors remained unpaid; (b) Interest on long-term loans not being reflected in the balance sheet; (c) Non-inclusion of the advance money received against Preference Shares (Rs 1.51 cr) in TNW; (d) Substantial increase in miscellaneous expenses over the last five years; and (e) Cost of production being higher than the industry average.

The Company gave a point by point reply to all our objections.

At the onset of the lean season when outstanding in the account had come down to Rs 1.54 crore, a *decision to freeze the drawing power and not allow any further drawings in the account* was taken by the loan-originating branch (Commercial Branch, Mooradabad) on the ground that the promoters had withdrawn themselves from the directorship of the Company and the Company's financials had become very weak, with TNW turning negative.

The Company submitted a settlement-cum-restructuring proposal to IDBI Bank envisaging restructuring of the principal amount of Rs 17.65 cr based on:

(1) issue of zero-coupon preference shares (Rs 3.53 cr); (2) issue of zero- coupon convertible preference shares (Rs 1.77 cr); (3) issue of equity shares at par (Rs 3.53 cr); and (4) two term loans (repayable over 3 and 7 years respectively) aggregating Rs 8.82 cr with varying rate of interest over the period such that they give a yield to maturity (YTM) of 8.50%, overall. This would have led to the Company's TNW turning positive.

I sent a team of Restructuring Cell officials to the loan-originating branch for detailed discussions, with the branch officials, on all aspects of the case. After getting inputs from my team officials, I re-examined the facts and held discussions with both the Company, as well as the loan-originating branch, officials. This led me to the conclusion that we had gone overboard in ordering a clampdown on drawing power in the loan account; the Company's situation perhaps did not merit that.

The consequences of the clampdown had *not* been positive for SBI, either. Since no other bank in the consortium had imposed the drawing power (DP) restriction, the Company started routing all its sale proceeds only through their other bank accounts – and none from the SBI account. This turned their loan in our bank into a non-performing asset (NPA) even as loans of other banks remained "Standard". A Cost-Benefit Analysis of the decision to freeze the outstanding amount in loan account is presented below.

Cost-Benefit Analysis

Costs:

- Since freezing of the outstanding loan amount, we had not recovered any interest;
- The account had turned NPA ("Doubtful" category), so we had to make a provision for Rs 1.54 crore;
- We had also been losing the exchange/ commission income from the account;
- Since the Company had stopped routing transactions through our account, we were unable to exercise any control over it.

Benefits:

- The only 'benefit' from freezing the outstanding amount in the loan account had presumably been restricting the Bank's exposure to the Company.

In the face of other banks in the consortium not going along with us and the unit's performance showing visible improvements, it was clear that continuing with this policy would be counter-productive for us. But, in the aftermath of the decision, toeing the same line had acquired a momentum of its own. Thus, in the face of an Advance Value of Security (our share) of Rs 5.19 crore and a Drawing Power of Rs 4.20 crore (as per the last stock statement), the financing branch averred that "unless the Company has a long-term strategy regarding the repayment of term liabilities, any increment in the present exposure at this juncture might jeopardize the bank's interest."

The Branch also put up a proposal to its Zonal Office recommending "approval for freezing the outstanding amount at Rs 1.54 crore", and the latter approved the same with the following stipulation: "Explore possibilities for obtention of good tangible security before recommending increase in exposure."

For quite some time, though, my view had been that continuing with the freeze on drawing power would not be in the best interests of the Bank. The analytical details that supported my view were:

a. As per the calculation of Commercial Branch Mooradabad, based on stock statement dated 28.02.05, the value of paid stocks was Rs 19.76 crore, after deducting the amount of Rs 5.93 lac owed to creditors (including milk creditors). The Drawing Power (DP) for the consortium thus worked out to Rs 12.00 crore, out of which our bank's share (at 35%) worked out to Rs 4.20 crore. Therefore, the argument that the drawing power computed after deducting the amount payable to "milk creditors" was not sufficient for allowing drawings up to the limit sanctioned to the Company was proven to be wrong.

b. The Company also advised us that "the commitment of the Promoters to the Company remained intact and there had been no dilution in their equity-holding, which had stood at 57.57 % since inception." They had also "funded losses of Rs 5.52 crore" by way of Inter-Corporate Deposits (ICDs) of Rs 1.93 cr and Preference Shares of Rs 3.59 cr. The Promoters had to resign from the directorship of the Company for technical reasons. Since the Company had defaulted in payment of its obligations to the debenture-holders, if they had continued to be on the Board they would have become ineligible for being on the Board of other group companies in terms of Section 274 (1)(g)(B) of the Companies Act 1956.

(Rs in crore)

				April-Dec (9 M)	
	2001–02	2002–03	2003–04	2003–04	2004–05
Net Sales	55.27	68.92	88.67	56.31	56.87
PBDIT	-1.49	1.72	2.08	-1.44	0.52
Cash Profit	-2.99	0.37	0.74	-2.46	-0.53
PBT	-6.03	-1.08	-0.95	-3.6	-1.54

c. The Company's performance had improved substantially over the last two years, as shown in the table above:

If the Rehabilitation Scheme submitted by the Company to IDBI was implemented, the Company's TNW would turn positive.

Since freezing of the drawing power (and the outstanding amount in the loan account), our bank had not made any headway – either in terms of regularizing the loan account, or bringing it back to health, or in terms of initiating recovery proceedings against the borrower. In fact, we could not initiate any legal action for recovering our dues, simply because the Company was a BIFR case and, in terms of Sec.22 of SICA, we were prevented from taking any legal action.

In order to break the stalemate, I held two meetings at my office with the Director of the Company, Shri Girish Sharma, and asked him to address the Bank's two major concerns arising from: one, Promoters relinquishing themselves from the post of directors and two, not agreeing to give their personal guarantees for the loan.

Shri Sharma's response was placid. He said that since the Company had defaulted in payment of its obligations to the debenture-holders, if Promoters had continued to be on the Board, in terms of Section 274 (1)(g)(B) of the Companies Act 1956, they would have become ineligible to remain on the Board of other group companies; and secondly, as a matter of policy, the Promoters had not given their personal guarantees to any bank in respect of the loans taken by any group companies – including an exposure of Rs 384 crore taken by the Bank's Corporate Accounts Group (CAG) Branch, Kolkata.

We persisted with our argument and said that, in such a case, the Company should consider giving us some other comfort. We suggested that, since the Company would need to avail of withdrawals over and above the frozen level only during the peak period, it should give us some fixed deposits at least for the period of such withdrawals. Shri Sharma said that he would check on this matter with the Promoters and get back to us.

In the next meeting, it was conveyed to us that the Promoters had agreed to give Inter-Company Deposits (ICDs) of Rs 1.00 crore to cover the peak period of 3 months during which withdrawals from the loan account will reach the maximum level. Promoters had also agreed that, if the Bank allowed the Company to avail of the sanctioned limits, the accrued but unpaid interest (amounting to Rs 20 lac) will be paid up front, paving the way for the loan account to become 'Standard' again.

The Rehabilitation Scheme proposed herein consisted essentially of de- freezing the drawing power, in lieu of the Company pledging ICDs of Rs 1 crore and making payment of the overdue interest; it did not involve any sacrifice on the part of the Bank – neither in the form of any concession in the interest rate nor by way of waiver of any past interest.

A monitoring system for keeping a close eye on the drawing power, as well as on the loan outstanding amount over the year, was also stipulated. During the lean season (April to September), the drawing power in the cash credit account (and the outstanding amount therein) should gradually come down and not go up. In order to monitor this closely, over this period the financing Branch would submit to the Stressed Assets Management Branch (SAMB), Lucknow, every month, a monthly comparative statement – showing the actual DP and outstanding amount at the end of the month, as against the average outstanding amount for the month during the last two years.

Before implementing the Scheme, the Company would have to give an undertaking that withdrawal of the ICDs of Rs 1 crore would be permitted only after the outstanding amount in the cash credit account falls to the freezing point level of Rs 1.54 crore and would be re-introduced at the beginning (October) of every busy season thereafter (before the outstanding starts going up again).

Based on the above, on March 21, 2005, the financing branch's Zonal Office approved lifting of the freeze on Drawing Power (DP) imposed on the cash credit account of the Company and permitting Drawing Power up to the sanctioned limit of Rs 4.20 crore.

Key Achievements

Stressed Assets Management Branches were launched by SBI for managing every Circle's large-value stressed assets (more than Rs 5 crore) by effecting turnarounds through Rehabilitation/ Restructuring and recovery through Compromise Settlements, Legal Recourse and Cash Sale. As the head of SAM Branch, Lucknow, my key achievements were:

a.   Reduction of 54% in the stressed assets under management, over a period of one and a half years;

b.   Highest recovery of Rs 105 crore among all nine SAM branches of SBI;

c.   Sensational turn-around in a case of rehabilitation of sick unit (ASP Sealing Products), with the company surpassing the turnover budgeted for the fifth year in future in the first year itself;

d.   Turned it into a case study and presented it at the Indian Institute of Management, Lucknow;

e.   Realized 21.13% of the outstanding amount in a cash sale of NPAs, as against the industry average of 10 to 12%.

FACTORING (2006–08)

Essentially, factoring is purchase of trade receivables, either with or without recourse. Against assignment of the accounts receivable in its favour, a Factor funds it so as to generate instant liquidity for the seller without disruption. In simple words, it is a receivables management and financing service designed to accelerate the seller's cash flow. In the process, its purchasing power increases, production moves up and sales turnover and profitability improve.

It covers both Domestic as well as Export Receivables, either with or without recourse. In 'with recourse' factoring, if the buyer fails to pay on maturity, seller will have to pay back the advance received from the Factor. In 'without recourse' factoring, the Factor provides finance and bears the risk of default in case of non-payment by the buyers.

It is a specialized and evolved product that caters specifically to the needs of SMEs (Small Scale Enterprises), and differs from bank finance as the *receivables are purchased, not financed*.

With its focus on managing receivables, it delivers four things in one package: *Collection; Risk Insurance, Sales Ledger Maintenance; and Financing*. It also monitors buyers by: (a) Evaluating the buyer's track record; (b) Setting up sub-limits on buyers; and (c) Implementing invoice-by-invoice tracking.

Domestic Factoring

Domestic Factoring relates to account receivables generated for sales in India. Its main characteristics are: Seller assigns the accounts receivables to the Factor on "open account" terms; receives payment to the extent of 80-90%; there is continuous sales flow on an ongoing basis with the same buyer or set of buyers; and the credit terms range between 30 to 180 days.

The advantages that seller gets from Domestic Factoring, are: assets are taken off the balance sheet; there is higher flexibility on account of a grace period of 60 days and lower risk because collection becomes the factor's responsibility; ease of operation because payment is made against a copy of the invoice; and faster decision-making due to specialized nature of the product.

It is very different from bank finance because: one, *receivables are purchased, not financed*; and two, it can be either *with or without* recourse whereas bank finance is always with recourse.

Since its focus is on managing receivables, it monitors buyers by constantly evaluating their track record through invoice-by-invoice tracking and, then, sets up sub-limits on them.

Export Factoring

In Export Factoring, FCI (earlier, Factors Chain International), the Global Representative Body for Factoring, plays a pivotal role through a two-factor system, with the following process flow: after receiving purchase order from the importer, exporter sends importer's information to the Export Factor for credit approval; Export Factor checks the importer's creditworthiness through an FCI partner; Import Factor evaluates the importer and approves a credit limit to Export Factor; exporter makes shipment to the importer and submits invoice details and supporting documents to the Export Factor; Export Factor makes *cash advance up to 90% of factored invoices* to the exporter; Import Factor collects the invoice amount from the importer and remits funds to Export Factor; Export Factor remits 10% remaining balance to the exporter's account less any charges.

With import factor covering the risk of default, the two-factor system spawns better management for non-LC exports. More importantly, it helps even smaller companies succeed in an environment where undue delay in payment is the norm.

This happens because of the advantages that they get from Export Factoring: 100% cover for default risk, as against 80% under an Export Credit Agency (in most cases, Export Credit Guarantee Corporation); higher flexibility as Import Factor makes payment in foreign currency; seamless functioning in a foreign environment; lower cost on account of non-L/C transactions; transactions do not show up on the company's balance sheet; accelerates cash flow – from about 4 months to a few days; company receives 90% of the invoice amount within a few days of submission (and the balance, minus fee, after customer pays it upon maturity of the invoice); and, finally, SMEs qualify for Export Factoring more easily because no collateral is needed.

Dealership Factoring is extended to the dealers (buyers) of industry majors (sellers) within India, based on strong recommendations of the Seller (Industry Major) by way of a comfort letter, backed by tripartite agreement. It is a without recourse facility offered to the Seller but, in case of any commercial or quality dispute between the Seller and the Buyer (Dealer) or if the invoice is not accepted by the Buyer (Dealer), the facility would become with recourse to the Seller.

Vendor Factoring is a facility for small players (sellers) in the market who supply goods to corporates (buyers) having strong financials/ credit rating. Supported by an undertaking of the Buyer (usually an Industry Major) to settle the dues on the due date, it is extended to the Vendor (Seller) on 'with recourse' basis, with the Buyer having the primary liability to pay the invoices. It is a facility that was launched specifically to help the SME/MSME sector in India.

In a factoring transaction, the client (seller) sells goods or services on "open account" terms (which means no fixed due date for receiving payment from the buyer – a norm in case of a Letter of Credit transaction) and assigns invoices to the Factor who makes prepayment of up to 80-90% of the invoice value, *immediately*. This is the advantage that the seller gets from factoring.

In "with recourse" factoring, if the buyer fails to pay the dues on maturity, the seller will have to pay back the advance received from the Factor. In "without recourse" factoring, the Factor bears the risk of default in case of non-payment by the buyer.

Other benefits that the seller gets from factoring are: no collateral security for advance payment of 80 to 90% of the invoice value; credit protection against buyer's default under export transactions; MIS Reports & Sales Ledger Administration without additional costs; follow-up with buyers on payment of receivables; and online access (24X7) to Clients to view their accounts.

The documents required under Factoring are simple whereas, in case of LC backed transactions, they are generally much more complicated. So, availing factoring facility, by simply handing over of normal trade documents to the Factor and receiving money, makes good economic sense. The other benefits are: immediate availability of cash to the extent of 90% of invoice value (while banks fund generally to the extent of 70-75% of the invoice value); lower administration and collection cost of debts; and savings arising out of reduction in invoice collection period.

Factoring transfers the risk from weaker SME sellers to relatively stronger corporate buyers, thereby offering a less-risky option for funding credit sales of SMEs.

Factoring at a Glance

Factoring was innovated so that the risk – and the drudgery – of collecting upon bills could be taken off the operational menu of the small guy in business. A factor factors invoices raised by a seller on the buyer, making a *pre-payment* (invoice amount, less retention money), and takes over the responsibility of collecting the same. You may ask: What's so great about it? A commercial bank renders the same service to its borrower, doesn't it – making an advance against the bill/ receivable and collecting the same from the borrower's customer?

Well, it may appear to be the same but there are crucial differences between the services rendered by a banker and those rendered by a factor. First and foremost, a banker makes an advance against the security of a bill/ receivable, whereas *a factor purchases the invoice, either with recourse or without recourse* – ideally, without recourse. Second, a banker collects upon the invoice *on behalf of its client* (the borrower), whereas a factor collects upon it *on its own behalf, thus permitting the asset (receivables) to be taken off the client company's balance sheet.* Third, since the underlying philosophy of a bank is to lend upon the security of an underlying asset – it operationalizes systems and procedures designed to ensure that the amount remaining outstanding, at any point of time, is within the "drawing power" (value of receivables pledged, less margin). In working capital finance, the mechanism for doing so is the "stock statement", submitted every month, based upon which the drawing power is computed and compared with the loan amount outstanding. If the amount drawn is higher than the drawing power, the borrower is called upon to rectify the "irregularity" (difference between the amount and drawing power). In case of receivables, bills that remain unpaid beyond the maturity date are promptly "removed from cover", or disallowed for computation of drawing power.

Not only does a factor not do any such thing but it allows a grace period of 60 days over and above the credit period. Is the factor being extra generous and less prudent? Far from it, for it tracks each and every invoice, almost on a daily basis, exerting itself to constantly assess the payment risk by computing average realization periods and follow up with the buyer for collecting payment. That is why it is said that administering the sales ledger on behalf of its client is what a factor actually does.

A factor conducts due diligence not only on the prospective client (the seller) but on the buyer as well – something which a banker does not do because of its different orientation. Ideally, for a factor, due diligence on the buyer is more important than due diligence on the client. Because of this basic difference in approach – as also the fact that the factor focusses exclusively on one part of the client's working capital cycle, the *last* part – the factor adds value to the service it offers to the seller.

The margin stipulated (or, retention money as it is termed) is also generally lower, and the factor's offerings and operations are characterized by flexibility, ease of operation and faster delivery – simply because it has a smaller set-up, it focusses on just one area (receivables) and its systems and procedures are different from those of a bank. In case of non-recourse factoring, the asset can be taken off the balance sheet of the seller, boosting its productivity ratios, which is considered a big advantage.

In case of export factoring, the route taken by the factor results in the following advantages for the exporter: 100% credit cover (as against 80% available under an export credit agency (ECA) guarantee usually taken by banks), invoice-by-invoice follow-up with buyer (service not available elsewhere), settlement of claim in foreign currency (an ECA settles in rupees), and availability of an intermediary ("import factor") in the country of the importer for performing due diligence, mediation work, etc.

Therefore, a factor's services are not a substitute for, but supplemental to, the services rendered by a working capital banker.

Market Intervention for SMEs

Factoring is a market intervention designed to bring about efficiency gains and address the issue of risk management and customers' needs satisfaction in a manner different from, for instance, banks. Such interventions are a natural corollary to the evolution of financial markets. In the nineteen sixties, securitization of home loans by specialist agencies in the U. S. brought about a transformation of the home mortgage market in that country. In the developed countries, factoring has done the same for SMEs.

Since collection of receivables is the area SMEs are most vulnerable in, factors and SMEs are natural partners. To the SMEs, the attractions of factoring are many – financial gain resulting from the receivables being taken off the balance sheet, reduction in risk on account of the transaction being without recourse and, of course, the joy of not being subjected to the rigmarole of a bank's systems and procedures. What accounts for the slow uptake of factoring in our country, as compared to other countries, then?

There are several reasons for this but, without doubt, the most important reason is non-enactment of factoring law. The RBI Study Group Report referred to earlier had flagged this issue in clear terms: "Indian law does not, at present, comprehensively deal with various aspects involved in factoring business. As such, it would be necessary to promote special legislation to support the establishment and operations of efficient and viable factoring organizations...To make factoring economically viable, it is essential that assignment of book debts in favour of a factor is exempted from stamp duty...."

In India, up to 2010, we didn't have a factoring law and RBI regulations did not clearly recognise the rights of factors over the assets of a buyer in case of non-payment. So, factoring was done with recourse. Although the Sale of Goods Act did allow "assignment" of invoices to the factor, it required payment of high stamp duties and, more importantly, existing laws in India did not give a legal right to factors to force buyers into the system. Developed countries had a factoring law in place which we badly needed, too.

ASSET RECONSTRUCTION (2009–2013)

Asset reconstruction was evolved as an answer to the distressed debt management problem faced by banks and financial institutions in this country.

The SARFAESI (Securitisation And Reconstruction of Financial Assets and Enforcement of Security Interest) Act, 2002 was legislated at the behest of the Narasimham Committee Report, for tackling the bad loans problem of banks. Before enactment of the Act, if a borrower had defaulted in making payment to the lending bank and the bank initiated action to take possession of the borrower's assets that had been pledged to it, the borrower would immediately file a petition against the bank in a civil court to counter the move. This would put a virtual stop to the bank's action. The case would keep lingering in the court for so many years that the assets pledged would either disappear or lose most of their value.

This happened because, at that time, banks and financial institutions in India did not have the power to take possession of the secured assets and sell them to recover their dues, without the court's intervention.

It is the SARFAESI Act that brought about this reform. Under Section 9, the Act lays down the following measures that a *"securitization company or reconstruction company"*, i.e. an *ARC*, is entitled to take: (a) proper management of the business of the borrower, by change in, or takeover of, the management of the business of the borrower; (b) the sale or lease of a part or whole of the business of the borrower; (c) rescheduling of payment of debts payable by the borrower; (d) enforcement of security interest in accordance with the provisions of this Act; (e) settlement of dues payable by the borrower; (f) taking possession of secured assets in accordance with the provisions of this Act.

ARC Operations in India: Challenges

But what needs to be emphasized is that no other country in the world operates an ARC model like we do. Internationally, ARCs were set up as centralized government agencies for tackling the bad debts problem in a banking crisis. Funded by the government, they generally enjoyed special powers to cut short legal procedures and engaged in wholesale purchase of banks' bad loans.

By contrast, Indian ARCs are private sector entities that operate under a tightly controlled regulatory regime and enjoy *no special powers*. They acquire NPAs through a transparent bidding process by paying only 5 to 15% of the acquisition price in cash, with the balance unpaid amount getting converted into the seller bank's investment in Security Receipts (SRs). Every NPA asset acquired by an ARC is held in a separate trust and Security Receipts representing investments by entities (the ARC itself, the selling bank, or other investors) in the acquired asset are issued by the ARC trust to its asset holders.

Indian ARCs face four challenges: debt aggregation (in case of corporate loans) so as to be able to put pressure on the borrower; sourcing funding from co-investors so as to be able to make acquisitions in cash; working out the acquisition price to be paid; and finding a way to speed up the resolution/recovery process.

The first one is a challenge which can get transformed into value addition if we are able to find a solution to it within our system. Finding a long-term solution to the second is imperative. The *third and fourth are core asset reconstruction challenges* and the way these are addressed would pretty much determine whether the ARC's gamble in a given case will pay off or not, since *the law does not grant to them the special powers that they need, something which the ARC models in several countries have given them.*

ARCs Vs. Banks: The Conundrum

When, in a continually rising NPA scenario, even large banks such as State Bank of India and IDBI Bank sell merely 3 and 2 NPAs, respectively, in a whole year to ARCs, what could one guess about business coming the way of ARCs in a given year?

That was a time when banks simply did not want to sell NPAs which had any value left in them. They wanted to sell only the most worthless, age-old NPAs – cases where they had already exhausted almost all recovery possibilities. And they wanted ARCs to pay a substantial price for such NPAs. *They based their 'reserve price' on the 'going concern' valuation they obtained from valuers, which might have been appropriate if you were financing a new unit but was totally irrelevant in case of a sick unit which had been closed for years.* It was inappropriate because *the assets of such a unit can be sold only on 'scrap sale' basis, at a fraction of the 'going concern' valuation.* If an ARC paid the price banks wanted, it would not have been able to recover the same from the sale of assets and was sure to incur a loss.

Moreover, while fixing the reserve price, banks did not factor in the cash outgo on account of statutory liabilities (unpaid statutory dues of the borrower company). In fact, in most cases, negative information that would affect the price adversely was not made available. One bank refused to show any papers, other than the loan documents, to ARC officials in the course of due diligence on cases put up for auction. Yet it expected ARCs to bid for the NPAs on an "as is where is and whatever there is" basis. An ARC was neither allowed to contact the borrower nor visit the factory to take a look at the land, building and plant and machinery before it submitted the bids. So, in such a case, all that the ARC knew at the time of submitting the bid was the name and address of the company and its promoters and the bank's dues.

Clearly, it was a sad case of failure of the market mechanism. Market mechanism means there must be a seller with an intention to sell and a buyer with an intention to buy – at a price determined by the market. If a bank keeps auctioning the same NPA over and over again without ever selling it to the highest bidder, it is clear that either it doesn't want to sell or it doesn't believe in market mechanism. In every auction, one found so many repeat cases. Every time you asked a bank why it had not sold the NPAs even after more than one auction, you would get the same answer: "Bid was below our 'reserve price'" which, of course, was never disclosed.

There is only one explanation for this. Banks, particularly public sector banks, don't lose anything if they allow NPAs to rot for years. Management pressure on their officials, if at all, comes only when a "standard" asset turns NPA. After that, no one is liable if the loan keeps rotting as NPA. All that the official in charge of the NPA has to do is create a record that he tried to recover in every possible way – writing letters to the borrower, attempting to take SARFAESI action, initiating legal action, and attempting to sell the NPA to an ARC. In the public sector, usually there is accountability only for doing and "no accountability for not doing". No wonder if public sector banks' NPA level shoots up (with the ghost of "restructured standard" loans – which had been allowed by RBI, earlier, on a one-time and exceptional basis – sitting on their heads), they will seek refuge in some ploy and keep sitting on the NPAs without doing anything. The banks will, thus, take care of their NPA problem in the most ingenious manner!

Another important issue that is pushed under the carpet is this. The real value from NPAs can get unlocked only if banks allow ARCs to revive Revivable Sick Unit cases and tackle Recalcitrant Borrower/ OTS (One- Time Settlement) cases.

As things stand in India, rather than helping a sick unit to revive, banks actually compound their problems by: (a) Debiting term loan installments in cash credit account, thus blocking the company's working capital; (b) Going on debiting interest (on both term loan and working capital loan) in cash credit account till it becomes NPA; and (c) Refusing to infuse fresh funds, even in a revivable case, because the company's loan is an NPA.

In a restructuring case, banks agree, at best, only to reschedule their loans and/ or convert a part of it into equity. Which is not of much use in most cases since, in the absence of adequate funds (working capital funds in most cases, and capex in some), the company simply cannot survive. In case after case after case, one sees the phenomenon of accumulated interest resulting in a doubling of the debt burden within 3 to 4 years' time. It is this excessive debt burden that pushes a sick unit so deep into a hole that it can never come out of it.

There are certain basic issues that ARCs in India face: no extra powers to aggregate debt (in order to be able to take action under SARFAESI Act), tackling recalcitrant borrowers (who use the legal system to their advantage), and take over incompetent managements (the RBI Guidelines in place make it un-workable), etc.

Regulatory reforms are also needed to ensure: one, accountability for letting the NPAs rot for years and the loss that a bank suffers on account of this (for, if an NPA has rotted for 10 years, its assets will fetch a very low price as compared to the price in the 1st, 2nd or 3rd year); and two, fair valuation guidelines so that there is no mix-up in valuation formula between guidelines on sale to a bank (in cash) and sale to an ARC (in cash or against Security Receipts); etc.

Secondary market for Security Receipts (SRs) is a utopia, since the primary market itself is not robust.

ADB REPORT ON ARCs IN INDIA, FEBRUARY 2004

Volume I (*"Recommendations for Changes in the Existing ARC Framework February 2004", TA No. 3943-IND)* of the *Asian Development Bank Report* on *"Developing the Enabling Environment for and Structuring Asset Reconstruction Companies in India"* is based an in-depth analysis of the NPA situation, as well as the existing legal and operational framework for ARC operations, in India. ADB had, in consultation with the Ministry of Finance, Government of India, appointed PricewaterhouseCoopers (PwC) as a Consultant charged with the responsibility to conduct the work in associa-tion with two reputed law firms - Amarchand & Mangaldas & Suresh A. Shroff & Co. (AM), an Indian law firm, and Blake Dawson Waldron, an international law firm.

The team reviewed NPAs of six banks (four public sector banks and two private banks) and one financial institution, aggregating Rs 422 bn, which worked out to about 47% of the Gross NPAs of the Indian Financial System (Rs 899 bn) as on March 31, 2003.   Nearly 76% of the sample NPAs (by gross value) had an average age of more than 2 years. Small NPAs (individual gross value less than Rs 10 million) comprised 99.9% of the sample NPAs by number, but only about 21% of the sample NPAs by gross value. Which means nearly 79% of sample NPAs (by gross value) were NPAs larger than Rs 10 million (Large NPAs).

2.1.6 Industry-Wise Distribution

The top 5 industries with maximum Large NPAs (by gross value) for the participant lenders were Textiles (14.7%), Iron & Steel (14%), Chemicals (9%), Engineering (7.6%) and (non-ferrous) Metals (5.3%). The Large NPAs of these 5 industries comprised approximately half of the total Large NPA portfolio (by gross value) of the participating lenders.

2.1.8 Operating Status

48% of Large NPAs in the sample were loans to non-operating entities, whereas a very small proportion of Large NPAs (4% by gross value) were in the form of loans to projects under implementation. So, rehabilitation of the NPAs would have involved longer workouts as well as injection of fresh capital.

2.1.9 Collateral

Nearly 93% of the sample NPAs were secured loans, 90% of which were secured against fixed assets.

Of the 46 collateral sales for which information had been provided, 40 involved sale of real estate. Average realization from collateral sales was about 83% of the value of collateral recorded in the books of the lenders at the time the loan was declared NPA. Value realization from sale of real estate collateral was 85%, as against 34% in the case of current assets.

2.2.4 Resolution Strategies

As of now, RBI's *"Master Circular – Asset Reconstruction Companies"*, issued on April 1, 2022 and updated on August 12, 2022, lays down a "planning period" of not more than six months for formulating a plan for realization and a maximum resolution time-frame of five years (including the planning period), from the date of acquisition of the assets. An ARC may, within the planning period, formulate a plan for realization of assets by taking action under one or more of the measures of asset reconstruction under Section 9 of SARFAESI Act ("Measures for Asset Reconstruction") *(6.C.(i))*, and put in place the policy for realization of financial assets under which the period for realization shall not exceed five years (which may be extended up to eight years by its Board of Directors) from the date of acquisition of the financial asset concerned *(6.C.(ii)) [Substituted vide Notification No. DNBS.PD(SC/RC).8/ CGM(ASR)-2010 dated April 21, 2010]*.

The measures that can be undertaken by an ARC for asset reconstruction include: a) enforcement of security interest; b) taking over or changing the management of the business of the borrower; c) sale or lease of the business of the borrower; d) entering into a settlement for payment of the dues; and e) restructuring or rescheduling of debt.

ARCs and the secured creditors cannot enforce security interest under SARFAESI unless secured creditors holding at least 60% of the secured creditors of the outstanding SRs agree to such action (6B(1)(iii)(b)) of the "Master Circular – Asset Reconstruction Companies").

The Master Circular also specifies that: "No ARC shall take the measures specified in Section 9(1)(b) of the SARFAESI Act, until the Bank issues necessary guidelines in this behalf" (paragraph 6B.(2), "Sale or Lease of a Part or Whole of the Business of the Borrower").

Although these measures have been laid down, the guidelines in respect of powers under "Sale or Lease of the Business of the Borrower" are still awaited from RBI and until these are issued, ARCs are not permitted to use them.

Recommendations for Changes in the Existing ARC Framework

As part of this TA, we have reviewed working of the following AMCs:

- *Danaharta in Malaysia*
- *KAMCO in Korea*
- *Thai Asset Management Company in Thailand*
- *Private sector AMCs in Taiwan*
- *Resolution Trust Corporation in USA*
- *Securum in Sweden*

- *FOBAPROA in Mexico*
- *Bank based restructurings in Poland*

We have found that AMCs have witnessed varying degrees of success across countries. While Danaharta in Malaysia, KAMCO in Korea, Securum in Sweden and RTC in USA are recognised as successful AMCs, TAMC in Thailand and FOBAPROA in Mexico have exhibited only mixed results. A combination of factors seems to have contributed to the success of the AMCs. Notable among these are the Government strategy and the role of AMCs in the overall financial reforms/ restructuring programme, legal environment prevailing in the country, the regulations and incentives instituted to facilitate asset transfer, the special legal powers conferred on AMCs with regard to resolution, the extent of funding support from both the Government and NPA investors and the tax benefits accorded to the AMCs.

On the basis of the review of the international best practices, we have identified the following as the critical success factors for the effective functioning of private ARCs in India.

- *Requirement of a strong legal framework for facilitating resolution of NPAs · Regulatory support and incentives to facilitate the transfer of NPAs by banks/financial institutions to ARCs*
- *Establishment of clear valuation guidelines and acceptance of NPA valuation methodology*
- *Availability of requisite funding and involvement of independent NPA investors, i.e. parties other than originating banks and financial institutions*
- *Flexibility to ARC in determination of resolution strategies*
- *Availability of special legal powers for the achievement of specific objectives*
- *Elimination/Minimisation of taxes and costs relating to NPA transfers*
- *Rationalisation of the tax regime incentivising investments in NPAs*
- *Use of professional management teams with expertise in financial restructuring*

In our experience of working of AMCs in the other countries, AMC structures used world-wide can be classified in the following broad categories:

- *Government owned/ supported AMCs*
- *Bank owned AMCs – Workout Units and Bad Bank models*
- *Private sector AMCs.*

3.2.1 Government Owned/ Supported AMCs

Governments in Malaysia, Korea, Thailand, USA and Mexico have relied upon the centralized, Government owned AMC model for effecting resolution of NPAs in those countries. While in Malaysia, Government guaranteed the Danaharta bonds, in Korea, an NPA Fund was set up for enabling KAMCO to acquire NPAs from various Korean banks.

The current policy thinking in the Indian Government proposes limited direct involvement by Government in the NPA resolution process.

3.2.2 *Bank Owned AMCs*

There are two bank based AMC approaches: Workout Units and Bad Bank model. In the case of Workout Units, the NPAs are moved to a separate bank department, but remain in the banks' books. In the case of a Bad Bank, the NPAs are transferred to separate affiliated organizations, usually wholly or majority owned subsidiaries of the transferring banks, which specialise in managing distressed assets. In this context, we have focused on the 'bad bank' model.

However, in the Indian environment, 'bad bank model' may also be subject to vigilance and audit related issues.

Further, in the Indian context, NPA ownership is quite fragmented and debt aggregation appears to be the key requisite for achieving an early and effective NPA resolution. Bank based AMCs would fail to address the fragmentation issue, as under the existing environment, bank based strategies may conflict with each other.

The existing ARC framework and guidelines envisage non-Government supported multiple ARCs, which may be set up inter-alia by lenders, NPA investors or corporates. A similar model was adopted in Taiwan, where many domestic banks collectively formed the Taiwan Asset Management Corporation ("TAMCO"). This AMC was in addition to the AMCs set up by NPA investors. Based on experience with AMCs in other countries, the requirement to achieve debt aggregation for effective functioning of ARCs in India, valuation and transfer issues including vigilance concerns in public sector banks transferring NPA to non-government supported/ private sector ARCs, we expect multiple category ARCs to emerge:

Multi-Bank owned ARCs: *These ARCs could effect aggregation of lenders' stakes and other value additions to facilitate induction of, or transfer to, NPA investors who might be in a position to provide services and obtain higher recoveries for the originating lenders. These ARCs may be particularly suited to:*

- *Focussing on value addition in a short time-frame (and) acting as rapid disposition vehicles (after aggregation and packaging), these ARCs can acquire interests of various secured creditors, achieve the required aggregation and involve other private parties, including NPA investors in actual day-to-day management of these NPAs. Given existing ownership limitations, involvement of external investors may be achieved through transfer of these NPAs to specific schemes in which majority/ 100% security receipts are owned by the external private parties. These external private parties can have an active role in management of NPAs transferred to that particular scheme.*

- *Carry out deep restructurings involving substantial sacrifices. In the recent past, the CDR mechanism has been quite successful in achieving financial restructurings and the lenders appear comfortable with the ongoing restructuring process. However, a few NPAs are likely to require complex business and financial restructurings involving substantial sacrifices. Aggregation of financial interests in*

---

8   *Though Security Receipt is an instrument, which is neither a debt instrument nor an equity instrument and represents the beneficial interest in a scheme, RBI notifications appear to classify these instruments in the nature of debt instruments.*

the ARC and consequent strengthening of its capacity to undertake negotiations with the debtor and the proposed powers regarding management/ business takeover can enable ARCs to effect complex restructurings in a timely and efficient manner.Further, transfer of financial stakes to these lender-owned ARCs would facilitate involvement of third party investors in these complex restructurings.

Privately owned and Public-Private partnership ARCs: *The introduction of NPA investors, both domestic and overseas, into the NPA resolution process has clearly been a key driver of success in other countries. They bring a combination of skills, experience, objectivity and commercialism to the resolution process. Importantly, they represent a significant source of capital that can be injected not just into the financial sector (through acquisition of NPAs), but also into the commercial/ real estate sector via capital infusion into distressed businesses as part of a restructuring.*

Existing ARC framework in India envisages multiple ARCs promoted inter-alia by lenders, corporates, service providers and NPA investors. Further, in absence of direct Government involvement, commercial objective of profit maximization is expected to be the primary objective of private sector ARCs and would govern level and nature of activities undertaken by various ARCs.

While multi-lender ARCs appear best placed to acquire NPAs from majority of banks/ financial institutions and focus on debt aggregation and their resolution, especially in case of large and complex cases, ARCs owned by NPA investors/ service providers may be more efficient in actual resolution activities, especially in small cases, in which debt aggregation is not a large issue and which require one-time settlements, sale of collateral assets, reschedulement decisions. To dissuade entry of non-serious players, in section 4.1 of this Volume of our Report, we have recommended granting of registration to ARCs promoted by reputed parties with adequate financial substance to ensure orderly growth of ARC activities.

However, in view of the existing geographical spread, quantum, diverse industry nature of NPAs, differing classification of NPAs in India, a multi- pronged approach may be more appropriate to achieve NPA resolution.

At the same time, we recommend that multiple "resolution focussed" ARCs be encouraged under this framework and investors should be allowed to set up ARCs if they so desire. Multiple investor ARCs being in operation would, in our assessment, speed up the transfer of NPAs from banks.

In the above context, we believe that RBI/ Government should not decide on any appropriate number/ types of ARCs and should leave it to market forces. We believe that once three or four multi-lender ARCs are in place and majority lenders associate with one of these ARCs, remaining lenders would see limited benefits in setting up/associating with the other multi-lender ARCs and this would allay the concerns regarding difficulties in debt aggregation in case there are too many multi-lender ARCs.

---

9   *27 public sector banks hold over 80% of the NPAs in India.*

10   *Currently, ARCs are required to obtain consent of secured creditors holding 75% (now, 60%) of the amount outstanding for security enforcement. It is understood that RBI may similarly prescribe a threshold level requiring aggregation for enabling ARCs to exercise powers to take over management or business of the borrower.*

3.3.3 *Illustrative Transactions*

Overall ARC operations and their success in tackling the NPA problem of the banking sector depends, first and foremost, on the lenders' willingness to transfer NPAs to the ARCs. The absence of any Government or regulatory direction and/or incentivisation, the requirement for upfront adjustment in the financial statements and attached accountability issues are likely to act as deterrents to NPA transfers.

In our various interactions, lenders have mentioned very high principal recovery figures (please see sub-section 2.7.4 of Volume III of the Report). However, if observed closely, time value of money is usually not accounted for in these recovery experiences.

In addition, in view of likely issues in effecting NPA-transfers at fair value, lenders may also engage the services of ARCs on an agency basis. In such cases, NPAs shall continue on the lenders' balance sheets and the ARC will manage such NPAs on a fee basis.

3.3.4 *Activities of ARCS in India*

In reviewing possible activities of ARCs in India, we have discussed the services offered by the international AMCs and their relevance in the Indian context.

3.3.4.1 *Acquisition and Aggregation of NPAs*

Although the acquisition of NPAs is a critical activity of every AMC, the actual acquisition process is governed by the specific objectives of the AMC and the Government objective with regard to financial restructuring. For instance, Danaharta in Malaysia is established as a restructuring agency and thus has focused on the acquisition of large NPAs with significant scope for value enhancement.

In India, in the absence of a systemic financial crisis and any specific Government pressures to transfer NPAs to the ARCs, market dynamics govern transfer of NPAs to ARCs. Banks are likely to transfer NPAs as per their own financial requirements, capacity to book losses and capital raising and other plans. In view of valuation concerns, requirement of upfront adjustment in financial books of the transferring lenders and other related issues, ARCs would need to market themselves aggressively to acquire adequate financial interest in NPAs from the existing lenders in order to be effective in NPA resolution/ recovery. In initial days, in the absence of any track record on value realizations from NPAs, this acquisition task becomes more difficult and equally more important. This activity may involve the following:

- Identification of NPAs including identifying respective lenders and their stakes, ascertaining security details and other relevant information
- Carrying out detailed financial, legal and technical due diligence
- Value analysis including possible resolution options, resolution timeframe and recovery estimates
- Structuring transaction and negotiating valuations, agreeing to valuations and consideration
- Making offers, allocating envisaged value among lenders with different status, rights and priorities.

3.3.4.2 *Resource Mobilisation*

Since Danaharta in Malaysia, KAMCO in Korea and TAMC in Thailand are centralised Government-owned AMCs, they have typically relied on the Government to meet their funding requirements for acquisition of NPAs.

Government support has enabled Danaharta to provide zero coupon Government guaranteed redeemable bonds in consideration of the NPAs acquired by it. KAMCO has sourced its acquisition funding from an NPA fund established by the Government. In Taiwan, while the investor-owned AMCs have primarily secured funding from their head office/parent company, some AMCs have also procured loans from commercial banks to fund the purchase of NPAs.

In India, since limited Government involvement is envisaged, ARCs will need to mobilize resources for funding acquisition of NPAs, which may be obtained from lenders or independent investors. Funding by originating lenders would mean replacement of NPA assets with NPA asset backed bonds. This suggests a requirement for funding from independent NPA investors for taking forward the overall AMC process.

Given existing ARC ownership limitations, investments in security recei-pts appear to be the most appropriate route for NPA investors to invest in the Indian NPA market. In the initial stages, we expect independent NPA investors to adopt a cautious attitude towards investments in Indian NPAs. However, involvement of independent NPA investors is very critical in achieving a clean-up of lenders' balance sheets. This activity may involve the following:

- Preparation of an offer document specifying NPA information, terms and structuring of the scheme and proposed tiering of rights of different investors

- Market making including approaching NPA investors, holding road shows, negotiating terms of investments and allocation of rights

- Investor servicing including NAV declaration, meeting compliance requirements and filing returns.

3.3.4.3 *Determination of Resolution Strategy*

Along with the disposition of NPAs, ARCs will need to determine NPA resolution strategies. International AMCs like Danaharta in Malaysia have specialised work groups that analyse specific characteristics of the loan including security details, the operational and financial performance of the borrower and his track record in debt servicing and the future prospects for both the industry and the borrower's business. Based on this analysis, Danaharta then determines the recovery strategy for each loan and the expected recovery rate. Similarly, KAMCO in Korea, while initially acting as a rapid disposition vehicle, has also determined resolution strategies appropriate to the type of loan and has thus shifted its focus to corporate restructuring to resolve the large number of workout loans in its portfolio. In Taiwan, the strong security enforcement regime and concerns about deterioration in value of assets and carrying cost to investors have directed AMCs to use foreclosure and debt settlement routes.

3.3.4.4 Loan Workouts

Restructuring agencies like Danaharta in Malaysia and TAMC in Thailand have effected business and financial restructurings as part of their resolution strategies. These AMCs prepare debt restructuring plans for borrower companies after conducting feasibility analyses and thereafter monitor and enforce borrower compliance with debt repayment schedules by employing debt collecting agents for this purpose. Danaharta has also engaged in the recovery of loans on behalf of the Government on a fee basis.

Out-of-Court restructuring mechanisms such as corporate debt restructuring committees ("CDRCs") have been employed in several countries like Thailand and India to facilitate negotiations between debtors and creditors and resolution of inter-creditor issues that often impede speedy resolution of NPAs. International experience suggests that AMCs can be an effective medium to supplement the restructuring efforts of such committees. In Malaysia, Danaharta had a "Corporate Debt Restructuring" division that was established to support the CDRC in its role of facilitating restructuring of large corporate debts in Malaysia. (This division was dissolved in August 2002 upon the closure of the CDRC in July 2002.)

In India, while the CDR mechanism has been quite successful in achieving financial restructuring, ARCs, with their private sector nature and commercial objectives of profit maximization, may be better placed to carry out complex business and financial restructurings. These restructurings may take place either as preparatory to NPA disposition, i.e. involvement of independent NPA investors or as part of overall resolution efforts being undertaken by the ARCs.

3.3.4.5 Security Enforcement/ Settlements

International AMCs have extensively resorted to foreclosure and collateral enforcement to effect recovery. For example, Danaharta has successfully used the tender route to carry out private treaty property sales. This has been possible due to extensive marketing of tenders via a wide range of media, communication with investors and establishment of links with and direct marketing to members of trade organisations. Danaharta has also managed to generate adequate buyer interest by providing requisite information through tender packages containing property valuation reports and copies of the sale and purchase agreements. These have been sold to buyers through specialised real estate agents employed for this purpose. Danaharta has also effected property sales through private contracts after entering into one-to-one negotiations with buyers. KAMCO in Korea has also employed both competitive bidding and private contract methods to dispose real-estate properties through public auctions. In Taiwan, lenders are not required to have any minimum stake in the principal outstanding to take enforcement action and this appears to have facilitated security enforcement by the AMCs.

Security enforcement is expected to be a key resolution strategy for ARCs in India as over two thirds of NPAs are in 'loss' and 'doubtful' categories and offer limited potential for their revival. Security enforcement may be the only option for ARCs to realise cash from such cases. It is thus essential that a market for sale of acquired assets be created to enable ARCs to improve their recovery levels. Annex 7 in Volume IV of the Report discusses our recommendations in this regard.

3.3.4.6 *Taking Over of Management*

Internationally, AMCs have been active in the reorganisation of borrower companies to harness more value from their NPA portfolios. KAMCO has recently established a corporate restructuring department that analyses and selects companies for restructuring, plans the restructuring process by establishing guidelines for reasonable and systematic management of companies and devises strategies for recovering investment. Joint venture CRCs (Corporate Restructuring Companies) established by KAMCO in collaboration with foreign investors provide foreign capital and advanced technology to improve operations of the companies and thereafter sell these businesses at profitable values. The TAMC in Thailand has coordinated with both local and international investors and the Stock Exchange of Thailand to mobilise funds for restructuring of borrower companies. In Taiwan, AMCs have not resorted to reorganisation of borrower businesses due to the inter-creditor and inter-party conflicts in the agreement of reorganisation plans and the long delays observed in the reorganisation process.

In India, ARCs may take over the business/ management of the defaulting company while implementing preferred resolution strategies. Though RBI guidelines for exercise of this power are still awaited, we feel that the proposed management/ business takeover power is very important and would help an ARC realise value in cases in which a) promoters are not co-operating or b) change in management has significant potential to improve the borrower's performance. In this regard ARCs may engage the services of independent professionals. Further, while the Act does not expressly permit ARCs to inject funds to facilitate business restructurings, we believe that this may be necessary to enable ARCs to exercise more control over the resolution process and to obtain higher value recovery. Sub-section 4.5.4 of this Report carries our recommendations in this regard.

3.3.4.7 *Collateral management and NPA collection*

As part of their recovery efforts, AMCs have been required to manage collateral assets taken over from the defaulting borrowers. KAMCO in Korea has not only engaged in preservation and maintenance of collateral attached to NPAs acquired but has also managed and disposed properties held by the Government and non-business real estate held by financial institutions, public companies and companies aiming to de-leverage their balance sheets.

Elements of our scope of work in this TA identify valuation of assets as one possible activity for ARCs in India. Since ARCs in India are likely to be private sector organizations (NARCL is not) guided by their own objectives including that of profit maximisation, their valuations may not be considered 'independent valuations'.

A key issue relates to the level and type of activities which would be undertaken by the ARCs themselves and activities which would be outsourced. In view of the private sector nature of ARCs, they are unlikely to be large organizations (KAMCO has over 1500 employees and Danaharta has over 250 employees).

On one side of the continuum, the ARC may end up providing coordinating and ancillary services to the scheme investors, on the other side, the ARC may be required to carry out all activities relating to NPA resolution, in which originating banks continue to be the security receipt holders. An ARC may carry out these activities only for part of the duration of a scheme as investors owned asset management companies may like to takeover resolution/ recovery efforts after NPA investors purchase security receipts from the originating lenders.

4. Recommendations for Changes in the Existing ARC Framework

Based on our analysis and assessment of the ARC framework in India, we have identified the following issues as critical for the effective functioning of ARCs in India.

- *Structural/ownership issues*

  Control and ownership issues, requirement of clarity on role and involvement of NPA investors in day-to-day management, capital adequacy requirements and different Directions applicable to ARC and trust.

- *Acquisition and Valuation Issues*

  Reluctance of lenders to transfer NPAs to ARCs in view of transfers being envisaged only at fair or market value, due to absence of market and lack of benchmarks, differences in fair value perceptions, inadequate provisioning and consequent upfront financial losses (particularly in absence of any amortization provisions) and concerns about possible criticism for having undersold.

- *Transaction Costs*

  Deterrents to transfer of financial assets include high transaction costs, comprising of expenses such as stamp duty payable on assignment of financial assets, which may be prohibitive in case of many states.

- *NPA Funding*

  Difficulty in attracting funding from sources other than the originating lenders in the absence of a well-developed market and clarity on permissible investments and structures, which allow returns commensurate with risk and appropriate flexibility in structuring and remittances.

- *Resolution Issues*

  Hindrances to effective resolution by way of limitations on the kind of NPAs to be acquired by ARCs, lack of clarity on how various resolution mechanisms are to be effected.

Elements of the TA scope require the Consultants to recommend changes to the existing ARC framework to make their operations effective and achieve Government objectives of NPA resolution. It is realised that amendments to SARFAESI may take time and relying upon such changes should not be allowed to delay the entire NPA resolution process. Therefore, while we recommend certain changes to the SARFAESI legislation, we have also tried to address the issues as best as possible through suggested clarifications, modifications or supplementation to the existing RBI Guidelines, rules and directions and changes in other laws and policy where appropriate.

However, there are certain legislative changes relating to the fiscal/ tax regime and applicability of transaction costs, which need to be made before independent investors invest in the Indian NPAs.

Recommendations Summary

4.1.1 Control And Ownership

"Act be amended to enable a single party to control an ARC subject to RBI prescribing safeguards to prevent warehousing of NPAs."

"Ministry of Finance/ RBI clarify that a single NPA investor including foreign entities be allowed to hold entire 100% of security receipts issued under any scheme."

4.1.2 Capital Adequacy

"Directions be modified to remove applicability of capital adequacy requirements to financial assets acquired by the ARCs."

Section 3(1)(b) of SARFAESI prescribes a capital adequacy requirement of 15% of financial assets acquired by the ARCs in addition to a minimum net owned fund of Rs. 2 crore.

"RBI may consider granting registration to ARCs promoted by reputed parties with adequate financial substance/ resources possibly with minimum net owned fund criterion of Rs 50 million."

4.1.3 Trust Structure

"Act be amended to recognize trust structure."

The Directions prescribe that requirements relating to capital adequacy, asset classification, provisioning and income recognition, though applicable to ARC, shall not be applicable to financial assets held in the trusts set up by the ARCs. Since the Act itself does not specifically mention trust structure, there is a need to recognize the trust structure in the Act.

4.2.1.1 Asset Acquisition/ Transfer

a. *"RBI review the asset classification norms to make them consistent across different lender categories."*

b. *"RBI ensure consistency in application of classification norms across lenders through measures such as permitting lenders/ARCs with at least 25% stake in a loan asset, classified as NPA, to request for review of classification of such a loan across all lenders."*

Differing application of asset classification and provisioning norms across lenders, either due to differential treatment in debt servicing by the borrowers or due to inconsistent application of these guidelines by lenders, has led to different classification and provisioning levels across lenders.

c. *"RBI direct lenders to make adequate provisions in a given time-frame and ensure compliance through stringent inspections."*

Internationally, NPAs are usually recognized as loss assets after one year of their classification as NPAs and lenders are required to make provision for the entire amount. Current Indian norms allow a time gap of five years after default takes place and before loan assets are recognized as loss assets. Even after these five years, some discretion is still available with the lender not to recognize an NPA as a loss asset.

4.2.1.2 Specifying target NPA levels

"Ministry of Finance/ RBI prescribe the desired NPA levels and timeframe for the financial system (including banks and financial institutions)"

In India, existing NPA levels are higher than those considered acceptable internationally. In view of the need for upfront loss adjustments upon transfer, vigilance issues ...., the lenders are likely to transfer NPAs to ARCs as per their own financial restructuring plans.

4.2.2 NPA Valuation

"RBI/Ministry of Finance prescribe a procedure for banks and financial institutions to determine transfer value of NPAs. Such a procedure should recognize negotiated transactions and encourage involvement of independent valuers and consultation among lenders".

Despite a clear provision in the Guidance Notes that NPA transfer should take place at fair value in a well-informed market, lenders' unwillingness and inability to absorb upfront financial losses leads to widely differing perspectives of parties, i.e. the lenders and the ARCs. It is difficult to expect private sector ARCs to acquire NPAs at prices higher than their assessment of "fair value".

4.2.3.1 Widening of definition of secured creditors

"Act be amended to include lenders other than banks and financial institutions"

Under the existing legal framework, the definition of secured creditors does not include lenders such as multilateral and bilateral agencies (except IFC - W and ADB), Non-Banking Financial Companies (unless notified) and foreign banks and institutions who are not recognized as banks for the purposes of applicable law in India.

4.2.3.2 Transfer of non-revivable assets to ARCs

"Guidelines to Banks be clarified to encourage banks/financial institutions to transfer non-revivable NPAs to ARCs"

The Guidelines to Banks seem to suggest that ARCs should not normally acquire the non-revivable assets and these NPAs should remain in the books of banks and financial institutions and ARCs should act as an agent for recovery on fee basis.

This has been reportedly interpreted by banks and financial institutions to suggest that transfer of non-revivable assets is not considered desirable by RBI. However, our NPA analysis shows that majority of NPAs are over 2 years old and approximately half of them are non-operating units/businesses (please see sub- section 2.3.3 and para 2.4.2.3 of Volume III of our Report). This suggests that majority of these NPAs may be non-revivable.

4.2.3.3 *Mandatory Transfer of NPAs to ARCs*

a. "Guidelines to Banks be modified to provide guidance on timeline and pricing of NPAs to be transferred to ARCs after 75% of financial stake has already been transferred"

b. "Guidelines to Banks be modified to reduce the above 75% in line with the proposed reduction in consent threshold level for security enforcement under SARFAESI".

Guidelines to Banks suggest a mandatory transfer of NPAs to ARCs in cases where 75% of the banks/ FIs (by value) have agreed to accept the ARC offer. This appears to have been suggested as 75% is the prescribed consent threshold criterion and an ARC with 75% financial stake can proceed with security enforcement. Hence, the requirement for transfer of financial stakes to ARCs after 75% of banks/ FIs (by value) transfer their stake to ARCs

4.2.3.4 *Customary Representation and Warranties*

"Guidelines to Banks be clarified to permit customary representation and warranties"

Guidelines to Banks suggest that no known liability should devolve on banks and financial institutions after they transfer financial assets to ARCs. RBI clarify that the giving of customary representations and warranties by the selling lender is not in violation of its guidelines, leaving it to the parties to decide on warranties and guarantees depending on their perspective and the market situation.

4.3 *Transaction Costs*

a. "Act be amended to provide for a clear vesting of title to assets acquired by issue of bonds and debentures"

b. "Central Government to encourage rationalization of stamp duty regime in various states"

c. "Act be amended to clarify that ARCs are required to register only with Central Registry on acquisition of financial assets"

High transaction costs involved in acquisition of financial assets is one of the biggest deterrents to asset reconstruction activities in India. Transfer of financial assets in some states could attract ad valorem stamp duty of up to 14% of either the consideration paid or the market value of the financial assets being assigned. Such high transaction costs may impede the commercial efficacy of the Act to the extent that it is intended to encourage the resolution of NPAs. Stamp duty is a 'state' subject; so, many stamp duty legislations need to be amended to reduce the stamp duty payable on the assignment / conveyance of financial assets to an ARC.

4.4.1 *Equity Investments in ARCS*

"Asset reconstruction be recognized as a separate category without any foreign equity linked capital requirements under Annexure B of Foreign Exchange Management (Transfer of issue of Security by a Person resident outside India) Regulations, 2000 with foreign ownership permitted up to 100%".

Since 'asset reconstruction' is not recognized as an activity under the foreign direct investment guidelines ("FDI Guidelines") and the Foreign Exchange Management Act, 1999 ("FEMA"), it is not clear whether the business of 'asset reconstruction' would be within the ambit of Annexure A (list of activities for which automatic route is not available) or Annexure B (list of activities for which there are sectoral caps on investments by persons resident outside India) of Foreign Exchange Management (Transfer of issue of Security by a Person resident outside India) Regulations, 2000.

4.4.2 Investment in Debt Securities

a. **"Investments in debt instruments of ARCs, whether issued in their capacity as trustees or otherwise, be given flexibility to structure tenor, coupon, end-use of funds as per their requirements beyond those provided in the ECB guidelines."**

b. **"SEBI (Foreign Institutional Investors) Regulations, 1995 be modified to ensure that debt FII's investments in debt instruments (including security receipts) issued by ARCs, whether in their capacity as trustees or otherwise, shall not be considered for determination of its individual ceiling. Further, a separate country level sub-ceiling shall be made available for total investment by debt FIIs in debt instruments, including SRs issued by the ARCs."**

SARFAESI permits ARCs to acquire financial assets by issue of debentures, bonds and other securities. So, ARC will have the option of acquiring the NPAs on its balance sheet basis and attempting resolution of the same, or retaining trusteeship and management in the assets (for a fee) and transferring all beneficial right, title and interest in such assets to QIBs, using a trust structure. Accordingly, investment from foreign distressed asset funds and others may be sought in

- *bonds/ debentures issued by ARCs incorporated in India;*
- *SRs issued by Indian ARCs in respect of various schemes managed by such ARCs.*

4.4.3 Widening of QIB Definition

"Government to notify process and net owned fund requirement for recognition of entities, including NBFCs, not covered under existing definition of QIBs"

The existing definition of 'QIBs' ("Qualified Institutional Buyers: QIB means a financial institution, insurance company, bank, state financial corporation, state industrial development corporation, trustee or any asset management company making investment on behalf of mutual fund or provident fund or gratuity fund or pension fund or a foreign institutional investor registered under the Securities and Exchange Board of India Act, 1992 (15 of 1992) or regulations made thereunder, or any other body corporate as may be specified by the Board.") does not cover NBFCs which have considerable presence in the Indian financial sector, including subsidiaries of reputed global financial sector companies. Under the existing legal framework, these NBFCs would need to be notified and recognized as financial institutions under SARFAESI to be able to invest as QIBs in NPA acquired by ARCs.

Clarity on Recognition of SRs as Unlisted Non-SLR Security

a. *"RBI guidelines (12 November, 2003) to be modified to clarify non- applicability of rating requirements for banks' investment into debt securities issued by ARCs, either as trustees or otherwise."*

b. *"RBI guidelines (12 November, 2003) to be modified to clarify non-inclusion of debenture and bonds issued by ARCs in non-SLR instruments for computing banks' compliance with 20% limit."*

Recent RBI guidelines restrict banks' investments in non-listed non-SLR securities to 20% of their total investments in non-SLR securities. These guidelines also appear to suggest that banks shall invest in listed non-SLR securities of only those companies which comply with Disclosure and Investor Protection ("DIP") guidelines issued by SEBI. Banks have also been prohibited from investing in "unrated" and "rated but non-investment grade" non-SLR securities. These guidelines effectively restrict banks from investing in debt securities of ARCs, including security receipts. It needs to be recognized that in the absence of adequate independent NPA investor interest, banks are initially likely to invest in debt instruments issued by ARCs. The inability of banks to invest in these debt instruments due to the above regulatory restrictions could be a serious impediment in the overall NPA resolution process, having economic implications in terms of value lying locked in the unproductive assets.

4.5.1 Simplification of Consent Requirement for Security Enforcement

a. *"Act be amended to make consent of secured creditors a default option in the absence of an inter-creditor agreement"*

The current legal framework[42] requires the ARCs[43] to obtain consent of secured creditors holding 60% (earlier 75%) of the amount outstanding before taking any security enforcement action. The existing definition of secured creditors is restrictive and does not include lenders such as multilateral and bilateral agencies (except IFC-W and ADB), Non-Banking Financial Companies (unless notified) and foreign banks and institutions who are not recognized as banks for the purposes of applicable law in India[44].

---

[42]   *Requirement for enforcement of security interest*

13(9) of SRFAESI : In the case of financing of a financial asset by more than one secured creditor or joint financing of a financial asset by secured creditors, no secured creditor shall be entitled to exercise any or all of the rights conferred on him under or pursuant to sub-section 4 unless the exercise of such right is agreed upon by the secured creditors representing not less than three-fourth in value of the amount outstanding as on a record date and such action shall be binding on all secured creditors.

[43]   *Enforcement of security interest by ARC*

Section 9 of SRFAESI specifies that an ARC shall exercise the security enforcements rights in accordance with the provisions of the Act. Section 13 of SRFAESI deals with exercise of security enforcement rights by the secured creditors.

[44]   *Definition of secured creditors*

2 (1.zd) of SRFAESI: secured creditor means any bank or financial institution or any consortium or group of banks or financial institution and includes - (i) debenture trustee appointed by any bank or financial institution; or (ii) securitization company or reconstruction company; or (iii) any other trustee holding securities on behalf of a bank or financial institution, in whose favour security interest is created for due repayment by any borrower of any financial assistance.

b. "Act be amended to enable RBI to prescribe lower consent threshold subject to a minimum of 51%"

We believe that the stipulated consent requirement at 60% (earlier 75%) of the secured creditors is an unduly high threshold requirement and may be a serious impediment in a large number of enforcement situations as ownership of NPAs is quite fragmented across lenders, on average spread over four-five lenders for a medium size NPA.

c. "Act be amended to ensure consent requirement only from senior and pari-passu charge holders for security enforcement action"

The Current legal environment requires an ARC to obtain consent of secured creditors holding 60% (earlier 75%) of the outstanding amount before taking any security enforcement action. The Act appears not to differentiate between lenders with different classes of securities and secured creditors, as defined in the Act, are likely to include holders of subordinate charges. There needs to be a clear distinction between 'recovery' and 'reconstruction' efforts as priority of charges, relevant for distribution of proceeds in recovery efforts, is not proposed to be changed. SARFAESI does not, in any manner, modify rights available to various classes of creditors.

a. "Act be amended to prescribe that acquired assets shall pass free of all encumbrances and charges of all secured creditors would shift to sale proceeds"

Under SARFAESI, especially in the context of provisions in the Enforcement Rules[46], it is possible to take a view that upon a sale under SARFAESI, the secured assets shall pass subject to the encumbrances of the other creditors, particularly those who are not subject to the provisions of SARFAESI. Continuance of charges of subsequent creditors over the secured assets shall dissuade potential buyers from investing in these assets and can impede the entire security enforcement process. It is recommended that the SARFAESI Act be amended to provide that upon a sale of the secured assets in accordance with SARFAESI and the Enforcement Rules, the secured assets would pass free of all encumbrances and the charges of all creditors, having a security interest over the secured assets would shift to the sale proceeds.

b. "Enforcement Rules requiring borrower's consent for effecting sale of acquired assets at a price lower than reserve price, be amended to permit use of step down auction method"

The current provision in the Enforcement Rules requires the secured creditor (on the basis of an independent valuation) to fix a reserve price in case of sale of immovable assets. Further, it requires the borrower's consent for proceeding with the sale in case the offer price is lower than the reserve price, which can stall the entire enforcement process.[48] We feel that this requirement should be removed and a market-driven pricing arrived at through use of an appropriate transparent means be accepted for such sales.

c. "Act be amended to ensure that no liability be imposed on secured creditors, an ARC, its staff or agencies acting on its behalf for actions taken in good faith in the course of NPA resolution."

The Enforcement Rules[49] clarify that any manager appointed by the secured creditors shall act as an agent of the borrower, which implies that the manager acting on behalf of secured creditors shall not be subject to any liability for action taken by them in good faith.

"RBI guidelines on sale/ takeover of business/ management should clarify the manner, extent, pre-conditions for exercise of these powers by ARCs."

We understand that RBI is in the process of framing guidelines for enabling ARCs to take over management/ business of the borrower and putting in place appropriate safeguards in respect of the exercise by ARCs of the special powers contained therein. We believe that these special powers are critical to the success of ARCs and therefore recommend that RBI ensure that safeguards provided do not, while checking the possibility of abuse, unduly curtail the exercise of these special powers conferred on ARCs.

a. *"Act be amended to clarify that asset reconstruction activity under SARFAESI includes provision of additional funding, if required."*

b. *"Priority rights in debt servicing be provided to the additional fund providers through approval in the CDR forum or otherwise."*

Genuine sustainable business restructuring often requires an injection of funds into a business. Provision of financial assistance such as availability of working capital finance to a few projects may facilitate higher value recovery and ARCs may realise better value than that considered achievable under the security enforcement route. It is unlikely that existing promoters and the originating lenders would provide this much-needed financing to borrowers with NPAs. However, independent NPA investors, investing in Indian NPAs (through bonds and debentures issued by ARCs or using security receipt route), may agree to provide/ arrange additional funds as part of their overall resolution strategy.

"Government consider setting up a rehabilitation fund to provide additional funding to potentially viable cases"

Independent NPA investors will most likely adopt a cautious attitude before investing in Indian NPAs. They may enter the market after ARCs establish a track record in NPA resolution. Given the possibility of making projects viable by incurring capital expenditure or through provision of additional working capital and limited availability of such funding, the Government may consider instituting measures to facilitate extension of financial assistance to potentially viable NPA cases until the independent NPA investors come in.

This may require Government setting up a 'Rehabilitation Fund' to extend additional funding to the potentially viable cases.

a. *"ARCs/ schemes controlled by foreign parties be permitted a grace period of 5 years on acquisition of equity shares in sectors in which FDI guidelines limit management control or provide for sectoral ceilings for investment by foreign entities".*

The prevailing FDI policy prohibits foreign investment in a few sectors such as real estate and retail and in addition limits foreign ownership/ management control for certain sectors like telecom, insurance, defence and media. It is possible that a debt conversion effected by an ARC controlled by foreign investors or its scheme in which the majority SR holders are of foreign origin, may come in conflict with the current FDI restrictions on ownership stake/ management control.

b. *"Government should notify ARCs under section 81(3) of the Companies Act so that ARCs do not require existing shareholders' approval under Companies Act for acquisition of shares on debt conversion, as part of their NPA resolution strategies"*

Section 81(1) of the Companies Act requires approval of existing shareholders before issue of fresh share capital to parties other than existing shareholders. In this context, acquisition of equity stake by an ARC/ scheme in a company pursuant to debt conversions undertaken as part of NPA resolution strategy would need to be approved by the existing shareholders. However, institutions specified by the Government do not require this approval u/s 81(1) of the Companies Act and institutions notified by the Government include PFIs (Public Financial Institutions) also.

"Directions be modified to permit a scheme structuring a realization period of more than five years in case majority SR holders agree"

The Directions stipulate that ARCs shall prepare the reconstruction scheme and shall realise the assets in a stipulated time frame, which shall not in any case exceed five years from the date of acquisition. However, it is possible that resolution strategy for a few financial assets may involve reschedulement/ restructuring scheme that goes beyond five years. Though, it is critical to ensure that NPAs are not warehoused, such a shortened term may limit restructuring opportunities

"Provision for abatement from BIFR to be made applicable to NCLT also (subject to consent threshold requirement for security enforcement)"

Another impediment to the actions of secured creditors in the current legal framework is the potential for conflict between enforcement actions taken under SARFAESI and the general law and any restructuring action before the National Company Law Tribunal ("NCLT"). In the past, the borrowers of banks and financial institutions have often taken shelter under the provisions of SICA[50], thereby preventing the banks and financial institutions from initiating enforcement proceedings.

"RBI clarify that funding brought in/ arranged by SR holders shall be deemed as funding by ARCs in accordance with CDR provisions"

Currently, the CDR mechanism provides an alternative platform to secured creditors to effect business and financial restructuring. Though, there does not seem to be any prohibition against an ARC participating in the CDR mechanism[51], ARCs taking up CDR membership would need to comply with any CDR decision, including provision of additional financing[52].

"A new clause (23DA) be inserted in Section 10 of the Income Tax Act, 1961"

Income Tax Act, 1961 recognizes pass through nature of trusts in mutual funds and exempts income of the mutual funds from Income Tax u/s 10(23D) and from Tax Deduction at Source (TDS) u/s 196. Income accruing to the unit holders is directly taxed as investment income or capital gains on redemption in the hands of the unit holders.

The same principle should apply to income earned by the ARCs, whether acting as trustees or otherwise, as income earned by such ARCs/ trusts will be passed through to the SR holders. SR holders should be assessed, subject to any exemptions, in respect of such income in accordance with their respective tax status. As such there would be no taxable income at the ARC/ trust level. Accordingly, a new clause (23DA) be inserted in Section 10 of the Income Tax Act, 1961. This could read as follows:

"... the income of any asset reconstruction company or securitisation company registered under the Securitisation and Reconstruction of Financial Assets and Enforcement of Security Interest Act, 2003, or of any scheme/ trust set up by such company, whether in its capacity as trustee or otherwise, arising from any securitisation or asset reconstruction activity undertaken by it."

"A new clause (23GA) be inserted in Section 10 of the Income Tax Act, 1961"

Investments in asset reconstruction activities are high risk investments and need to be incentivised. We recommend that SR holders should be given an incentive similar to the one provided to attract investments in the infrastructure projects and that the income from investment schemes of the ARC be exempted, including capital gains arising on transfer of SRs.

A new clause (23GA) be inserted in Section 10 of the Income Tax Act, 1961. This could read as follows:

"Any income or long term capital gains from investment made in an asset reconstruction company or securitisation company registered under the Securitisation and Reconstruction of Financial Assets and Enforcement of Security Interest Act, 2002 or in any scheme/trust set up by such company."

"A new section be inserted in Chapter XII – E of the Income Tax Act, 1961"

U/s 115R of Income Tax Act, 1961, any income distributed by an entity falling u/s 10(23D) can be subject to a distribution tax @ 12.5%, as applicable to income distributed by the mutual funds. Investments in asset reconstruction activities carry more than normal equity risk on account of high risk inherent in investment in the underlying assets which are already non-performing. To promote investments in SRs, which are akin to equity instruments on account of risk being undertaken by the SR holders, as in case of equity oriented mutual funds, trusts set up by the ARCs may be exempted from dividend distribution tax.

A new section 115RA be inserted in Chapter XII – E of the Income Tax Act, 1961 to exclude trust/scheme from liability of distribution tax to read as under: Tax on income distributed by ARCs and SCs

"115 RA Notwithstanding anything contained in any other provision of this Act, the provisions of this Chapter XII – E shall not apply to any distribution made on or after the 1st day of April 2004 by any asset reconstruction company or securitisation company registered under the Securitisation and Reconstruction of Financial Assets and Enforcement of Security Interest Act, 2002 or any scheme/trust set up by such company, which is eligible for the exemption under section 10(23 DA)."

"A new clause (v) be inserted in section 196 of the Income Tax Act, 1961"

As income being a return on investment from trust/scheme (set up by ARCs) is recommended to be exempt from tax, no tax should be deducted at source on such income.

A new clause (v) be inserted in section 196 of the Income Tax Act, 1961 for non-deduction of tax at source on any payments made by any person to such ARC/trust.

"(v) an asset reconstruction company or securitisation company registered under the Securitisation and Reconstruction of Financial Assets and Enforcement of Security Interest Act, 2002, whether in its capacity as trustee or otherwise," and the words "financial assets" be added to the remainder of the section such that it reads as follows: "where such sum is payable to it by way of interest or dividend in respect of any **financial asset***, securities or shares owned by it   "(emphasis supplied)*

Also an explanation be added to Section 196 as follows: "Explanation.- For the purposes of this section the words "financial asset" shall have the same meaning given to such term in the Securitisation and Reconstruction of Financial Assets and Enforcement of Security Interest Act, 2002."

Amendment to Section 36 (viia) of Income Tax act, 1961

U/s 36 (viia) of the Income Tax Act, 1961, in any year, provision for bad and doubtful debts is permitted to be claimed as a tax deductible expense only to an extent of 7.5% of income of banks and financial institutions and banks are required to write-off debts to claim income tax deduction. Such a restriction on provisioning amount encourages banks to manage provisioning levels[53] at any point of time as provisioning in excess of the above specified limit will not be allowed as a tax deductible expense. Lenders should be permitted to claim deduction for making adequate and appropriate provisioning as this would have only timing implications on tax collections from the banks.

"The limits prescribed in section 36(viia) of Income Tax Act, in respect of tax-deductible provisioning of bad and doubtful debts, be deleted and it be provided that any provisions in accordance with RBI norms shall be allowed as deduction."

4.6.6 Non-Recognition of Contingent Income

The Directions permit the lenders to transfer these non-performing loans to ARCs with provision for upside sharing, which may include banks sharing in the proceeds from non-performing assets in case these exceed a particular level. RBI Guidelines to banks also recognize uncertainty in assessing value of such 'upside sharing' provision and suggest that banks should not take any credit for expected profit until the profit is actually realised.

4.6.7 Clawback of Income Recognized in Earlier Years

Investments in SRs carry more than normal equity risk as underlying assets are non-performing assets from the very beginning. Some scheme/trust may have income in the initial period (tax year) but may result in loss in subsequent periods due to earlier realization of more liquid and healthy assets. In such circumstances, recognition of income in the initial period merely on the basis of transactions undertaken till then without taking cognizance of the likely future loss in the portfolio, would result in lopsided tax liability. It is therefore recommended that the losses in the hands of SR holder be allowed to be claimed back till 5 years[54].

---

[54] *This recommendation may not be required if the recommendation in sub-section 4.6.2 is accepted by the Revenue authorities. ("Investments in asset reconstruction activities are high risk investments and need to be incentivised. We recommend that SR holders should be given an incentive similar to the one provided to attract investments in the infrastructure projects and that the income from investment schemes of the ARC be exempted, including capital gains arising on transfer of SRs.")*

4.6.8 *Other Issues*

The Act and the SARFAESI Rules/ Guidelines taken together suggest acquisition of NPAs at fair price in an informed market in an arm's length transaction and consequently, the transfer price is likely to be lower than book value in the books of banks/financial institutions. As per Guidelines to Banks, the banks/ financial institutions are required to recognize this loss in the profit and loss account of the current year. Though, the existing Income Tax regulations suggest that such loss shall be recognized as a trading loss and can be carried forward, like other business losses, up to a period of 8 years, a confirmation in this regard by way of clarification from Income Tax authorities would be desirable.

4.7 *Regulation*

Elements of the TA scope also require the Consultants to recommend appropriate regulations to govern the operations of ARCs, including recommendation on appropriate regulatory authority. RBI has been identified as the regulatory authority for ARCs' operations and has already issued Directions and Guidance Notes in April 2003 for regulating functioning of the proposed ARCs and these Directions/ Guidance Notes cover various aspects relating to registration, operations and funding of ARCs and resolution of NPAs by ARCs. Additionally, it has issued guidelines to banks and financial institutions on issues relating to transfer of assets to ARCs, consideration for the same and valuation of instruments issued by the ARCs. Additionally, the Central Government has issued the Security Interest (Enforcement) Rules, 2002 ("Enforcement Rules"), which lay down the procedures to be followed by a secured creditor while enforcing security interests pursuant to the Act. All these rules, directions and guidelines referred to in this paragraph are collectively referred to as "SARFAESI Rules/ Guidelines". Given the fact that RBI has already been identified as the regulatory authority in the existing ARC framework, our recommend-ations focus only on modifying/ improving the existing regulatory framework, i.e. SARFAESI and SARFAESI Rules/ Guidelines.

After NPA acquisition, ARCs step into the shoes of originating lenders and are entitled to take certain special remedies, including takeover/ sale of management/ business. During our discussions with various stakeholders on possible activities of ARCs in India, concerns have been expressed that ARCs, as private sector organisations, would be driven by their commercial objectives. Further, funding of NPAs would involve participation of various banks and financial institutions, by investments in 'pass through certificates' issued by the ARCs. In this context, NPA resolutions activities carried out by the ARCs shall have substantial implications for the entire banking system and business community. In this context, questions have been raised - whether existing structures would be able to address the concerns relating to abuse of powers available to ARCs including issues relating to right pricing of deals, selling assets back to the original borrower, precautions against public interests and protection of labour participants.

Simultaneously, concerns have been repeatedly expressed that private sector ARCs, as envisaged in India, would like maximum flexibility in their decision making. With their objectives of maximizing shareholders' wealth, ARCs may identify resolution strategies which may involve a few tough decisions that cannot be wished away such as business restructuring involving sale of a part of the business or closure of business rendering labour surplus.

Similarly, an ARC may consider it appropriate to sell the acquired assets back to the original borrower to arrest rapid deterioration in value of those assets in case it does not find an alternative suitable party.

RBI may consider putting in place appropriate guidance notes to enable an individual ARC to frame their internal guidelines/ policies on various aspects of its operations, at the same time ensuring that these guidance notes are not prescriptive and do not lead to direct management of an ARC's affairs.

Under the existing ARC framework, the working of Board of Directors of an ARC would influence the nature and type of activities undertaken by it and the above guidance notes may include provisions to make the ARCs' boards more effective to address the above concerns. In this connection, RBI may consider extending the recommendations made by the Expert Group[55] constituted by RBI to improve functioning of the Boards of Banks and Financial Institutions in critical areas of corporate governance, transparency and compliance, to ARCs, with modifications as deemed appropriate.

Further, we understand that RBI has already set up a committee, consisting of certain individuals well known in the financial sector, representative from the Banking Division, Government of India and Senior Functionaries from RBI, to screen registration applications of ARCs, with the objective of allowing registration only to ARCs promoted by the parties serious in resolution of NPAs. The Board of Financial Supervision of RBI is responsible for supervising activities of NBFCs, including ARCs. Further, RBI may consider setting up a grievance redressal system and specify the process for receipt of complaints against ARCs and their disposal. This grievance redressal system can take up issues relating to takeover of business/ management affecting stakeholders other than secured creditors, valuation of NPAs and grievances caused by activities of various ARCs.

RBI is yet to issue its guidelines for exercise of ARC's powers on management/ business takeover. These guidelines and the Supreme Court judgement in Mardia Chemicals case, which is expected shortly, is likely to influence the role of the above referred grievance redressal system. RBI may consider these while framing scope and process for such grievance redressal system.

5 Priority of Recommendations During our various discussions with RBI, Ministry of Finance and ADB, it was suggested that recommendations be prioritized distinguishing between recommendations which are essential and those which are desirable for ARCs to function effectively to help the Government and RBI in examining them. The table below lists all our recommendations and attempts to cover the following aspects:

- *Suggested manner of implementing various recommendations*
- *Authority who can effect these recommendations*
- *Priority of these recommendations (TABLE)*

---

55 *RBI had constituted an expert group to review the supervisory role of Boards of banks and financial institutions and to make recommendations to improve functioning of the Board vis -à-vis compliance, transparency, disclosures, audit committees, etc. As issues relating to transparency, public interest, corporate governance are equally important in activities undertaken in the ARCs, RBI may examine extending above expert group recommendations, a summary of which has been presented in Exhibit 11 to this Report, to ARCs to make their boards more effective in ensuring that concerns relating to transparency, public interest, corporate governance in ARC's activities are addressed.*

2.2.1 Allow investment – from both Indian and foreign NPA investors – with a combination of skills, experience, objectivity and commercialism crucial for the resolution process and remove the provision that any person holding 10% or more of the paid-up equity capital can be a sponsor.

2.2.1 For ringfencing of investments made by QIBs (Qualified Institutional Buyers), as well as of the financial assets acquired by ARCs using such investments, set up different schemes under the trust structure with ARC acting both as the trustee as well as the manager of the scheme.

2.2.2 Allow a private investor to subscribe to all security receipts issued under a particular scheme so that it may take up management of the financial assets held under the scheme through contractual arrangements. This investor could operate under a power of attorney to be granted by the ARC, and in turn indemnify the ARC against any loss that may arise as a result of any course of action/ resolution strategy recommended by it.

2.2.3 Make the requirement – that an ARC has to maintain a capital adequacy ratio of 15% of its risk weighted assets – non-applicable to the financial assets held in trusts.

2.2.2 In addition to issuing security receipts to investors, allow ARCs to issue bonds and debentures to the QIBs for meeting their funding needs.

2.2.3 Amend the law to recognize foreign banks as banks for the purposes of applicable law in India and NBFCs and multilateral agencies as secured creditors.

2.2.4 ARCs should value the acquired assets in an objective manner and use uniform process for all assets of the same profile.

2.2.3 Once an asset is acquired by it, the ARC becomes a party to all the contracts/ deeds/ agreements as well as all the suits and appeals applicable to the acquired financial asset.

2.2.4 ARCs have a maximum resolution time-frame of five years (including a one-year planning period) from the date of acquisition of the assets. Of the five measures of asset reconstruction that can be undertaken by an ARC under the SARFAESI Act, guidelines for the sale or lease of business of the borrower are still awaited from the RBI. Until these are issued, ARCs are not permitted to use them.

RECOMMENDATIONS SUMMARY

Reference	Recommendation	To be effected through	Initiating Authority	Priority
4.1	**Structural/Ownership Framework**			
4.1.1.a	A single party be allowed to control an ARC subject to safeguards to prevent warehousing of NPAs	Amendment in the Act	Government (safeguards-RBI)	Essential
4.1.1.b	A single NPA investor including foreign entities be allowed to hold entire 100% of security receipts issued under any scheme.	Clarification	RBI/Ministry of Finance	Essential
4.1.1.c	SR holders/ARCs can appoint a manager to respective scheme to perform all activities for asset reconstruction under SRFAESI	Clarification	RBI	Essential
4.1.2.a	Applicability of capital adequacy requirements to financial assets acquired by the ARCs be removed	Modification in Directions	RBI	Essential
4.1.2.b	ARC registration requirements be framed to ensure that only ARCs sponsored by reputed parties with adequate financial substance/ resources are granted registration possibly with minimum net owned fund criterion of Rs. 50 million.	Modification in Directions	RBI	Desirable
4.1.3	Trust Structure in the Act be Recognized	Amendment in the Act	Government	Essential
4.2	**Acquisition and Valuation**			
4.2.1.1.a	Asset classification norms be made consistent across different lender categories	Modification in RBI norms on Income Recognition & asset classification	RBI	Essential
4.2.1.1.b	Consistency in application of asset classification norms across lenders be ensured through measures such as permitting lenders/ARCs with at least 25% stake in a loan asset, classified as NPA, to request for review of classification of such a loan across all lenders	Modification in RBI norms on income recognition and asset classification	RBI	Essential

(Contd.)

Reference	Recommendation	To be effected through	Initiating Authority	Priority
4.2.1.1.c	Lenders be directed to make adequate provisions in a given timeframe and compliance be ensured through stringent inspections.	Modification in RBI norms on income recognition and asset classification	RBI	Essential
4.2.1.2	The desired NPA levels and timeframe for banks and financial institutions be specified.		RBI/Ministry of Finance	Essential
4.2.1.3	Banks and financial institutions be allowed to amortise losses over five years for capital adequacy computations.	Modification in RBI norms on capital adequacy computations	RBI	Essential
4.2.2	A procedure for banks and financial institutions to determine transfer value of NPAs be prescribed. Such a procedure should recognize negotiated transactions and encourage involvement of independent valuers and consultation among lenders.	Modification in Guidelines to Banks	RBI/Ministry of Finance	Essential
4.2.3.1	Definition of secured creditors be widened to include lenders other than banks and financial Institutions	Amendment in the Act	Government	Desirable
4.2.3.2	Transfer of non-revivable NPAs by banks/financial institutions to ARCs be encouraged.	Clarification in Guidelines to Banks	RBI	Essential
4.2.3.3.a	Guidance on the timeline and pricing of NPAs to be transferred to ARCs (after 75% of financial stake has already been transferred) be provided.	Modification in Guidelines to Banks	RBI	Desirable
4.2.3.3.b	Reduction in the above 75% limit in line with the proposed reduction in consent threshold level for security enforcement under	Modification in Guidelines to Banks	RBI	Desirable

Reference	Recommendation	To be effected through	Initiating Authority	Priority
	SARFAESI.			
4.2.3.4	Customary representation and warranties by the selling lender be permitted.	Clarification in Guidelines to Banks	RBI	Desirable
4.3	**Transaction Costs**			
4.3.a	Rationalisation of the stamp duty regime be encouraged in various states.	Amendment in various State legislations	Government	Essential
4.3.b	Clear vesting of title to assets acquired by issue of bonds and debentures by the ARC.	Amendment in the Act modifying the language	Government	Essential
4.3.c	ARC be required to register only with the Central Registry on acquisition of financial assets.	Amendment in the Act providing for this	Government	Desirable
4.4	**NPA Funding**			
4.4.1	Asset reconstruction be recognised as a separate category without any foreign equity linked capital requirements under Annexure B of Foreign Exchange Management (Transfer of issue of Security by a Person resident outside India) Regulations, 2000 with foreign ownership permitted up to 100%.	Modification in Foreign Exchange Management (Transfer of issue of Security by a Person resident outside India) Regulations, 2000	Government	Essential
4.4.2.a	Investments in debt instruments of ARCs, whether issued in their capacity as trustees or otherwise, be given flexibility to structure tenor, coupon, end-use of funds as per their requirements beyond those provided in the ECB guidelines	Modification in ECB Guidelines	Ministry of Finance	Essential
4.4.2.b	Debt FII's investments in debt instruments (including security receipts) issued by ARCs, whether in their capacity as trustees or otherwise, shall not be considered for determination of its individual	Modification in SEBI (Foreign Institutional Investors) Regulations, 1995	SEBI	Essential

(Contd.)

Reference	Recommendation	To be effected through	Initiating Authority	Priority
	ceiling. Further, a separate country level sub-ceiling be made available for total investment by debt FIIs in debt instruments (including security receipts) issued by the ARCs."			
4.4.3	Process and net-owned fund requirement for recognition of entities, including NBFCs, not covered under existing definition of QIBs be notified.	Notification	Government	Desirable
4.4.4.a	Non-applicability of rating Requirements for banks' investment into debt securities issued by ARCs, either as trustees or otherwise, be clarified.	Modification in RBI guidelines (12 November, 2003)	RBI	Essential
4.4.4.b	Non-inclusion of debenture and bonds issued by ARCs in non-SLR instruments for computing banks' compliance with 20% limit be clarified.	Modification in RBI guidelines (12 November, 2003)	RBI	Essential
4.4.5	Disclosure requirements in respect of security receipts, which would be issued under the scheme structure, be made for the respective scheme, in which security receipts are being issued, not for all the schemes in relation to which the ARC, the issuer company is acting as a trustee.	Clarification in SEBI, September 30, 2003 guidelines	SEBI	Desirable
4.5	**Resolution Strategies**			
4.5.1.a	Consent of secured creditors for security enforcement be a default option in absence of an inter- creditor agreement.	Amendment in the Act	Government	Essential
4.5.1.b	Lower consent threshold level for security enforcement may be prescribed by RBI subject to a minimum of 51% of secured creditors.	Amendment in the Act	Government	Essential

Reference	Recommendation	To be effected through	Initiating Authority	Priority
4.5.1.c	Consent be required only from senior and *pari-passu* charge holders for security enforcement action.	Amendment in the Act	Government	Essential
4.5.2.a	Acquired assets to pass free of all encumbrances and charges of all secured creditors to shift to sale proceeds.	Amendment in the Act	Government	Desirable
4.5.2.b	Requirement to obtain borrower's consent for effecting sale of immo- vable assets at a price lower than reserve price be removed and a step down auction method be permitted.	Amendment in the Enforcement Rules	Government	Desirable
4.5.2.c	No liability be imposed on secured creditors, an ARC, its staff or agencies acting on its behalf for actions taken in good faith in the course of NPA resolution.	Amendment in the Act	Government	Essential
4.5.3	The manner, extent and preconditions for exercise of powers of sale/ takeover of business/ management by ARCs be clarified.	Issuance of Guidelines	RBI	Essential
4.5.4.a	Asset reconstruction activity under SRFAESI to include provision of additional funding, if required.	Amendment in the Act	Government	Essential
4.5.4.b	Priority rights in debt servicing be provided for additional fund providers through approval in the CDR forum or otherwise.	Amendment in the Act	Government	Essential
4.5.5	A rehabilitation fund be considered to provide additional funding to potentially viable cases.		Government	Desirable
4.5.6.a	ARCs/ schemes controlled by foreign parties be permitted a grace period of 5 years on acquisition of equity shares in sectors in which FDI guidelines limits management control or provide for sectoral ceilings for investment by foreign entities.	Modification in FDI Guidelines	Government	Essential

(Contd.)

Reference	Recommendation	To be effected through	Initiating Authority	Priority
4.5.6.b	ARCs be notified under section 81(3) of the Companies Act so that ARCs do not require existing shareholders' approval under Companies Act for acquisition of shares on debt conversion, as part of their NPA resolution strategies.	Notification by the Central Government in accordance with sub-section (3) of Section 81 of the Companies Act.	Government	Essential
4.5.7	A scheme be permitted a realization period of more than five years in case majority SR holders agree	Modification in the Directions	RBI	Desirable
4.5.8	Provision for abatement from BIFR be made applicable to NCLT also subject to the consent threshold requirement for enforcement of security.	Amendment in the Act	Government	Desirable
4.6	**Taxation**			
4.6.1	Income of an ARC or of any scheme/trust set up by it, whether in its capacity as trustee or otherwise, arising from any asset reconstruction activity undertaken by it be exempted.	Insertion of a new clause (23DA) in Section 10 of the Income Tax Act, 1961.	Government	Essential
4.6.2	Any income in the hands of the SR holders including long term capital gains arising on transfer of SRs be exempted.	Insertion of a new clause (23GA) in Section 10 of the Income Tax Act, 1961.	Government	Essential
4.6.3	Any distribution made by any ARC or any scheme/trust set up by it be exempted from dividend distribution tax.	Insertion of a new section 115RA in Chapter XII – E of the Income Tax Act, 1961.	Government	Desirable
4.6.4	Any income being a return on investment made in an ARC or trust/scheme (set up by ARC) be exempted from deduction of tax at source.	Insertion of a new clause (v) in section 196 of the Income Tax Act, 1961.	Government	Essential

Reference	Recommendation	To be effected through	Initiating Authority	Priority
4.6.5	The provision to allow banks and financial institutions to claim provision for bad and doubtful debts as a tax deductible expense only to an extent of 7.5% of income of banks and financial institutions be deleted and lenders be permitted to claim deduction for making adequate and appropriate provisioning.	Amendment to section 36 (viia) of Income Tax Act, 1961	Government	Desirable
4.6.6	Any profits/income of banks on account of upward sharing provision in NPA transfer be recognised only in the year in which they are ascertainable and quantifiable.	Issuance of CBDT circular	Government	Essential
4.6.7	Losses in the hands of SR holder be allowed to be claimed back till 5 years.		Government	Desirable
4.6.8	The loss incurred by banks and financial institutions on transfer of financial assets be recognized as a trading loss and be carried forward, like other business losses, up to a period of 8 years.	Clarification by issuance of circular	Government	Desirable

MY VIEW ON COURSE CORRECTION NEEDED

As per data as of 2003, whereas IBRA (Indonesian Bank Restructuring Agency), the Indonesian ARC, acquired assets at practically zero value and KAMCO, the Korean ARC, at an average discount of 64% to the appraised value, the acquisition price-to-face value ratio for India's largest ARC (ARCIL) worked out to 25.7%.

In its February 2004 *Report on "Recommendations for Changes in the Existing ARC Framework"*, the *Asian Development Bank* had *identified the following **critical success factors** for the effective functioning of private ARCs in India: strong legal framework for facilitating resolution of NPAs; regulatory support and incentives to facilitate transfer of NPAs to ARCs; clear valuation guidelines for NPAs; promoting investment by independent investors; innovating new resolution strategies; special legal powers for specific objectives; eliminating tax on NPA transfers; tax incentives for investment in NPAs; setting up professional management teams with expertise in financial restructuring.*

India paid no heed to these recommendations, sowing the seeds for what happened thereafter.

Reserve Bank of India issued its first guideline on ARCs – *"The Securitisation Companies and Reconstruction Companies (Reserve Bank) Guidelines and Directions, 2003"* - on April 23, 2003. It took 7 years for RBI to issue the "Guidelines on Change in or Take Over of the Management of the Business of the Borrower by Securitisation Companies and Reconstruction Companies (Reserve Bank) Guidelines, 2010" on April 21, 2010.

This was followed by a Notification on takeover of the borrower's business titled "Notification as amended up to June 30, 2010 - The Securitisation Companies and Reconstruction Companies (Reserve Bank) Guidelines and Directions, 2003", issued on July 1, 2010.

Paragraph 7(2) of this Notification said: "(2) *Change or take Over of Management/ Sale or Lease of Business of the Borrower: No Securitisation Company or Reconstruction Company shall take the measures specified in Sections 9(1)(a) and (b) of the Act (SARFAESI Act), until the Bank (i.e., RBI) issues necessary guidelines in this behalf."*

This was followed by paragraph 7(6)(i)(d): "*Every Securitisation Company or Reconstruction Company may, within the planning period, formulate a plan for realization of assets, which may provide for one or more of the following measures: (a)... (b)...(c)...(d) Change or take-over of the management, or sale or lease of the whole or part of business of borrower after formulation of necessary guidelines in this behalf by the Bank (i.e., RBI) as stated in paragraph 7(2) herein above."*

By then, the *"Guidelines on Change in or Take Over of the Management of the Business of the Borrower by Securitisation Companies and Reconstruction Companies (Reserve Bank) Guidelines, 2010"* had already been issued on April 21, 2010. But, even 12 years later, Guidelines on the Sale or Lease of the Business of the Borrower are still awaited.

In paragraph 6B(2) (*"Sale or Lease of a part or whole of the business of the borrower"*), the *Master Circular - Asset Reconstruction Companies,* issued by RBI on April 1, 2022, clearly says that: "No ARC shall take the measures specified in Section 9(1)(b) of the Act, until the Bank issues necessary guidelines in this behalf." These guidelines are yet to be issued. (The revised Guidelines - Notification as Amended up to June 30, 2015, dated July 01, 2015 - also mentions that: Paragraph 7(2) of the guidelines ("2003 Guidelines for ARCs": (2) Change or take Over of Management/ Sale or Lease of Business of the Borrower: No Securitis-ation Company or Reconstruction Company shall take the measures specified in Sections 9(a) and (b) of the Act, until the Bank issues necessary guidelines in this behalf.) shall be substituted as under: "(2) **(i) Change or Take Over of Management of The Securitisation Company or Reconstruction Company** shall take the measures specified in Sections 9(a) of the Act, in accordance with instructions contained in Circular DNBS/PD(SC/RC) No.17/26.03.001/2009-10 dated April 21, 2010 as amended from time to time. **(ii) Sale or Lease of a part or whole of the business of the borrower** No Securitisation Company or Reconstruction Company shall take the measures specified in Section 9(b) of the Act, until the Bank issues necessary guidelines in this behalf.)

With banks auctioning only portfolios, not single NPAs, not allowing ARCs to do full due diligence on them, and the ARCs having neither a strong legal framework for resolution of NPAs nor the regulatory support for transfer of NPAs by banks/ financial institutions, Indian ARCs were only getting short-changed. With all ARCs as a group earning a sub-8% IRR (Internal Rate of Return) on investments made at that time, they were actually fighting for survival.

ARCs must look beyond cleaning up banks' balance sheets. One area they may turn their attention to is corporate restructuring and rehabilitation/ work- out.

These two measures – restructuring and rehabilitation – can be powerful tools in the hands of ARCs for tackling difficult, going concern cases. A case of successful rehabilitation/ revival, to which the second measure applies, could add much greater value than, say, seizure & sale action and the right to sell or lease business under the first can be an effective antidote to recalcitrant management.

Together, these two measures have the potential to reconstruct asset reconstruction. But that will happen only when objective conditions for successful rehabilitation are created.

Corporate restructuring invariably needs infusion of fresh funds (debt and equity) and conversion of a part or whole of the borrower company's debt into equity and it is imperative that the final RBI Guidelines contain explicit enabling provisions for both. Certain legal cobwebs – such as precipitate action by a statutory authority after action for revival has been initiated, long- winded procedure for debt-equity conversion, etc. – also need to be cleared.

Reconstructing asset reconstruction would involve making progress on two fronts in the case of corporate bad debts: one, transforming the process of acquisition so that ARCs can get out of the quagmire of holding only a small part of the bad loan; and two, facilitating corporate restructuring/ rehabilitation and opening up the opportunity for equity upsides.

Master Circular 2022

On April 1, 2022, RBI issued a *"Master Circular - Asset Reconstruction Companies"* with the objective of having "all current instructions/ guidelines on the subject at one place."

A comprehensive document on Asset Reconstruction, it not only covers all the notifications and guidelines issued by RBI on this subject over the last 22 years but combines them into one simple code. So, now, one doesn't need to examine multiple guidelines or notifications to figure out what is relevant – and what is not relevant – in respect of any issue.

The most important measures of asset reconstruction are: change in or takeover of the management of the business of the borrower (eligibility conditions, grounds, policy and procedure for it are all covered in the Master Circular); sale or lease of a part or whole of the business of the borrower (as of now, this measure cannot be taken because RBI guidelines on it are yet to be issued); rescheduling of debts (applicable to restructuring); enforcement of security interest; settlement of dues payable by the borrower; conversion of any portion of debt into equity of a borrower company; plan for realization of financial assets; and securitization.

This circular not only inserts all the relevant details from the notifications and guidelines issued – from 2002 to March 31, 2022 – at the right place but, at the end, displays a full list of the links for accessing all these notifications and guidelines. There are 48 links in the list and, by clicking on any one of them, one can immediately access the full notification or guidelines from the RBI website.

Important excerpts from the Master Circular 2022 are furnished below:

6. *Asset Reconstruction*

    A. *(1) Acquisition of Financial Assets*

        i. Every ARC shall frame, with the approval of its Board of Directors, a 'Financial Asset Acquisition Policy', within 90 days of grant of Certificate of Registration, which shall clearly lay down the policies and guidelines covering, inter alia,

           a. norms and procedure for acquisition either on its own books or directly in the books of the trust;

           b. types and the desirable profile of the assets;

           c. valuation procedure ensuring that the assets acquired have realizable value which is capable of being reasonably estimated and independently valued;

           d. in the case of financial assets acquired for asset reconstruction, the broad parameters for formulation of plans for their realisation.

ii. The Board of Directors may delegate powers to a committee comprising any director and/ or any functionaries of the ARC for taking decisions on proposals for acquisition of financial assets;

iii. Deviation from the policy should be made only with the approval of the Board of Directors.

iv. Before bidding for the stressed assets, ARCs may seek from the auctioning banks adequate time, not less than two weeks, to conduct a meaningful due diligence of the account by verifying the underlying assets.

2. *Permission to acquire financial asset from other ARCs*

ARCs will acquire financial asset from other ARCs on the following conditions:

a. The transaction is settled on cash basis;

b. Price discovery for such transaction shall not be prejudicial to the interest of Security Receipt (SR) holders;

c. The selling ARC will utilize the proceeds so received for the redemption of underlying SRs;

d. The date of redemption of underlying SRs and total period of realization shall not extend beyond eight years from the date of acquisition of the financial asset by the first ARC.

3. *Acquisition of financial assets by ARCs from sponsors and lenders*

ARCs shall not acquire financial assets from the following on a bilateral basis, whatever may be the consideration:

i. a bank/ financial institution (FI) which is the sponsor of the ARC;

ii. a bank/ FI which is either a lender to the ARC or a subscriber to the fund, if any, raised by the ARC for its operations;

iii. an entity in the group to which the ARC belongs.

However, they may participate in auctions of the financial assets provided such auctions are conducted in a transparent manner, on arm's length basis and the prices are determined by market forces.

6 B. Measures of Asset Reconstruction

1. *Change in or Takeover of the Management of the Business of the Borrower*

i. The objective of these guidelines is to ensure fairness, transparency, non- discrimination and non-arbitrariness in the action of ARCs and to build in a system of checks and balances while effecting change in or takeover of the management of the business of the borrower by the ARCs under Section 9(1)(a) of the Act. The ARCs shall follow these instructions while exercising the powers conferred on them under Section 9(1)(a) of the Act.

ii. An ARC may resort to change in or takeover of the management of the business of the borrower for the purpose of realization of its dues from the borrower subject to the provisions of these guidelines. The ARCs resorting to takeover of management of the business of the borrower shall do so after complying with the manner of takeover of the management in accordance with the provisions of Section 15 of the Act. On realization of its dues in full, the ARC shall restore the management of the business to the borrower as provided in Section 15(4) of the Act; provided that if any ARC has converted part of its debt into shares of a borrower company and thereby acquired controlling interest in the borrower company, such ARC shall not be liable to restore the management of the business to such borrower.

iii. **Eligibility conditions to exercise power for change in or takeover of management** In the circumstances set forth in paragraph (iv) below

    a. An ARC may effect change in or takeover of the management of the business of the borrower, where the amount due to it from the borrower is not less than 25% of the total assets owned by the borrower; and

    b. Where the borrower is financed by more than one secured creditor (including ARC), secured creditors (including ARC) holding not less than 60% of the outstanding SRs agree to such action.

    Explanation: 'Total Assets' means total assets as disclosed in its latest audited Balance Sheet immediately preceding the date of taking action.

iv. *Grounds for effecting Change in or Takeover of Management*

Subject to the eligibility conditions set forth in paragraph (iii) above, ARC shall be entitled to effect change in management or takeover of the management of business of the borrower on any of the following grounds:

    a. the borrower makes a wilful default in repayment of the amount due under the relevant loan agreement/s;

    b. the ARC is satisfied that the management of the business of the borrower is acting in a manner adversely affecting the interest of the creditors (including ARC) or is failing to take necessary action to avoid any event which would adversely affect the interest of the creditors;

    c. ARC is satisfied that the management of the business of the borrower is not competent to run the business resulting in losses/ non-repayment of dues to the ARC or there is a lack of professional management of the business of the borrower or the key managerial personnel of the business of the borrower have not been appointed for more than one year from the date of such vacancy which would adversely affect the financial health of the business of the borrower or the interests of the ARC as a secured creditor;

    d. the borrower has without the prior approval of the secured creditors (including ARC), sold, disposed of, charged, encumbered or alienated 10% or more (in aggregate) of its assets secured to the ARC;

    e. there are reasonable grounds to believe that the borrower would be unable to pay its debts as per terms of repayment accepted by the borrower;

    f. the borrower has entered into any arrangement or compromise with creditors without the consent of the ARC which adversely affects the interest of the ARC or the borrower has committed any act of insolvency;

    g. the borrower discontinues or threatens to discontinue any of its businesses constituting 10% or more of its turnover;

v. *Policy regarding Change in or Takeover of Management*

    a. Every ARC shall frame policy guidelines regarding change in or takeover of the management of the business of the borrower, with the approval of its Board of Directors and the borrowers shall be made aware of such policy of the ARC.

    b. Such policy shall generally provide for the following:

        i. The change in or takeover of the management of the business of the borrower should be done only after the proposal is examined by an Independent Advisory Committee to be appointed by the ARC consisting of professionals having technical/ finance/ legal background who after assessment of the financial position of the borrower, time frame available for recovery of the debt from the borrower, future prospects of the business of the borrower and other relevant aspects shall recommend to the ARC that it may resort to change in or takeover of the management of the business of the borrower and that such action would be necessary for effective running of the business leading to recovery of its dues;

       ii. The Board of Directors including at least two independent directors of the ARC should deliberate on the recommendations of the Independent Advisory Committee and consider the various options available for the recovery of dues before deciding whether under the existing circumstances the change in or takeover of the management of the business of the borrower is necessary and the decision shall be specifically included in the minutes.

vi. *Procedure for Change in or Takeover of Management*

    a. The ARC shall give a notice of 60 days to the borrower indicating its intention to effect change in or takeover of the management of the business of the borrower and calling for objections, if any.

    b. The objections, if any, submitted by the borrower shall be initially considered by the IAC and thereafter the objections along with the recommendations of the IAC shall be submitted to the Board of Directors of the ARC. The Board of Directors of ARC shall pass a reasoned order within a period of 30 days from the date of expiry of the notice period, indicating the decision of the ARC regarding the change in or takeover of the management of the business of the borrower, which shall be communicated to the borrower.

2. *Sale or Lease of a part or whole of the business of the borrower*

   No ARC shall take the measures specified in Section 9(1)(b) of the Act, until the Bank issues necessary guidelines in this behalf.

3. *Rescheduling of Debts*

   i.   Every ARC shall frame a policy, duly approved by the Board of Directors, laying down the broad parameters for rescheduling of debts due from borrowers;

   ii. All proposals should be in line with and supported by an acceptable business plan, projected earnings and cash flows of the borrower;

   iii. The proposals should not materially affect the asset liability management of the ARC or the commitments given to investors;

   iv. The Board of Directors may delegate powers to a committee comprising any director and / or any functionaries of the company for taking decisions on proposals for re-schedulement of debts;

   v.   Deviation from the policy should be made only with the approval of the Board of Directors.

   vi. In cases where ARCs have exposure to a borrower in respect of which a resolution plan is under implementation in terms of the Prudential Framework for Resolution of Stressed Assets dated June 7, 2019, as amended from time to time, ARCs shall also sign the inter-creditor agreement (ICA) and adhere to all its provisions.

4. *Enforcement of Security Interest*

   i.ARCs are required to obtain, for the purpose of enforcement of security interest, the consent of secured creditors holding not less than 60% of the amount outstanding to a borrower as against 75% hitherto.

   ii. While taking recourse to the sale of secured assets in terms of Section 13(4) of the Act, an ARC may itself acquire the secured assets, either for its own use or for resale, only if the sale is conducted through a public auction.

5. *Settlement of dues payable by the borrower*

   i.   a. Every ARC shall frame a policy duly approved by the Board of Directors laying down the broad parameters for settlement of debts due from borrowers;

        b. The policy may, inter alia, cover aspects such as cut-off date, formula for computation of realizable amount and settlement of account, payment terms and conditions, and borrower's capability to pay the amount settled;

        c. Where the settlement does not envisage payment of the entire amount agreed upon in one installment, the proposals should be in line with and supported by an acceptable business plan, projected earnings and cash flows of the borrower;

        d. The proposal should not materially affect the asset liability management of the ARC or the commitments given to investors;

e. The Board of Directors may delegate powers to a committee comprising any director and/ or any functionaries of the company for taking decisions on proposals for settlement of dues;

f. Deviation from the policy should be made only with the approval of the Board of Directors.

ii. Promoters of the defaulting company/ borrowers or guarantors are allowed to buy back their assets from the ARCs provided the following conditions are met:

a. Such a settlement is considered helpful in

   i. minimizing or eliminating the cost of litigation and the attendant loss of time;

   ii. arresting the negative impact of diminution in the value of secured assets which are likely to rapidly lose value once a unit becomes non- operational;

   iii. where the recovery/ resolution process would appear to be rather uncertain and;

   iv. where such settlement will be beneficial for restructuring purposes.

b. The valuation of the asset is worked out by the ARCs after factoring in the following components:

   i. The current value of the proposed settlement (valuation of the asset not more than six months old) vis-à-vis the net present value of the recoveries under the alternative mode of resolution taking into consideration the timelines involved therein.

   ii. likely positive or negative changes in the value of the secured asset on account of passage of time.

   iii. likely diminution in realization due to accumulation of statutory dues, liability to employees etc.

   iv. other factors, if any, which may affect recoveries.

c. ARCs shall frame a Policy duly approved by the Board of Directors, which should include the above aspects besides those already contained in clause 6(B)(5)(i)(a) mentioned above.

6. *Conversion of any portion of debt into equity of a borrower company*

   i. Every ARC shall frame a policy, duly approved by the Board of Directors, laying down the broad parameters for conversion of debt into shares of the borrower company;

   In cases of the Financial Assets which have turnaround potential after restructuring but normally with huge default and unsustainable level of debt, it will be necessary to arrive at sustainable level of debt, on the basis of evaluation of detailed business plan with projected level of operations, which can be serviced by the company. A part of residual unsustainable debt may have to be converted to equity for an optimal debt equity structure. While ARCs are permitted to have significant influence or have a say in decisions surrounding the borrower company's turnaround through conversion of debt into shares, they should not be seen to be running the companies. The shareholding of the ARC shall not exceed 26% of the post converted equity of the company under reconstruction.

Provided that ARCs meeting the criteria set out in sub-paragraph (a) below shall be exempted from the cap of 26% subject to compliance with the provisions of the Act, Guidelines/ Instructions issued by the Bank from time to time as applicable to ARCs as well as Foreign Exchange Management Act, 1999, Reserve Bank of India Act, 1934, Companies Act, 2013, SEBI Regulations and other relevant Statutes. The extent of shareholding post conversion of debt into equity shall be in accordance with permissible Foreign Direct Investment (FDI) limit for that specific sector.

a. ARCs that meet the conditions mentioned below are exempted from the limit of shareholding at 26% of post converted equity of the borrower company:

   i. The ARC shall be in compliance with NOF (Net Owned Funds) requirement of Rs.100 crore on an ongoing basis;

   ii. At least half of the Board of Directors of the ARC comprises of independent directors;

   iii. The ARC shall frame policy on debt to equity conversion with the approval of its Board of Directors and may delegate powers to a Committee comprising majority of independent directors for taking decisions on proposals of debt to equity conversion;

   iv. The equity shares acquired under the scheme shall be periodically valued and marked to market. The frequency of valuation shall be at least once in a month.

b. The ARC shall explore the possibility of preparing a panel of sector- specific management firms/ individuals having expertise in running firms/ companies which could be considered for managing the companies.

C. *Plan for realization of financial assets*

i. Every ARC may, within the planning period, formulate a plan for realization of assets, which may provide for one or more of the following measures:

   a. Rescheduling of payment of debts payable by the borrower;

   b. Enforcement of security interest in accordance with the provisions of the Act;

   c. Settlement of dues payable by the borrower;

   d. Change in or take-over of the management, or sale or lease of the whole or part of business of borrower as stated in paragraphs 6(B)(1) and 6(B)(2) herein above;

   e. Conversion of any portion of debt into shares of a borrower company.

ii. ARC shall formulate the policy for realization of financial assets under which the period for realization shall not exceed five years from the date of acquisition of the financial asset concerned.

iii. The Board of Directors of the ARC may increase the period for realization of financial assets so that the total period for realization shall not exceed eight years from the date of acquisition of financial assets concerned.

iv. In case the ARC is one of the lenders in an account where a resolution plan has been finalised and the same extends beyond the maximum resolution period allowed for ARCs as per clause (iii) above, the ARC may accept a resolution period co-terminus with other secured lenders.

v. The Board of Directors of the ARC shall specify the steps that will be taken by the ARC to realise the financial assets within the time frame referred to in clause (ii) or (iii) above as the case may be.

vi. The Qualified Buyers (QBs) shall be entitled to invoke the provisions of Section 7(3) of the Act only at the end of such extended period, if the period for realization is extended under clause (iii) above.

7. *Securitisation*

1. ***Issue of SRs*** - An ARC shall give effect to the provisions of Sections 7(1) and 7(2) of the Act through one or more trusts set up exclusively for the purpose. The ARC shall transfer the assets to the said trusts at the price at which those assets were acquired from the originator if the assets are not acquired directly on the books of the trust:

   i. The trusts shall issue SRs only to QBs; and hold and administer the financial assets for the benefit of the QBs;

   ii. The trusteeship of such trusts shall vest with the ARC;

   iii. The ARC proposing to issue SRs, shall, prior to such an issue, formulate a policy, duly approved by the Board of Directors, providing for issue of SRs under each scheme formulated by the trust;

   iv. The policy referred to in clause (iii) above shall provide that the SRs issued would be transferable / assignable only in favour of other QBs.

2. ***Investment in SRs issued by the trusts floated by ARC***

   ARC shall by transferring funds, invest a minimum of 15% of the SRs of each class issued by them under each scheme on an ongoing basis till the redemption of all the SRs issued under such scheme.

3. ***Restructuring Support Finance***

   An ARC can utilize a part of funds raised under a scheme from the QBs for restructuring of financial assets acquired under the relative scheme subject to following conditions:

   i. ARCs with acquired assets in excess of Rs.500 crore can float the fund under a scheme which envisages the utilization of part of funds raised from QBs in terms of Section 7(2) of the Act, for restructuring of financial assets acquired out of such funds.

ii. The extent of funds that shall be utilized for reconstruction purpose should not be more than 25% of the funds raised under the scheme in terms of Section 7(2) of the Act. The funds raised to be utilized for reconstruction (within the ceiling of 25%) should be disclosed upfront in the scheme. Further, the funds utilized for reconstruction purposes should be separately accounted for.

iii. Every ARC shall frame a policy, duly approved by the Board of Directors, laying down the broad parameters for utilization of funds raised from QBs under such a scheme.

11. Asset Classification

1. Classification

i. Every ARC shall, after taking into account the degree of well-defined credit weaknesses and extent of dependence on collateral security for realization, classify the assets [held in its own books] into the following categories, namely :

   a. Standard assets

   b. NPAs

ii. The NPAs shall be classified further as

   a. 'Sub-standard asset' for a period not exceeding twelve months from the date it was classified as NPA;

   b. 'Doubtful asset' if the asset remains a sub-standard asset for a period exceeding twelve months;

   c. 'Loss asset' if (A) the asset is non-performing for a period exceeding 36 months; (B) the asset is adversely affected by a potential threat of non- recoverability due to either erosion in the value of security or non-availability of security; (C) the asset has been identified as loss asset by the ARC or its internal or external auditor; or (D) the financial asset including SRs is not realized within the total time frame specified in the plan for realization formulated by the ARC under paragraph 6(C)(ii) or 6(C)(iii) and the ARC or the trust concerned continues to hold those assets.

iii. Assets acquired by the ARC for the purpose of asset reconstruction may be treated as standard assets during the planning period, if any.

2. Asset Reconstruction: Renegotiated / Rescheduled assets

i. Where the terms of agreement regarding interest and/ or principal relating to standard asset have been renegotiated or rescheduled by an ARC (otherwise than during planning period) the asset concerned shall be classified as sub-standard asset with effect from the date of renegotiation/ reschedulement or continue to remain as a sub-standard or doubtful asset as the case be.

ii. The asset may be upgraded as a standard asset only after satisfactory performance for a period of twelve months as per the renegotiated / rescheduled terms.

3. *Provisioning requirements*

Every ARC shall make provision against NPAs, as under: -

Asset Category	*Provision Required*	
Sub-standard Assets	A general provision of 10% of the outstanding;	
Doubtful Assets	(i)	100% provision to the extent the asset is not covered by the estimated realizable value of security;
	(ii)	In addition to item (i) above, 50% of the remaining outstanding.
Loss Assets		The entire asset shall be written off.
		(If, for any reason, the asset is retained in the books, 100% thereof shall be provided for).

(RBI T&P REPORT 2020-21)

A REVIEW OF THE WORKING OF ARCs

RBI's "REPORT ON TREND & PROGRESS OF BANKING IN INDIA,

2020-21": Report of the Committee to Review the Working of Asset Reconstruction Companies (ARCs): Excerpts

The ARC framework is designed to allow originators to focus on lending, by removing sticky stressed financial assets from their books. Experience so far, however, shows that ARCs' performance has been lacklustre, both in terms of ensuring recovery and revival of businesses. The Reserve Bank had set up a Committee (Chairperson: Shri Sudarshan Sen) to review the existing legal and regulatory framework applicable to them and to recommend measures to improve their efficacy. The Committee's report was released on November 2, 2021 for public comments.

Key recommendations of the Committee are set out below:

1. In order to incentivise lenders to sell NPAs at an early stage of stress, it has recommended the amortization of loss on sale of stressed assets over a period of two years.

2. To determine reserve price of financial assets worth Rs 500 crore and above, assessment by two valuers and for assets between Rs 100 crore and Rs 500 crore by one valuer is recommended.

3. In order to enhance ARCs' ability to acquire all related debt pertaining to a borrower, Reserve Bank may be empowered to specify the entities from which ARCs can acquire financial assets under Securitisation and Reconstruction of Financial Assets and Enforcement of Securities Interest (SARFAESI) Act, 2002. Further, using these powers, the Reserve Bank may consider permitting ARCs to acquire financial assets from all the regulated entities and retail investors.

4. For financial assets under consortium/multiple banking arrangements, if 66 per cent of lenders (by value) decide to accept an offer by an ARC, the same may be made binding on the remaining lenders and it must be implemented within 60 days of approval by majority of lenders.

5. Given that additional funding to the stressed borrowers is the key in reviving their businesses, ARCs should be allowed to use Securities and Exchange Board of India (SEBI) registered Alternative Investment Funds (AIFs) as an additional vehicle for facilitating restructuring/ recovery of debt acquired by them.

6. For better value realization and enhancing the effectiveness of ARCs in recovery, even the borrower's equity may be allowed to be sold to ARCs.

7. ARCs may be allowed to participate under IBC as a resolution applicant either through their SR trust or through the AIF sponsored by them.

8. To give impetus to listing and trading of SRs, the list of eligible qualified buyers may be expanded to include high net-worth individuals (HNIs), corporates, NBFCs/HFCs, trusts, family offices, pension funds and distressed asset funds with suitable safeguards.

9. To balance the need of protecting the interest of SR investors along with distribution of risk among willing and sophisticated investors, the minimum investment in SRs by an ARC may be specified at 15 per cent of the lenders' investment in SRs or 2.5 per cent of the total SRs issued, whichever is higher.

10. Considering the wider role envisaged for ARCs in the resolution of stressed assets, the minimum net owned fund requirement for ARCs may be increased to Rs 200 crore.

RBI's "REPORT ON TREND & PROGRESS OF BANKING IN INDIA, 2021-22":

Table IV.11: NPAs of SCBs Recovered through Various Channels

(Amount in Rs crore)

Recovery Channel	2020–21				2021–22 (P)			
	No. of cases referred	Amount involved	Amount recovered	Col 4 as % of Col 3	No. of cases referred	Amount involved	Amount recove-red *	Col 4 as % of Col 3
1	2	3	4	5	6	7	8	9
Lok Adalats	19,49,249	28,084	1,119	4	85,06,648	1,19,005	2,777	2.3
DRTs	28,182	2,25,361	8,113	3.6	29,487	47,165	12,114	25.7
SARFAES I	57,331	67,510	27,686	41	2,49,475	1,21,642	27,349	22.5
IBC@ #	536	1,35,319	27,311	20.2	885	1,99,250	47,421	23.8
Total	20,35,298	4,56,274	64,229	14	87,86,495	4,87,062	89,661	18.4

Notes: 1.   P: Provisional.

2.   *: Refers to the amount recovered during the given year, which could be with reference to the cases referred. during the given year as well as during the earlier years.

3.   DRTs: Debt Recovery Tribunals.

4.   @: Data in column no. 2 and 6 are the cases admitted by National Company Law Tribunals (NCLTs) under IBC.

5.   #: Data in column no. 3, 4 and 5 are with respect to 121 cases, and in column no. 7, 8 and 9 are with respect to 143 cases, where in resolution plans were approved during 2020-21 and 2021-22, respectively.

Source: Off-site returns, RBI and Insolvency and Bankruptcy Board of India (IBBI).

This Table shows that, in the year 2021-22, the total number of cases referred for resolution had jumped to more than 4 times the number in 2020-21 but the total amount involved saw an increase of only 6.7%. The number of Lok Adalat cases saw a jump of over 4 times, signaling a huge increase in small loans. SARFAESI cases also saw a jump of more than 4 times, both in terms of the number as well as the amount involved. The number of DRT cases increased by a miniscule 4.6% whereas the amount involved decreased by 20.9%. And the number of IBC cases increased by 65.1% and the amount involved, by 47.2%. In terms of both the amount involved as well as the amount recovered, IBC is the leader. The Pre-Packaged Insolvency Resolution Process (PPIRP) window for MSMEs was promulgated by IBBI on June 30, 2021 to assuage the mounting pressure of pending cases before NCLTs, reduce haircuts and improve declining recovery rates.

Table IV.12: Details of Financial Assets Securitised by ARCs

(Amount in Rs crore)

Item	Mar-20	Mar-21	Mar-22
Number of Reporting ARCs	28	24	28
1. Book Value of Assets Acquired	4,35,122	4,71,204	5,65,683
2. Security Receipt issued by SCs/ RCs	1,53,239	1,33,755	1,22,130
3. Security Receipts Subscribed to by:			
a. Banks	1,02,005	87,897	83,190
b. SCs/RCs	30,167	23,359	22,105
c. FIIs	10,367	10,156	4,548
d. Others (Qualified Institutional Buyers)	10,700	12,343	12,288
4. Amount of Security Receipts Completely Redeemed	18,213	23,131	23,396
5. Security Receipts Outstanding	1,09,168	85,298	69,219

Source: Quarterly statements submitted by ARCs.

The above Table shows that the share of SRs subscribed by banks in total SRs issued increased to 68 per cent in 2021-22. The share of ARCs also increased to 18.1 per cent from 17.5 per cent a year ago. Redemption of SRs issued by ARCs, which is an indicator of recovery through this mode, also increased during the year, resulting in a decline in the total SRs outstanding.

The pre-pack insolvency resolution process is yet to gain traction. Up to September 2022, only two cases had been admitted, so far, under the channel. Sales of stressed assets to ARCs have also gradually decreased; in 2021-22, only 3.2 per cent of the previous year's GNPAs were sold to ARCs (Chart IV.22a).

Un-Implementable Measures

There are three types of cases in the non-performing loans universe – Revivable Sick Unit Cases (Category 1), Recalcitrant Borrower/ OTS (One-Time Settlement) Cases (Category 2) and Seizure & Sale Cases (Category 3) – the first two, i.e. Category 1 and Category 2 cases, have the highest potential for unlocking value.

Under section 9, the SARFAESI Act lists seven measures for asset reconstruction: (*a*) proper management of the business of the borrower, by change in, or takeover of, the management of the business of the borrower; (*b*) sale or lease of a part or whole of the business of the borrower; (*c*) rescheduling of payment of debts payable by the borrower; (*d*) enforcement of security interest in accordance with the provisions of this Act; (*e*) settlement of dues payable by the borrower; (*f*) taking possession of secured assets in accordance with the provisions of this Act; and (*g*) conversion of any portion of debt into shares of a borrower company.

Of these, the first three asset reconstruction measures are suitable for tackling the two types of cases which have the highest potential for unlocking value – Category 1 and Category 2 cases. In the pre-IBC code era, our fixation with SARFAESI being a foreclosure law had ensured that *all* these three measures remained virtually unimplementable – the first one, on account of the stipulation that, after recovering its dues in full, the secured creditor will restore the management of the business to the borrower; the second one, for want of guidelines; and the third one, because it can be taken only if one is confident of implementing either any one of the first two, or the fifth one.

The restoration of management clause was stipulated under the take- over of management measure because, SARFAESI being a foreclosure law, does not address the issue of ownership. Company's ownership always remains with the borrower. People who wrote the law did not, perhaps, understand that a bank or an ARC is not in the business of running companies. They can, at best, find another company to take over a sick one. But such deals require you to have the legal right to transfer the ownership of the defaulter company. It is exactly this right that is available to a secured creditor in the U. S. under Reorganization Law but is not available here.

Fixing the Loopholes

An ARC can tackle the Revivable Sick Unit and Recalcitrant Borrower/ OTS cases only if we incorporate such a provision in the SARFAESI Act. We must also evolve a suitable structure for: (a) one-on-one negotiation between bank and ARC for sale of such NPAs; (b) extra- legal powers for ARC, including powers to aggregate debt, post- acquisition; (c) a new investor taking control of, and implementing a scheme of arrangement for, a company without going through the long- winded Company Court procedure, etc.; (d) enforcing market mechanism in sale of NPAs to ARCs; and (e) accountability for loss incurred by a bank when it rejects the highest bid offered as too low but is not able to recover *even that much, for years.*

The current stipulation that an ARC can take up a Revivable Sick Unit case *only* if it is an NPA and, that too, only after it has *acquired* at least one of the Company's NPAs from a bank first, needs to be changed. Most of the CDR (Corporate Debt Restructuring) cases fall outside the purview of ARCs simply because they are not NPA. Even where the target company's debt is an NPA, an ARC is obliged to put that much extra money at risk, which gives it no value-add.

We, therefore, need to transform SARFAESI from a foreclosure law into a foreclosure-cum-reorganization law. The role of ARC must be to sift sands for finding diamonds – the Category 1 and Category 2 cases – rather than merely disposing of garbage (Category 3 cases).

Mere cosmetic changes in the law and the regulation will not do. It is high time we took courage in both our hands and brought about systemic changes.

Some time back, RBI issued draft guidelines in respect of one asset reconstruction measure (out of a total of six stipulated under SARFAESI Act) that can be taken only by ARCs – "proper management of the borrower's business by effecting a change in, or take-over of, its management".

Guidelines for the second one – sale or lease of a part or whole of the business of the borrower – are still awaited.

These two measures can be powerful tools in the hands of ARCs for tackling difficult, going concern cases. A case of successful rehabilitation/ revival, to which the first measure applies, could add much greater value than, say, seizure & sale action and the right to sell or lease business under the second can be an effective antidote to recalcitrant management.

Together, these two measures have the potential to reconstruct asset reconstruction. But that will happen only when objective conditions for successful rehabilitation are created.

Corporate restructuring invariably needs infusion of fresh funds (debt and equity) and conversion of a part or whole of the borrower company's debt into equity and it is imperative that the final RBI Guidelines contain explicit enabling provisions for both. Certain legal cobwebs – such as precipitate action by a statutory authority after action for revival has been initiated, long- winded procedure for debt-equity conversion, etc. – also need to be cleared.

Reconstructing asset reconstruction would involve making progress on two fronts – one, correcting the balance in case of portfolio auctions; and two, facilitating corporate restructuring/ rehabilitation and opening up the opportunity for equity upsides.

Letter to the Prime Minister

On November 16, 2014 – barely six months after Modi had taken oath as the Prime Minister of India for the first time – his Government proposed to bring in two new reforms through amendments in the Micro, Small and Medium Enterprises Development (MSMED) Act; one, it would promote revival for the fit and proper companies; and two, for unfit companies, it would provide easier exits through liquidation proceedings. The news item, *"Government Proposes Norms for Easier Exits, Revival of MSMEs"* appeared in India's leading newspapers, along with the comment that the government had invited suggestions on this.

So, on November 28, 2014, I wrote a letter to the Prime Minister on this issue. These were some of the points that I made in the letter:

My suggestions and comments emanate from my first-hand experience in *financing* of *SMEs, rehabilitation* of *sick units* and management of *stressed assets,* including conduct of *in-depth, Techno-Economic Viability* studies to formulate *Turnaround Plans* and then *implement* the same, at the country's premier bank, and in *asset reconstruction.*

1. Bankruptcy as an *Independent Law*

While having the long-awaited bankruptcy law in place will be a *big positive* for the financial services industry in general and forrevival of sick units in particular, its enactment by way of an amendment to the MSMED Act will raise two questions:

    a. Will such an amendment to MSMED Act mean that the law will not be applicable to businesses *not* falling in any of these three categories – *large corporates*, for instance?

    b. Since the Companies Act, 2013 and the SARFAESI (Securitisation And Reconstruction of Financial Assets and Reinforcement of Security) Act, 2002 already have provisions for revival and rehabilitation of sick companies, will it not add to the confusion if we enact a third law covering the same?

2. Pillars of Reorganization Law

The structure for revival outlined under the proposed amendment to the MSMED Act is very different from that stipulated under the Companies Act. Whereas the criterion for determining *sickness* under the Companies Act is *failure to pay debt within 30 days of a demand notice being served by the secured creditors,* the one proposed under the MSMED Act is *erosion of half or more of the Company's net worth.* The latter, incidentally, is the standard definition of sickness in finance.

Clearly, under the Companies Act, the process is designed to be *driven* by the *secured creditors,* whereas under the proposed amendment to the MSMED Act, it would be driven by the *debtor/ borrower.*

As against this, under the Chapter 11 Reorganization Law in the U.S., a petition may be filed either by the debtor or the creditors. Once the petition is filed, the debtor becomes a debtor in possession and has a 120-day period during which it has an exclusive right to file a plan.

Once the petition is filed, a committee consisting, normally, of the largest unsecured creditors having claims against the debtor is appointed by the U.S. trustee which: one, consults with the debtor in possession on administration of the case; two, investigates the debtor's conduct and operation of the business; and three, participates in formulating a plan. The court, the U.S. trustee, the committee, or another party in interest acts to ensure the case's timely resolution. The creditors' right to file a competing plan provides incentive for the debtor to file a plan within the exclusivity period and acts as a check on excessive delay in the case.

Our laws do not stipulate any of this.

Hence:

a. **The objective of *unlocking value from revivable sick units*, quickly, will not be realized if we have multiple laws with multiple objectives. The company promoter's rehabilitation plan prepared under the reorganization law will get mired in court proceedings if lenders choose to take action under the SARFAESI Act. So, what we need is one bankruptcy-cum-reorganization law, like in the U.S., which can drive *both*, the debtor as well as the creditor, towards revival of sick units and, if that is not feasible, then allow recovery of the secured creditors' dues through sale of assets under SARFAESI.**

b. **This law should be formulated *not* as a provision in an existing Act, but as an independent Bankruptcy-cum-Reorganization law, on the lines of the Bankruptcy Code in the U.S., with an appropriate check-and-balance system for investigating the debtor's conduct, formulating a rehabilitation plan, monitoring its implementation, etc.**

3. Tackling the Ghosts in our System

It would be unrealistic to expect, though, that the process of revival of sick units will take off once the new law is enacted. For, there are so many *ghosts* sitting in our system, today.

We have many deficient laws and the situation gets aggravated by a system that allows inordinate delays in courts for frivolous grounds.

Let us take the MSMED Act as an example. It stipulates a maximum period of 45 days for payment of a supplier's bill by the buyer but the law remains only on paper. Despite a new law, the reality of undue – and arbitrary – delays in payment of bills by the party who has an upper hand, the buyer, has not changed one bit. In the case of SARFAESI, only the smaller, retail borrowers feel the threat of bank action under it whereas the larger, corporate ones, who have the wherewithal to manipulate our legal and administrative system, don't. And while there is a provision in the SARFAESI Act giving a secured creditor the right to take over the management of a recalcitrant borrower, there is *not* a single instance where this has actually happened.

Liquidation cases have remained unresolved for decades. The Companies Act is stuck in the Supreme Court as its bedrock National Company Law Tribunal (NCLT) provisions have been challenged by the Madras Bar Association. And the apex court has also ruled that a secured lender cannot take SARFAESI action to evict a lessee from a mortgaged property.

For NCLT (National Company Law Tribunal) members, the term of office was restricted to five years so that no self-respecting and competent lawyer could apply, and it is hilarious that a person with experience in virtually any field, save and except one – *company law* – qualified for appointment as a technical member!

Banks have, all along, been facing inordinate delays in the courts of District Magistrate (DM)/ Chief Metropolitan Magistrate (CMM); yet, in a recent judgment, Supreme Court has mandated that the rights of lessee of the mortgaged properties be decided by the DM/CMM court.

Therefore what we badly need, today, are two corrective steps: one, a cleaning up of the mess of multiple, inefficient laws; and two, having in place an administrative system to tackle the menace of inordinate delays in courts.

Overhauling the PSB System:

The pile of bad loans (or Non-Performing Assets/ NPAs) accumulated at PSBs over the last seven years is posing an existential threat to them. One estimate puts the figure of All Banks Loans in Default plus Under Threat of Default at Rs 10 lakh crore, which is more than the All Banks' Total Net Worth. With the Gross NPA Ratio of PSBs being more than double that of private sector banks, the real pressure is on the former. Under Basel III norms, PSBs will need an additional capital of Rs 4 lakh crore. Even the possibility of this huge burden forcing the government to reduce its stake to minority cannot be ruled out.

This monumental failure is a result of obnoxious practices (capitulation to dictates from above, errors of omission and commission, cronyism with bad promoters and acquiescence to inflated project costs), management deficiencies (lack of expertise, inadequate due diligence and a mind-set of "no accountability for not doing") and regulatory forbearance (liberal norms for "Restructured Standard" loans which gave banks an excuse to hide the NPAs).

In many potentially good Revivable Sick Unit cases, banks have actually compounded the unit's problems by: (a) Not taking any resolution decision for years – either in favour of revival/ restructuring or recalling the loan; (b) Using the presumptive right to go on debiting term loan installments in the borrower's cash credit account, thus blocking whatever little working capital happened to be available to it under the sanctioned limit; (c) Going on debiting interest (on both term loan and working capital loan) in the cash credit account till the account became NPA; (d) Not differentiating between a case where the unit had fallen sick on account of external factors but promoter was honest and a case where promoter had duped the bank or siphoned off funds; and (e) Refusing to infuse fresh funds, even in a good revivable case, simply because the company's loan had turned NPA.

However, post the path-breaking RBI initiatives (the first one being the Guidelines on "Early Recognition of Financial Distress, Prompt Steps for Resolution and Fair Recovery for Lenders: Framework for Revitalising Distressed Assets in the Economy", effective since April 1, 2014), PSBs have become more amenable to options for tackling bad loans rather than simply sitting over them. They have sold NPAs of Rs 80,000 crore to ARCs (Asset Reconstruction Companies) in the last fifteen months (as against Rs 2,100 crore in the previous year) and are now open to sell even non-NPA, stressed loans.

In the coming months, RBI will need to take many more such corrective steps so as to keep PSBs under a tight leash and ensure that our system lands in the comfort zone.

4. Revival/ Rehabilitation: The Road Ahead

Given these ground realities, what can be the road ahead for turning around the revivable cases held either in the books of the banks or the ARCs?

Neither banks nor ARCs have the wherewithal or the inclination to undertake revival of distressed sick units.

When confronted with a sick unit case, PSBs are game, at the most, for a "restructuring" of the loans – if the promoter plays his cards well and is able to persuade the bank to lend its minimum support. Normally, this includes a rescheduling of the company's loans, converting a part of it into equity and, in some cases, an increase in the working capital limit, subject to the company and/or promoter fulfilling certain tough conditions. Some of the lender sacrifices that are a standard in rehabilitation – writing off a part of the existing debt, waiving the interest accrued but not realized, and sanctioning new term loans for capital expenditure – are a complete "no-no". The Restructuring Plan itself is based *not* on an in-depth, Techno-Economic Viability (TEV) study, the *sine qua non* for rehabilitation, but on what concessions and facilities would be acceptable to the bank. As a result, only such cases as are *stressed but not distressed* yet, or those whose promoters have deep pockets are able to steer their companies around; others simply get washed away.

ARCs would have been able to add value had they been modeled as turnaround specialists. Instead, solving the banks' bad loans problem became their *raison d'etre*.

They have smugly played the role of either a *savior* (turn banks' bad loans into an investment in banks' books through the magic wand of *acquisition at an unwarranted, high price against issue of security receipts (SRs) to the selling bank itself*, a structure under which the ARC has to pay only 5-10% of the price in cash) or a *self-shooter* (acquire dud NPAs by *paying a higher-than-warranted price in cash* so that the selling bank books a profit on the deal even as ARC prepares itself for booking a loss after the hand-holding period of seven years is over). Given the pile of bad loans they are sitting on, they have no choice but to focus on recovery rather than rehabilitation. Blaming it on inadequate capital is a mistake; morphing ARC into a turnaround specialist institution may, therefore, be a difficult proposition.

The road-map outlined in the RBI Guidelines on "Early Recognition of Financial Distress" referred to earlier, which proposes to allow:

a. PE firms, large NBFCs and other institutions with proven expertise in resolution of NPAs and in turnaround management to participate in NPA auctions and restructuring of troubled company accounts, respectively;

b. Banks to extend finance to 'specialized' entities put together for acquisition of troubled companies; and

c. A specialized institution, with equity/ quasi-equity participation of the above entities, or international institutions and Government of India, to be set up and allowed to participate in restructuring of borrowal accounts along with banks and other lenders, is a good idea.

However, since only PE firms and foreign investors have deep pockets, a pre-requisite for investment in troubled companies, we need to focus on attracting investments from them. (Investment by "Turnaround NBFCs" would be feasible only if the regulator allows a deviation in the NPA norm – by stipulating a time-line of, say, seven years for its realization as applicable to ARCs, as against 90 days stipulated for NBFCs.)

In order to attract such investments, we need to:

a. **Categorize all stressed and distressed cases above, say, Rs 50 cr, that have suffered an erosion of 50% or more in their net worth as "troubled" companies;**

b. **Set up duly approved 'specialized' entities (SEs) for undertaking turnaround management of troubled companies;**

c. **Allow both SEs and PE funds/foreign investors to invest in turnaround companies and acquire the same, if required;**

d. **Make investment in troubled companies, by way of both debt and equity, a feasible and an attractive proposition for foreign investors; and**

e. **Allow such investment in the security receipts held in an ARC trust, in case the debt, having been sold by the banks(s), is in the books of the ARC(s).**

Since our existing regulations [The SEBI FVCI (Foreign Venture Capital Investor) Regulations, 2000 and SEBI AIF (Alternative Investment Funds) Regulations, 2012] already have provisions for benefits (such as free entry and exit pricing, exemption under the Takeover Code, status of Qualified Institutional Buyer, etc.) as well as tax exemptions for foreign investors (in case of investment from a country which has a double taxation avoidance treaty with us), all we would need to do is tweak the provision under the FVCI Regulations which currently restricts the investment in a financially weak or sick company to only 33.33% of the investor's total investible funds and that, too, only in equity share, a restriction that is actually laughable and makes no sense.

In the proposed Bankruptcy-cum-Reorganization Law, we will also need to include a provision for acquisition of the company and/ or take-over of its management by the new investor, if warranted.

Although SARFAESI Act has a provision for change in or take- over of management of the borrower company, it has a ridiculous clause mandating its restoration to the original promoter once it generates enough cash, under the new management, to repay the debt. So, we need to be careful while drafting the provision in the Bankruptcy-cum-Reorganization Law.

Given the huge pile of bad loans accumulated at PSBs and the logjam in functioning of ARCs, it would be a good idea to set up a government-owned specialized institution with the mandate

to, first, acquire the bad loans from PSBs at the market price and, then, clean up the mess by: (a) undertaking corporate restructuring of revivable cases with the help of the registered and approved 'specialized turnaround entities', PE firms and foreign investors; and (b) selling the non-revivable bad loans or physical assets to ARCs/ other entities. Being government institutions, this is what the Asset Management Companies, KAMCO in Korea and Danaharta in Malaysia, have been able to achieve, while ARCs in India being private sector companies have not been able to.

5. Other Corrective Measures Needed

Over-valuation of company's assets – so as to ensure that the promoter does not have to bring in his contribution – has become a standard practice, which PSBs have, by and large, acquiesced to. This is a deadly menace that PSBs need to fight.

They also employ the services of "government approved valuers" for valuation and "empanelled consultants" for restructuring of loans; they neither follow any standards, nor work under a code of ethics.

Lack of expertise in handling term loans is also a common phenomenon, and so is 'ad-hoc-ism' such as: a bank taking seizure & sale action in a good revivable case; giving the long rope of 'restructuring' to a rogue promoter who had, in the past, diverted and misused funds; technically written-off cases going out of the bank officials' radars, etc.

Reserve Bank needs to specify certain minimum standards and a code of ethics for members of these two professional categories.

Letter to RBI Governor

I followed it up by writing another letter, on December 5, 2014, to Dr. Raghuram Rajan, Governor, Reserve Bank of India, attaching a copy of the letter I had written to the Prime Minister earlier. Following were the main points in this letter:

Enacting a Bankruptcy-Cum-Reorganization Law

I have the honour and privilege of sharing with you a letter I just wrote to our honourable Prime Minister, giving my comments and suggestions on enactment of a bankruptcy-cum-reorganization law, which could play a critical role in tackling the corporate bad loans problem we are currently facing and making revival of sick units a doable proposition.

Since I have first-hand experience in the two areas that the proposed amendments to the MSMED Act cover, I thought of sharing some of my thoughts on this with the government and, now, with you.

You might recall that, some 14 months back, I had written a letter to you explaining what lay at the root of the problem of bad loans that our banks were facing. Much water has flown down the river since then and some of the path- breaking initiatives taken by Reserve Bank under your leadership have resulted in a monumental change. Rather than simply sitting over the bad loans, public sector banks (PSBs) have, now, become amenable to options for tackling them.

But the bad debts monster has only grown in size and we need to take more steps.

I have mulled over the propositions mentioned in the nodal RBI Guidelines on *"Early Recognition of Financial Distress, Prompt Steps for Resolution and Fair Recovery for Lenders: Framework for Revitalising Distressed Assets in the Economy"* and would like to offer my comments on some of them:

1. PE firms and large NBFCs with proven expertise in resolution/recovery may be allowed to participate in NPA auctions and authorized to take action under SARFAESI Act on a selective basis: While enlarging the group of participants in NPA auctions will be a welcome change, my sense is that this alone will not lead to an improvement in the resolution process because of the two bugs that we have in our system: one, since action under SARFAESI can be taken only if the acquirer acquires minimum 60% of the NPA debt, any acquisition below this level is ineffectual; and two, the standard route for sale of NPAs – auction of the debt held by each participating bank, *individually*, rather than together and *jointly* – gives no option for debt aggregation to the acquirer.

2. 'Specialized' entities, having expertise in turnaround management and adequate capital resources of their own (partly funded by a bank, if necessary), may be allowed to acquire troubled companies in order to turn them around: This is an *excellent* idea but, in order to implement this, we will need a suitable provision in the Insolvency and Bankruptcy Code. (The current provision in the SARFAESI Act is non- implementable on account of the restoration cause.) We will also need a suitable framework for registration and approval of these 'specialized' entities by Reserve Bank.

   While such 'specialized' (turnaround) entities could well be set up as an ARC, imposing this as a condition may not be the best option. For, in that case, a PE firm or an NBFC desirous of playing the game (both find a mention in the *"Early Recognition of Financial Distress"* Guidelines) would need to obtain a licence for operating as an ARC, first.

   But whatever route we take, we *must* put at least a handful of such entities in place fast.

3. Reserve Bank would allow banks to extend finance to 'specialized' entities put together for acquisition of troubled companies: Again, an *excellent* idea, somewhat on the lines of the Entrepreneur Scheme that SBI had launched, for start-ups, over four decades back. The Scheme was, however, not a great success because: one, the cap on funding stipulated – Rs 2 lakh – was too low; and two, with promoter having zero capital, risk for the enterprise was high. With adequate capitalization and appropriate incentive structures for the 'specialized' entities being stipulated under the proposed arrangement, these weaknesses would be taken care of. If the law can ensure hassle-free acquisition of a good revivable company, the idea should work this time around.

   As mentioned in my letter to the Prime Minister, provisions of the law need to be changed so as to allow the 'specialized' entities to: one, invest in troubled companies by way of both debt and equity, including investment in the security receipts of ARCs (in case the debt has been acquired by an ARC); and two, attract investment from foreign investors.

Under current provisions of the SEBI FVCI (Foreign Venture Capital Investor) Regulations, 2000 and the SEBI AIF (Alternative Investment Funds) Regulations, 2012, investment in a financially weak or sick company is restricted to only 33.33% of the investor's total investible funds and that, too, only in equity share. Such a restriction makes no sense and we need to remove it.

4. Alternatively (or additionally), a specialized institution may be created with equity/ quasi-equity participation of the above entities or international institutions with the Government of India holding a part of the stake: This may well be the best way to fix the flawed ARC model we currently have in operation.

I am of the view that we are at an inflexion point insofar as the corporate bad loans problem of PSBs is concerned. And it is time we tackled the issue head- on – in the same manner in which it was tackled by ASEAN countries in the wake of the Asian Financial Crisis of 1997 and by the U.S. in the wake of the sub-prime crisis of 2007-08. We need to clean up the corporate bad loans mess from the books of PSBs.

As mentioned in my letter to the Prime Minister, under Indian conditions, sale of NPAs by PSBs, *at the market price*, would happen only if the institution buying it enjoys special powers as a government entity. In the case of both ASEAN countries (Thailand, Korea and Indonesia) and the U.S., such sale was facilitated through the intermediation of a government entity: AMCs (Asset Management Companies) set up by the government in the case of the former and government-launched TARP (Troubled Assets Relief Program) in the case of the latter.

We need such a specialized institution – either fully owned by, or with a majority stake of, the government – to act as an intermediary which will, first, acquire the corporate NPAs at the market price and, then, seek to resolve them either by re-selling the same to an ARC, or arranging sale of the underlying companies to one of the 'specialized' (turnaround) entities mentioned in sub- paragraphs (2) and (3) above, or selling the physical assets of these companies in the open market.

In which case, it will be an additional institution, and not an alternative to the 'specialized' (turnaround) entities.

Crony Capitalism

The Finance Minister, in his Budget Speech on February 28, 2015, outlined the first resolute step to break the back of crony capitalism by announcing that the government will bring a "comprehensive bankruptcy code that will meet global standards and provide necessary judicial capacity".

As the then RBI Governor, Dr. Raghuram Rajan, put it in a speech, at that time: "*....we have to ask if India's system of credit is healthy. Unfortunately, the answer is that it is not. We need fundamental reforms starting with a change in mind set....*

"*.... across the world, default means the borrower has to make substantial sacrifices, else he would have no incentive to repay. For instance, a defaulting banker in Barcelona in mediaeval times was given time to* *repay his debts, during which he was put on a diet of bread and water. At the end of the period, if he could not pay he was beheaded. Punishments became less harsh over time. If you defaulted in Victorian England, you went to debtor's prison. Today, the borrower typically only forfeits the assets that have been financed, and sometimes personal property too if he is not protected by limited liability, unless he has acted fraudulently.*

"Why should the lender not share in the losses to the full extent? That is because he is not a full managing partner in the enterprise. In return for not sharing in the large profits if the enterprise does well, the lender is absolved from sharing the losses when it does badly, to the extent possible. By agreeing to protect the lender from "downside" risk, the borrower gets cheaper financing, which allows him to retain more of the "upside" generated if his enterprise is successful.

".....the sanctity of the debt contract has been continuously eroded in India in recent years, not by small borrower but by the large borrower. And this has to change if we are to get banks to finance the enormous infrastructure needs and industrial growth that this country aims to attain.

"The reality is that too many large borrowers see the lender, typically a bank, as holding not a senior debt claim that overrides all other claims when the borrower gets into trouble, but a claim junior to his equity claim. In much of the globe, when a large borrower defaults, he is contrite and desperate to show that the lender should continue to trust him with management of the enterprise. In India, too many large borrowers insist on their divine right to stay in control despite their unwillingness to put in new money. The firm and its many workers, as well as past bank loans, are the hostages in this game of chicken -- the promoter threatens to run the enterprise into the ground unless the government, banks, and regulators make the concessions that are necessary to keep it alive. And if the enterprise regains health, the promoter retains all the upside, forgetting the help he got from the government or the banks – after all, banks should be happy they got some of their money back!

"Why do we have this state of affairs? The most obvious reason is that the system protects the large borrower and his divine right to stay in control.

"This is not for want of laws. The Debts Recovery Tribunals (DRTs) were set up under the Recovery of Debts Due to Banks and Financial Institutions (RDDBFI) Act, 1993 to help banks and financial institutions recover their dues speedily without being subject to the lengthy procedures of usual civil courts. The Securitization and Reconstruction of Financial Assets and Enforcement of Security Interests (SARFAESI) Act, 2002 went a step further by enabling banks and some financial institutions to enforce their security interest and recover dues even without approaching the DRTs. Yet the amount banks recover from defaulted debt is both meagre and long delayed. The amount recovered from cases decided in 2013-14 under DRTs was Rs. 30590 crore while the outstanding value of debt sought to be recovered was a huge Rs. 2,36,600 crore. Thus recovery was only 13% of the amount at stake.

"While these views have gained currency because of recent revelations of possible corruption in banks, my sense is that Occam's Razor suggests a more relevant explanation – the system renders the banker helpless vis-a- vis the large and influential promoter. While we should not slow our efforts to bring better governance and more transparency to banking, we also need to focus on reforming the system."

ROAD MAP FOR THE FUTURE

For recovering their dues from large, corporate borrowers (who had the wherewithal to manipulate our legal and administrative system), banks had only two workable options, then: either take action under the SARFAESI (Securitisation And Reconstruction of Financial Assets and Enforcement of Security Interest) Act or file an application under the Companies Act, 2013 for liquidating the borrower company. But, in both cases, the issue would remain stuck in the court for years, just as it used to happen in the earlier civil court cases.

So, enacting a bankruptcy code legislation, with a mechanism for time- bound, fast action under the supervision of a "Resolution Professional" – and not a civil court – was the biggest reform that could have been undertaken.

For, it was expected to have two positive outcomes: one, to facilitate a time- bound exit for lenders in non-revivable cases; and two, to ensure that the revivable ones get necessary attention for a quick turn-around.

But the Government's earlier proposal to bring this law through the back door – by way of an amendment to the MSMED (Micro, Small and MediumEnterprises Development) Act, 2006 – would have been a disaster because: one, it would have left large corporates – an important benefactor of crony capitalism – out of its purview; and two, the attempt to cobble together multiple laws in one place would, as it had happened in many cases in the past, have failed miserably.

This law should be formulated not as a provision in an existing Act, but as an independent Bankruptcy-cum-Reorganization law, on the lines of the Bankruptcy Code in the U.S., with an appropriate check-and-balance system for investigating the debtor's conduct, formulating a rehabilitation plan, monitoring its implementation, etc.

It would be a good idea to set up a government-owned specialized institution with the mandate to, first, acquire the bad loans from PSBs at the market price and, then, clean up the mess.

As mentioned in my letter to the Prime Minister, under Indian conditions, sale of NPAs by PSBs, at the market price, would happen only if the institution buying it enjoys special powers as a government entity. In the case of both ASEAN countries (Thailand, Korea and Indonesia) and the U.S., such sale was facilitated through the intermediation of a government entity: AMCs (Asset Management Companies) set up by the government in the case of the former and government-launched TARP (Troubled Assets Relief Program) in the case of the latter.

We need such a specialized institution – either fully owned by, or with a majority stake of, the government – to act as an intermediary which will, first, acquire the corporate NPAs at the market

price and, then, seek to resolve them either by re-selling the same to an ARC, or arranging sale of the underlying companies to one of the 'specialized' (turnaround) entities mentioned in sub-paragraphs (2) and (3) above, or selling the physical assets of these companies in the open market.

In the letter, I also offered my comments on the propositions mentioned in the nodal RBI Guidelines on *"Early Recognition of Financial Distress, Prompt Steps for Resolution and Fair Recovery for Lenders: Framework for Revitalising Distressed Assets in the Economy".*

On February 28, 2015, in his Budget Speech, the then Finance Minister, Mr. Arun Jaitley said: *"Bankruptcy law reform, that brings about legal certainty and speed, has been identified as a key priority for improving the ease of doing business. SICA (Sick Industrial Companies Act) and BIFR (Bureau for Industrial and Financial Reconstruction) have failed in achieving these objectives. We will bring a comprehensive Bankruptcy Code in fiscal 2015- 16, that will meet global standards and provide necessary judicial capacity."*

By then, a "Bankruptcy Law Reforms Committee" had already been constituted under the chairmanship of Dr. T. K. Viswanathan on 28 August, 2014. The Committee submitted its Report to the Government of India on November 4, 2015.

Letter to Ministry of Finance

In my letter of November 20, 2015 to the Ministry of Finance, Government of India, I made the following comments and suggestions on the Bankruptcy Law Reforms Committee Report:

For me, it is a matter of great satisfaction that the proposed bill is on the lines of what I had recommended, one year back, in terms of my letter of November 28, 2014 addressed to the Prime Minister (copy attached hereto for your ready reference).

The Draft Bill has crafted an innovative structure to push reforms. In fact, proposals like minimizing the role of the adjudicating authority (NCLT and DRT), establishing Insolvency and Bankruptcy Board of India as the new super regulator with a mandate to unleash reforms (ensuring high recovery rates in net present value (NPV) terms, low delays, coverage for all types of claims, etc.), spawning a set of virtually two new industries by nudging for the establishment of multiple private self-regulatory Insolvency Professional (IP) and Information Utility (IU) agencies, mandating that they work under a "regulated self-regulation" model (under which the agencies themselves have to lay down minimum standards for action and control of the entities registered with, and functioning under, them and ensure that these are strictly adhered to), strengthening the information infrastructure so to manage live databases on defaults and financials of all debtors, etc. go far beyond what one would have imagined as feasible, earlier.

The Report [Volume 1] rightly observes that:

1. *"A sound bankruptcy process is one that helps creditors and debtors realize and agree on whether the entity is facing financial failure or business failure...(If a viable, turnaround case is treated as a "failed business model", the value that could have been earned (by way) of keeping it as a going*

concern is lost... A sound bankruptcy process is one that (makes creditors and debtors agree) on a financial rearrangement to preserve the economic value of the business...Through (such) a financial rearrangement, the enterprise remains a going concern."

(3.2 The role that insolvency and bankruptcy plays in debt financing)

2. *"(A)...financial rearrangement...can earn the creditors a higher economic value than shutting down the enterprise. On the other hand, where the cost of the financial arrangement required to keep the enterprise going will be higher than the NPV of future expected cash flows, the enterprise is considered unviable or bankrupt and is better shut down as soon as possible."*

(3.2.1 Assessing viability)

3. *"However, the assessment of viability is difficult. There is no fixed or unique approach to answer this question. In an ideal environment, the assessment will be the outcome of a collective decision. Here, creditors and debtor will negotiate a potential new financial arrangement. Each of them will balance all available information, including all future possibilities of the economic environment under which the enterprise will operate, as well as all alternative investment opportunities available to the creditors as well as the debtor."*

(3.2.1 Assessing viability)

4. *"In the negotiation, the debtor is likely to request that creditors restructure their liabilities so as to ease the liquidity stress of future repayments. The proposal may contain the need for fresh financing, either from existing creditors or from new financiers. In exchange, the debtor may offer to reorganize the operations of the enterprise by giving up some rights in management or to change the size of operations. Creditors will evaluate the proposal and offer modifications on their own. If both sides see the possibility of value in the enterprise, these negotiations will settle on a new financial arrangement. On the other hand, if they cannot agreeon a solution, it will be optimal for the creditors to sell the assets available and shut down the enterprise."*

(3.2.1 Assessing viability)

5. *"From the viewpoint of the economy, some firms undoubtedly need to be closed down. But many firms possess useful organizational capital. Across a restructuring of liabilities, and in the hands of a new management team and a new set of owners, some of this organizational capital can be protected. The objective of the bankruptcy process is to create a platform for negotiation between creditors and external financiers which can create the possibility of such rearrangements."*

(3.2.3 What can a sound bankruptcy law achieve?)

6. *"Control of a company is not (a) divine right. When a firm defaults on its debt, control of the company should shift to the creditors. In the absence of swift and decisive mechanisms for achieving this, management teams and shareholders retain control after default. Bankruptcy law must address this."*

(3.2.3 What can a sound bankruptcy law achieve?)

7. *"The illegitimate transfer of wealth out of companies by controlling shareholders is malfeasance. When a company is sound, corporate governance ensures that the benefits obtained by every share are equal. When a company approaches default, managers may anticipate this ahead of time and illicit transfers of cash may take place. The bankruptcy process must be designed with a particular focus on blocking such behavior, which is undoubtedly malfeasance."*

(3.2.3 What can a sound bankruptcy law achieve?)

8. *"With regard to the two regulated industries (information utilities and insolvency professionals/ agencies), the Board will have legislative, executive and quasi-judicial functions."*

(4.1.4 Functions of the regulator)

9. *"In the case of insolvency resolution, a failure of the process may result from two main sources: collusion between the parties involved and poor quality of execution of the process itself."*

(4.4.1 Mandates for IPs)

10. *"In India today, there are professionals and intermediaries that offer services to resolve financial distress... These include lawyers, accountants and auditors, valuers and specialist resolution managers...(Given) the critical role that the Code envisages for these entities in the resolution process... the Board should set minimum standards for the selection of these professionals, along with their licensing, appointment, functioning and conduct under the Code."*

(4.4.1 Mandates for IPs)

11. *"The Indian experience on self-regulating professional bodies (such as Institute of Chartered Accountants of India (ICAI), Bar Council of India and Institute of Company Secretaries (ICSI)) has been reasonably positive in the development of their respective professions and professional standards. However, the experience on their role in regulating and disciplining their members has been mixed. In comparison, financial regulators (such as SEBI and RBI) have had greater success in preventing systemic market abuse and in promoting consumer protection."*

(4.4.3 IP Regulatory Structure)

12. *"This approach has many strengths:*

   - *Asset stripping by promoters is controlled after and before default.*
   - *The promoters can make a proposal that involves buying back the company for a certain price, alongside a certain debt restructuring.*
   - *Others in the economy can make proposals to buy the company, at a certain price, alongside a certain debt restructuring.*
   - *All parties know that if no deal is struck within the stipulated period, the company will go into liquidation. This will help avoid delaying tactics. The inability of promoters to steal from the company, owing to the supervision of the IP, also helps reduce the incentive to have a slow lingering death.*

> ■ *The role of the adjudicator will be on process issues: To ensure that all Financial Creditors were indeed on the creditors committee, and that 75% of the creditors do indeed support the resolution plan."*

(The Insolvency Resolution Process (IRP), Executive Summary)

Finally, the Report, most appropriately, lays down the role of the Board as "the supervisor of the industry of insolvency professionals (IPs), as well as the regulator for the overall insolvency and bankruptcy processes in the country."

(4.1.5 Statistical and research functions)

One crucial area which has been left uncovered, though, is turn-around management – the recipe for correcting, and unlocking value from, what the Report labels as cases of "financial failure" (a persistent mismatch between payments by the enterprise and receivables into the enterprise, even though the business model is generating revenues), as opposed to liquidation cases, which are cases of "business failure" (a breakdown in the business model of the enterprise, leading to inability to generate sufficient revenues to meet payments).

Since "examining company's viability for a revival" is one of the tasks assigned to IPs, they will need to incorporate turnaround management as one of the vital components of their package and include it in the list of their executive functions. Turnaround professionals will, thus, become a part of the collegium of professionals allowed to be registered as IPs. Alongside that, standards for ethics and for conducting the study and preparing and implementing the rehabilitation plan, etc. will need to be set under the Board's supervision.

But, on the lines of the Institute of Chartered Accountants of India (ICAI), Bar Council of India and Institute of Company Secretaries (ICSI), what we will also need is an autonomous institutional framework for registering the practicing turnaround professionals as members and stipulating minimum standards, including ethical ones, to be followed by them.

There are two reputed international organizations that have done seminal work in this field: Turnaround Management Society (TMS), which is headquartered in Hamburg, Germany; and Turnaround Management Association, which has its headquarters in Chicago, U.S.A. They offer many services, including consulting; have distinguished professionals on their rolls; and possess sound knowledge database. They also register turnaround professionals from across different countries.

We may invite them to set up an office in India and evolve a set of turnaround management standards, especially for professionals in this county.

Currently, many of the turnaround consultancies have engineers and experienced bankers on their panel. For an IP, an accountant may be a good choice for the task of checking company transactions and illegal diversion of assets and a lawyer, for handling liquidation proceedings. But, for the task of examining viability, a banking professional with experience and expertise in corporate finance and rehabilitation/ turnaround may be the best choice.

More so, because the proposed Code stipulates that it is the debtor – not the creditor – who must propose the name of a registered Insolvency Professional (IP) for managing the Insolvency Resolution Process (IRP). Since both the debtor and the creditor have to negotiate with each other, a banking professional representing the debtor may be a good choice.

Therefore, two more categories of professionals need to be added: experienced banking professionals registered with the Indian Institute of Bankers and engineers registered with the Indian Institute of Engineers.

INSOLVENCY & BANKRUPTCY CODE, THE KEY TO UNLOCKING VALUE

Both for the companies under stress and for their lenders, the earlier system was anarchic. Lenders faced numerous roadblocks to recovery from non- performing loans (i.e., NPAs) even as incompetent and dishonest promoters of willful defaulter companies remained in full control; recalcitrant borrowers used our clogged and dysfunctional legal system to their advantage leading to inordinate delays; and, in the absence of an effective structure for turnaround management, viable turnaround cases were driven to a slow, lingering death.

This was virtually a template for destroying economic value.

Promulgating the Insolvency and Bankruptcy Code, 2016 (IBC) was the biggest reform for tackling this menace and unlocking value from stressed assets/ bad loans.

It created a new legal system, by putting a bar on the jurisdiction of civil court "in any matter in which the Adjudicating Authority or the Board is empowered by, or under, this Code to pass any order and no injunction shall be granted by any court or other authority in respect of any action taken or to be taken in pursuance of any order passed by such Adjudicating Authority or the Board under this Code" (Section 231, IBC, 2016) and transformed the management structure for handling bad loans. A new regulatory authority – the Insolvency and Bankruptcy Board of India (IBBI) – was set up and the National Company Law Tribunal (NCLT), constituted under section 408 of the Companies Act, 2013, was designated as the Adjudicating Authority (Section 5).

Under the new law, Central Government appoints the Chairperson, three members of the Board (IBBI) from amongst the officers of the Central Government (representing the Ministry of Finance, Ministry of Corporate Affairs and Ministry of Law, *ex officio*), and five other members – of whom at least three will be whole-time members. One member is nominated by the Reserve Bank of India, *ex officio*. The appointment of the Chairperson and the members of the Board, other than the appointment of an *ex officio* member under this section, is made after obtaining the recommendation of a selection committee consisting of Cabinet Secretary, Secretary to the Government of India, Chairperson of IBBI, and three experts of repute from the field of finance, law, management, insolvency and related subjects. The guiding principle for selecting the Chairperson and other members of the Board will be: *"persons of ability, integrity and standing, who have shown capacity in dealing with problems relating to insolvency or bankruptcy and have special knowledge and experience in the field of law, finance, economics, accountancy or administration"*. (Section 189)

Framework for Insolvency Resolution

IBC code has put in place a robust legal and operational framework for insolvency resolution, both for corporates as well as for individuals and partnership firms. For corporates, the Adjudicating Authority is NCLT (National Company Law Tribunal) and for individuals and partnerships, it is DRT (Debt Recovery Tribunal).

The four pillars of the Corporate Insolvency Resolution Process (CIRP) are: one, minimum role for the Adjudicating Authority (NCLT); two, a new dominion of Insolvency Professional (IP) Agencies and Information Utility (IU) created for managing the insolvency process; three, an information infrastructure with strict rules for filing detailed information with IUs, both on defaults and on the financials of debtors, which IPs can easily access in the course of the insolvency process; and four, the Insolvency and Bankruptcy Board of India (IBBI) as the new super regulator. The mandate to all entities involved is to ensure high recovery rates in *net present value (NPV)* terms and low delays, and to complete the insolvency resolution process within the prescribed period of 180 days.

The basic structure of the IBC code conforms to international standards: a step- by-step procedure for insolvency resolution – from initiating the process, to examining the viability of reorganization/ turnaround, to forcing liquidation in case the turnaround option is not feasible; both debtor and creditor having the right to initiate the corporate insolvency resolution process; a clear time-line for completing every step; etc.

But its operationalization has been aligned to suit Indian conditions.

Thus: instead of being supervised by a Bankruptcy Court as in the U.S., in our country the insolvency process is almost entirely handled by the Insolvency Professional (IP), with NCLT (National Company Law Tribunal) being the Adjudicating Authority, or the judge (in place of the civil court), and IBBI (Insolvency & Bankruptcy Board of India), or the Board, playing a pivotal role; instead of the seven largest *unsecured creditors* forming the creditors committee, *all Financial Creditors* as well as *Operational Creditors* are part of it; and, as against only Corporate Debtor having an exclusive right to file a reorganization plan in the US, either a Financial Creditor, or an Operational Creditor, or the Corporate Debtor itself may initiate the Corporate Insolvency Resolution Process (CIRP), which will get approved only if at least 51 per cent of the creditors (Sec 21 (8), IBC Amended Up To 12-08-2021) support it, with the adjudicator's role being limited to supervision of the process followed. If creditors reach no agreement on a solution to the problem within the stipulated time, the liquidation process will get triggered, automatically, along with appointment of an IP as the liquidator.

Appointment of IRP

Where an application for Corporate Insolvency Resolution Process is made by a Financial Creditor or the Corporate Debtor (CD) to the Adjudicating Authority, the Resolution Professional proposed therein gets appointed as the "Interim Resolution Professional", or IRP, if no disciplinary proceedings are pending against him. Where the application for corporate insolvency resolution process is made by an Operational Creditor and no proposal for an interim resolution professional is made, the Adjudicating Authority makes a reference to the Board for the recommendation of an insolvency professional who may act as an interim resolution professional.

(Section 16, IBC Amended Up To 12-08-2021)

Duties of IRP

The IRP has to monitor the assets of the CD and manage its operations till either he himself or another Insolvency Professional is appointed as the Resolution Professional by the Committee of Creditors. The IRP collects all information relating to the assets, finances and operations of the CD for determining its financial position, collates all the claims submitted by creditors to him, pursuant to the public announcement made under sections 13 and 15, constitutes a Committee of Creditors (CoC), monitors the assets of the CD and manages its operations until either the IRP himself is appointed as the RP or another RP is appointed in his place by the CoC for the Corporate Insolvency Resolution Process (CIRP). The RP appointed takes control and custody of all the assets over which the CD has ownership rights.

The IRP has to make every effort to protect and preserve the value of CD's property and manage its operations on a going concern basis. His role gives him the authority to appoint accountants, legal and other professionals, enter into contracts on behalf of the CD, raise interim finance (without creating any security interest over CD's encumbered properties), issue instructions to CD's personnel and take all such actions as are necessary to keep it a going concern.

Committee of Creditors

After collating all claims received against the CD, the IRP constitutes a Committee of Creditors (CoC) comprising all Financial Creditors. Where the CD owes financial debts to two or more Financial Creditors as part of a consortium or agreement, all of them will be part of CoC, with their voting share getting determined on the basis of the financial debts owed to them. Where a creditor is both a Financial Creditor as well as an Operational Creditor, such person will be a Financial Creditor to the extent of the financial debt owed by the CD and shall be included in the CoC. The first meeting of the Committee of Creditors is to be held within seven days of the constitution of the CoC, at which the CoC may, by a majority vote of not less than sixty-six (Sec 22 (1) & (2), IBC Amended Up To 12-08- 2021) per cent of the voting share of the Financial Creditors, either resolve to appoint the IRP as the RP or to replace the IRP by another RP.

Corporate Insolvency Resolution Process

The RP appointed by the CoC conducts the entire Corporate Insolvency Resolution Process and manages the operations of the CD during the corporate insolvency resolution process period and even after its expiry, until an order approving the Resolution Plan or appointing a liquidator under it is passed by the Adjudicating Authority. The RP will also exercise all the powers and perform duties vested or conferred on the IRP. The IRP will provide all the information, documents and records pertaining to the CD in his possession and knowledge to the RP.

Ensuring continued business operations of the CD and preserving and protecting its assets is the prime duty of the RP. So, the RP will: (a) take immediate custody and control of all the assets of the CD, including its business records; (b) represent and act on behalf of the CD with third parties, exercise rights for the benefit of the CD in judicial, quasi-judicial or arbitration proceedings; (c) raise interim finances subject to the approval of the CoC under Section 28; (d) appoint accountants, legal or other professionals in the manner as specified by the Board; (e) maintain an updated list of claims; (f) convene and attend all meetings of the Committee of Creditors; (g) prepare the information memorandum in accordance with section 29; (h) invite prospective resolution applicants, who fulfil such criteria as may be laid down by him with the approval of committee of creditors, having regard to the complexity and scale of operations of the business of the CD and such other conditions as may be specified by the Board, to submit a resolution plan or plans; (i) present all resolution plans at the meetings of the CoC; (j) file application for avoidance of transactions in accordance with Chapter III, if any; and (k) such other actions as may be specified by the Board.

(Sec 25, IBC Amended Up To 12-08-2021)

Powers & Functions of the Board

The Board has the authority to: specify the eligibility for registration and register IP Agencies, IPs and IUs; renew, suspend or cancel such registrations; regulate their working, levy fee or other charges of insolvency professional agencies, insolvency professionals and information utilities, and specify regulations for their functioning; lay down the curriculum for IPs' examination for enrolment as members of the IP Agencies; carry out investigations on IP Agencies, IPs and IUs and pass orders as may be required; monitor the performance of IP Agencies, IPs and IUs; call for any information and records from the IP Agencies, IPs and IUs and publish the same; specify regulations for collecting and storing data by the IUs and for providing access to such data; collect and maintains records relating to insolvency and bankruptcy cases and disseminate information relating to such cases; constitute such committees as may be required, including committees for efficient discharge of Board's functions as laid down in section 197; promote transparency and best practices in its governance; maintain websites and such other universally accessible repositories of electronic information as may be necessary; enter into memorandum of understanding with any other statutory authorities; issue necessary guidelines to the IP Agencies, IPs and IUs; specify mechanism for redressal of grievances against IPs, IP Agencies and IUs and pass orders relating to complaints filed against the aforesaid for compliance of the provisions of this Code and the regulations issued hereunder; conduct periodic study, research and audit on the functioning and performance of the IP Agencies, IPs and IUs at such intervals as may be specified by the Board; specify mechanisms for issuing regulations, including the conduct of public consultation processes before notification of any regulations; make regulations and guidelines on matters relating to insolvency and bankruptcy as may be required under the Code, including mechanism for time-bound disposal of the assets of the Corporate Debtor or debtor; and perform such other functions as may be prescribed.

The Board may make model bye-laws to be adopted by the IP Agencies which may provide for: (a) minimum standards of professional competence of the members of IP Agencies; (b) the standards for professional and ethical conduct of the members of IP Agencies; (c) requirements for enrolment of persons as members of IP Agency which shall be non-discriminatory (in terms of religion, caste, gender or place of birth and such other grounds as may be specified); (d) the manner of granting membership; (e) setting up of a governing board for the internal governance and management of insolvency professional agency in accordance with the regulations specified by the Board; (f) the information required to be submitted by members including the form and the time for submitting such information; (g) the specific classes of persons to whom services shall be provided at concessional rates or for no remuneration by members; (h) the grounds on which penalties may be levied upon the members of insolvency professional agencies and the manner thereof; (i) a fair and transparent mechanism for redressal of grievances against the members of IP agencies; (j) the grounds under which IPs may be expelled from the membership of insolvency professional agencies; (k) the quantum of fee and the manner of collecting fee for inducting persons as its members; (l) the procedure for enrolment of persons as members of insolvency professional agency; (m) the manner of conducting examination for enrolment of insolvency professionals; (n) the manner of monitoring and reviewing the working of insolvency professionals who are members; (o) the duties and other activities to be performed by members; (p) the manner of conducting disciplinary proceedings against its members and imposing penalties; (q) the manner of utilising the amount received as penalty imposed against any insolvency professional.

Notwithstanding anything contained in any other law for the time being in force, while exercising the powers under this Code, the Board shall have the same powers as are vested in a civil court under the Code of Civil Procedure, 1908 (5 of 1908), while trying a suit, in respect of the following matters, namely: (i) the discovery and production of books of account and other documents, at such place and such time as may be specified by the Board; (ii) summoning and enforcing the attendance of persons and examining them on oath; (iii) inspection of any books, registers and other documents of any person at any place; (iv) issuing of commissions for the examination of witnesses or documents.

(Sec 196, IBC Amended Up To 12-08-2021)

The Board may, for the efficient discharge of its functions, constitute advisory and executive committees or such other committees, as it may deem fit, consisting of a Chairperson and such other members as may be specified by regulations. (Sec 197, IBC Amended Up To 12-08-2021)

Notwithstanding anything contained in this Code, where the Board does not perform any act within the period specified under this Code, the relevant

Adjudicating Authority may, for reasons to be recorded in writing, condone the delay.

(SEC 198, IBC Amended Up To 12-08-2021)

Insolvency Professionals

No person shall render his services as insolvency professional under this Code without being enrolled as a member of an insolvency professional agency and registered with the Board.

(SEC 206, Amended Up To 12-08-2021)

Every insolvency professional shall, after obtaining the membership of any insolvency professional agency, register themselves with the Board within such time, in such manner and on payment of such fee, as may be specified by regulations.

The Board may specify the categories of professionals or persons possessing such qualifications and experience in the field of finance, law, management, insolvency or such other field, as it deems fit.

(SEC 207, Amended Up To 12-08-2021)

Functions and Obligations of Insolvency Professionals

Where any insolvency resolution, fresh start, liquidation or bankruptcy process has been initiated, it shall be the function of an insolvency professional to take such actions as may be necessary, in the following matters, namely: (a) a fresh start order process under Chapter II of Part III; (b) individual insolvency resolution process under Chapter III of Part III; (c) corporate insolvency resolution process under Chapter II of Part II; (d) individual bankruptcy process under Chapter IV of Part III; and (e) liquidation of a Corporate Debtor firm under Chapter III of Part II.

(SEC 208 (1), IBC Amended Up To 12-08-2021)

Where the name of the insolvency professional proposed to be appointed as a resolution professional, is approved under clause (e) of sub-section (2) of section 54A, it shall be the function of such insolvency professional to take such actions as may be necessary to perform his functions and duties prior to the initiation of the pre-packaged insolvency resolution process under Chapter III-A of Part II.

Every insolvency professional shall abide by the following code of conduct: (a) to take reasonable care and diligence while performing his duties; (b) to comply with all requirements and terms and conditions specified in the byelaws of the insolvency professional agency of which he is a member; (c) to allow the insolvency professional agency to inspect his records; (d) to submit a copy of the records of every proceeding before the Adjudicating Authority to the Board as well as to the insolvency professional agency of which he is a member; and (e) to perform his functions in such manner and subject to such conditions as may be specified. *(SEC 208 (1A), IBC Amended Up To 12-08-2021)*

Where the name of the insolvency professional proposed to be appointed as a resolution professional, is approved under clause (e) of sub-section (2) of section 54A, it shall be the function of such insolvency professional to take such actions as may be necessary to perform his functions and duties prior to the initiation of the pre-packaged insolvency resolution process under Chapter III-A of Part II.

Every insolvency professional shall abide by the following code of conduct: (a) to take reasonable care and diligence while performing his duties; (b) to comply with all requirements and terms and conditions specified in the byelaws of the insolvency professional agency of which he is a member; (c) to allow the insolvency professional agency to inspect his records; (d) to submit a copy of the records of every proceeding before the Adjudicating Authority to the Board as well as to the insolvency professional agency of which he is a member; and (e) to perform his functions in such manner and subject to such conditions as may be specified.

Information Utilities

Information Utility (IU) is an institution that was created for providing accurate information on defaults, online, to persons eligible for it under the IBC code. IUs play a key role in insolvency and resolution by storing financial information in a universally accessible format and accepting electronic submissions of financial information from persons eligible for doing so, in the form and manner specified. They have to meet such minimum service quality standards as may be specified by regulations and get the information received from various persons authenticated by all concerned parties before storing such information. They provide access to the financial information stored by it to any person who intends to access such information in such manner as may be specified by regulations and publish such statistical information as may be specified by regulations. On top of all these, they have inter-operability with other information utilities.

(Section 214, IBC Amended Up To 12-08-2021)

Core Services

The Core Services rendered by an IU include accepting electronic submission of financial information, ensuring safe and accurate recording of the same, authenticating and verifying the ones submitted by a person and providing access to information stored with the IU to persons as may be specified.

(Sec 3 (9), IBC Amended Up To 12-08-2021)

An IU has the responsibility to provide the specified services only to a person who complies with the terms and conditions specified by the regulations.

(Sec 213, IBC Amended Up To 12-08-2021)

Eligibility for Registration

The prerequisite for carrying on business as an IU is grant of a certificate of registration by the Insolvency & Bankruptcy Board of India (IBBI).

(Sec 209, IBC Amended Up To 12-08-2021)

In order to be eligible for registration as an IU, the applicant is required to be a public company set up with the objective of providing core services and other services under the IBC Regulations; its shareholding and governance must conform to the regulations under Chapter III, and the bye-laws under Chapter IV, of *IBBI (Information Utilities) Regulations, 2017 (Amended Up To 25.07.2019)*; it should have a minimum net worth of fifty crore rupees; the person itself, its promoters, its directors, its key managerial personnel, and persons holding more than 5% of its paid-up equity share capital, directly or indirectly, or its total voting power, should be 'fit and proper' persons, the relevant considerations for which are integrity, reputation and character, absence of conviction by a court for an offence and absence of restraint order, in force, issued by a financial sector regulator or the Adjudicating Authority, and financial solvency.

A person who has been sentenced to imprisonment for a period of less than six months may be considered 'fit and proper'; a person shall not be considered 'fit and proper' if he has been sentenced to imprisonment for a period (a) of not less than six months but less than seven years and a period of five years has not elapsed from the date of expiry of the sentence, or (b) of seven years or more.

(Regulation 3, IBBI (Information Utilities) Regulations, 2017,
Amended Up To 25.07.2019)

Registration Process

A person eligible for registration as an information utility may make an application to the Board in Form A of the Schedule, along with a non- refundable application fee of five lakh rupees. An application for renewal of registration has to be made, at least six months before the expiry of its registration, also in Form A, along with a non-refundable application fee of *five lakh rupees*. The Board shall acknowledge an application made under this Regulation within seven days of its receipt.

(Regulation 4, IBBI (Information Utilities) Regulations, 2017,
Amended Up To 25.07.2019)

Disposal of Application

The Board shall examine the application, and give an opportunity to the applicant to remove the deficiencies, if any; submit, within reasonable time, additional documents or clarification that it deems fit; appear before the Board in person, or through its authorised representative, for clarifications. The Board may grant or renew a certificate of registration to the applicant as an IU in Form B of the Schedule, within sixty days of receipt of the application, excluding the time given by the Board for removing the deficiencies, or presenting additional documents or clarifications, or appearing in person, as the case may be, if it is satisfied, after such inspection or inquiry as it deems necessary, that: the applicant is eligible under Regulation 3; has the technical competence and financial capacity required to function as an IU; has adequate infrastructure to provide services; has, in its employment, persons having adequate professional and other relevant experience, to provide services in accordance with the Code; and has complied with the conditions of the certificate of registration if he has submitted an application for renewal under Regulation 4(2).

If, after considering an application made under Regulation 4, the Board is of the *prima facie* opinion that the registration ought not to be granted or ought not to be renewed, or be granted or renewed with additional conditions, it shall communicate the reasons for forming such an opinion within forty-five days of receipt of the application, excluding the time given by the Board forremoving the deficiencies, presenting additional documents or clarifications, or appearing in person, as the case may be.

The applicant shall submit an explanation as to why its application should be accepted within fifteen days of the receipt of the communication under sub- regulation (5), to enable the Board to form a final opinion.

After considering the explanation, the Board shall communicate its decision to accept the application, along with the certificate of registration, or reject it by an order, giving reasons thereof within thirty days of receipt of explanation.

The order rejecting an application for renewal of registration shall require the IU to discharge any pending obligations, continue its functions till such time as may be directed, to enable its users to transfer information stored with it to another information utility; and comply with any other directions as considered appropriate.

(Regulation 5, IBBI (Information Utilities) Regulations, 2017,
Amended Up To 25.07.2019)

Registration Period, Fee and Renewal of Certificate

The certificate of registration shall remain valid for a period of five years from the date of issue if the IU continues to abide by the Code and its bye- laws, keeps meeting all the requirements under Regulation 5 (4) (eligibility conditions, technical competence & financial capacity, adequate infrastructure, employment of professionals with relevant experience), continues to pay the annual fee of *fifty lakh rupees* every year, takes Board's prior approval for certain actions, such as: allowing acquisition of shares or voting power by a person which taken together with the paid-up equity share or voting power, if any, held by such person, entitles him to hold more than five per cent of the paid-up equity share capital or total voting power; a change of control, or a merger, amalgamation or restructuring; sale, disposal, or acquisition of the whole of its undertaking; voluntary liquidation, dissolution, or any similar action; intimate the Board if a person holding *more than five per cent* of its paid-up equity share capital or total voting power ceases to hold at least five per cent of its paid-up equity share capital or total voting power, within fifteen days from such cessation; take adequate steps for redressal of grievances; take over information stored with other information utilities as per the directions of the Board and provide core services to their users; and abide by such other conditions as may be stipulated by the Board).

(Regulation 6, IBBI (Information Utilities) Regulations, 2017,
Amended Up To 25.07.2019)

Registration of Information Utility

1. Every application for registration has to be made to the Board in such form and manner, containing such particulars, and accompanied by such fee, as may be specified by regulations:

    Provided that every application received by the Board shall be acknowledged within seven days of its receipt.

    (Section 210 (1), IBC Amended Up To 12-08-2021)

2. On receipt of the application under section *210 (1)* of IBC, the Board may, on being satisfied that the application conforms with all requirements specified under sub-section *(1)*, grant a certificate of registration to the applicant or else, reject, by order, such application.

    Provided that no order rejecting the application shall be made without giving an opportunity of being heard to the applicant;

    (Regulation 5, IBBI (Information Utilities) Regulations, 2017,
    Amended Up To 25.07.2019)

    Provided further that every order so made shall be communicated to the applicant within forty-five days of receipt of the application and the applicant shall submit an explanation as to why its application should be accepted within fifteen days of the receipt of the communication.

    (Regulation 5 (1), IBBI (Information Utilities) Regulations, 2017,
    Amended Up To 25.07.2019)

3. The Board may grant or renew the certificate of registration to the applicant as an information utility in Form B of the Schedule within sixty days of receipt of the application, excluding the time given by the Board for removing the deficiencies, or presenting additional documents or clarifications, or appearing in person, as the case may be.

    (Regulation 5 (4) (e), IBBI (Information Utilities) Regulations, 2017,
    Amended Up To 25.07.2019)

4. The Board may, by order, suspend or cancel the certificate of registration granted to an IU on any of the following grounds, namely: –

    a. that it has obtained registration by making a false statement or misrepresentation or by any other unlawful means;

    b. that it has failed to comply with the requirements of the regulations made by the Board;

c. that it has contravened any of the provisions of the Act or the rules or the regulations made thereunder;

d. on any other ground as may be specified by regulations:

Provided that no order shall be made under this sub-section unless the IU concerned has been given a reasonable opportunity of being heard:

Provided further that no such order shall be passed by any member except whole-time members of the Board.

(Section 210 (5), IBC Amended Up To 12-08-2021)

Appeal to NCLAT

An IU aggrieved by the Board's order to suspend or cancel its registration may prefer an appeal to the National Company Law Appellate Tribunal, within a period of *thirty days* of receipt of the order, in the manner prescribed in Part III of the National Company Law Appellate Tribunal Rules, 2016.

*(Section 202, IBC & Regulation 42, IBBI (Information Utilities) Regulations, 2017,
Amended Up To 25.07.2019)*

Governing Board of IU

Every IU will set up a Governing Board, with such number of independent members, as may be specified by regulations.

(Section 212, IBC Amended Up To 12-08-2021)

The Governing Board of an IU shall consist of: (a) managing director; (b) independent directors; and (c) shareholder directors, with more than half of the directors being citizens of India residing in India. The managing director will not fall in the category of either independent director or shareholder director.

An IU employee appointed as a director on its Governing Board in addition to the managing director shall be deemed to be a shareholder director and the number of independent directors shall not be less than the number of shareholder directors. No meeting of the Governing Board shall be held without the presence of at least one independent director.

A person of ability and integrity, with expertise in the field of finance, law, management or insolvency, will qualify for appointment as an independent director if he is not: a relative of the directors of the Governing Board, has no pecuniary relationship with the IU or any of its directors, or any of its shareholders holding more than ten per cent of its share capital, during the immediately preceding two financial years or during the current financial year; a shareholder of the IU; a member of the Board of Directors of any of the shareholders holding more than ten per cent of the share capital of the IU. An independent director shall be nominated by the Board from amongst the list of names proposed by the IU.

An individual may serve as an independent director for a maximum of two terms (the second term being subject to a satisfactory performance review of the first term by the Governing Board) of three years each or part thereof, or up to the age of seventy-five years, whichever is earlier.

For an independent director to become a shareholder director in the same or another IU, a cooling off period of three years will be required. The directors will elect an independent director as the Chairperson of the Governing Board.

A director, who has any interest, direct or indirect, pecuniary or otherwise, in any matter coming up for consideration at a meeting of the Governing Board or any of its Committees, shall as soon as possible after relevant circumstances have come to his knowledge, disclose the nature of his interest at such meeting and such disclosure shall be recorded in the proceedings of the Governing Board or the Committee, as the case may be, and the director shall not take part in any deliberation or decision of the Governing Board or the Committee with respect to that matter.

(Regulation 9, IBBI (Information Utilities) Regulations, 2017,
Amended Up To 25.07.2019)

Registration of Users

A person can register itself with an IU for (a) submitting information to; or (b) accessing information stored with any of the IUs. The IU verifies the identity of the person and examines its eligibility for registration. If found eligible, the IU registers and, then, intimates it of its unique identifier. A person registered once with an IU shall not register itself with any IU again. An IU provides a registered user a functionality to enable its authorised representatives to carry on the activities (submitting information to, or accessing information stored with, any of the IUs) on its behalf.

An IU shall maintain a list of the registered users, the unique identifiers of the registered users as well as the unique identifiers assigned to the debts, and make the list available to all IUs and the Board.

(Regulation 18, IBBI (Information Utilities) Regulations, 2017,
Amended Up To 25.07.2019)

Use of Different Information Utilities (IUs)

A registered user may submit information to any IU. Different parties to the same transaction may use different IUs to submit, or access information in respect of the same transaction. For example, a debt transaction has creditor A and debtor B. A may submit information about the debt to information utility X, while B may submit information about the same debt to information utility Y.

A user may access information stored with an IU through any IU.

(Regulation 19, IBBI (Information Utilities) Regulations, 2017,
Amended Up To 25.07.2018)

Acceptance and Receipt of Information

An IU shall accept information submitted by a user in Form C of the Schedule and, then: assign a unique identifier to the information, including records of debt, acknowledge its receipt, and notify the user of: (i) the unique identifier of the information; (ii) the terms and conditions of authentication and verification of information; and (iii) the manner in which the information may be accessed by other parties.

(Regulation 20, IBBI (Information Utilities) Regulations, 2017,
Amended Up To 25.07.2019)

Information of Default

On receipt of information of default, an IU shall expeditiously undertake the process of authentication and verification of the information of default. It will deliver the information of default to the debtor and seek debtor's confirmation of the same within the time specified in the Technical Standards. If the debtor does not respond, the IU will remind the debtor at least three times, seeking confirmation of information of default, and allow three days each time for the debtor to respond.

The IU shall deliver the information of default or the reminder, as the case may be, to the debtor either by hand, post or electronic means at the postal or e-mail address of the debtor: (i) registered with the IU by him, failing which, (ii) recorded with any other statutory repository as approved by the Board, failing which, (iii) submitted in Form C of the Schedule.

On completion of the processes of authentication and verification detailed above, the IU shall communicate the information of default, and the status of authentication to registered users who are: (a) creditors of the debtor who has defaulted; and (b) parties and sureties, if any, to the debt in respect of which the information of default has been received.

(Regulation 21, IBBI (Information Utilities) Regulations, 2017,
Amended Up To 11.10.2018)

Storage of Information

An IU can store all information only in a facility located in India and governed by the laws of India.

(Regulation 22, IBBI (Information Utilities) Regulations,2017,
Amended Up To 25.07.2019)

Access to Information

An IU can allow only the following persons to access information stored with it: (a) the user which has submitted the information; (b) all the parties to the debt and the host bank, if any, if the information pertains to Section 3(13)(a), (c) and (d) of IBC *[records of the debt of the person, or records of assets of person over which security interest has been created, or records, if any, of instances of default by the person against any debt]*; (c) the corporate person and its auditor, if the information is of the categories in section

3(13)(b) and (e) *[records of liabilities when the person is solvent; and records of the balance sheet and cash-flow statements of the person]* (d) the insolvency professional, to the extent provided in the Code; (e) the Adjudicating Authority; (f) the Board; (g) any person authorised to access the information under any other law; and (h) any other person who the persons referred to in (a), (b) or (c) have consented to share the information with.

An IU shall in all cases enable the user to view- (a) the date the information was last updated; (b) the status of authentication; and (c) the status of verification while providing access to the information.

An IU shall provide information to the Adjudicating Authority and Board free of charge.

(Regulation 23, IBBI (Information Utilities) Regulations, 2017,
Amended Up To 25.07.2019)

Accessing Information Stored with Other Information Utilities

An IU shall provide a functionality to enable users to access information stored with any information utility, which they are entitled to access.

This will enable other IUs to provide access to information to the user directly and ensure privacy and confidentiality of information.

(Regulation 24, IBBI (Information Utilities) Regulations, 2017,
Amended Up To 25.07.2019)

Claims by Operational Creditors

Any person who intends to submit financial information to the IU or access the information from the IU shall pay such fee and submit information in such form and manner as may be specified by the regulations.

A Financial Creditor shall submit financial information and information relating to assets in relation to which any security interest has been created, in such form and manner as may be specified by regulations.

An Operational Creditor may submit financial information to the IU in such form and manner as may be specified.

(Section 215, IBC Amended Up To 12-08-2021)

A person claiming to be an Operational Creditor, other than workman or employee of the Corporate Debtor, shall submit claim with proof to the IRP in person, by post or by electronic means in Form B of the Schedule. It may submit supplementary documents, or clarifications in support of the claim, before the constitution of the committee.

The existence of debt due to the Operational Creditor may be proved on the basis of - (a) the records available with an IU, if any; or (b) other relevant documents, including a contract for supply of goods and services with Corporate Debtor, an invoice demanding payment for the goods and services supplied to the Corporate Debtor, an order of a court or tribunal that has adjudicated upon the non-payment of a debt, and financial accounts.

(Regulation 7, IBBI Notification on CIRP Regulations, 2016, 30.11.2016)

Claims by Financial Creditors

(1) A person claiming to be a Financial Creditor, other than a Financial Creditor belonging to a class of creditors *(which means "a class with at least ten financial creditors", as per paragraph 2 (aa) of the IBBI Notification dated July 3, 2018)*, shall submit claim with proof to the IRP in electronic form in Form C of the Schedule. It may submit supplementary documents, or clarifications in support of the claim, before the constitution of the committee.

The existence of debt due to the Financial Creditor may be proved on the basis of the records available with an IU, or other relevant documents, including a financial contract supported by financial statements as evidence of the debt; a record evidencing that the amounts committed by the Financial Creditor to the Corporate Debtor under a facility has been drawn by the Corporate Debtor; financial statements showing that the debt has not been paid; or an order of a court or tribunal that has adjudicated upon the non- payment of a debt.

(Regulation 8, CIRP Regulations, 2016,
Amended Up To 28.11.2019)

Claims by Creditors in a Class

A person claiming to be a creditor in a class *(which means "a class with at least ten financial creditors", as per paragraph 2 (aa) of the IBBI Notification dated July 3, 2018)* shall submit claim with proof to the IRP in electronic form in Form CA of the Schedule.

The existence of debt due to a creditor in a class may be proved on the basis of: the records available with an information utility, if any; or other relevant documents, including an agreement for sale, a letter of allotment; a receipt for payment made, or such other document, evidencing existence of debt.

A creditor in a class may indicate its choice of an insolvency professional, from amongst the three choices provided by the IRP in the public announcement, to act as its authorised representative.

(Regulation 8 A, CIRP Regulations, 2016,
Amended Up To 28.11.2019)

Claims by Workmen and Employees

A person claiming to be a workman or an employee of the Corporate Debtor shall submit claim with proof to the IRP in person, by post or by electronic means in Form D of the Schedule. It may submit supplementary documents, or clarifications in support of the claim, on his own or if required by the IRP, before the constitution of the committee.

Where there are dues to numerous workmen or employees of the Corporate Debtor, an authorised representative may submit one claim with proof for all such dues on their behalf in Form E of the Schedule.

The existence of dues to workmen or employees may be proved by them, individually or collectively on the basis of records available with an information utility, or other relevant documents, including: a proof of employment such as contract of employment for the period for which such workman or employee is claiming dues; evidence of notice demanding payment of unpaid dues and any documentary or other proof that payment has not been made; or an order of a court or tribunal that has adjudicated upon the non-payment of dues, if any.

(Regulation 9, CIRP Regulations, 2016,
Amended Up To 28.11.2019)

Claims by Other Creditors

A person claiming to be a creditor, other than those covered under regulations 7, 8, or 9, shall submit its claim with proof to the IRP or RP in person, by post or by electronic means in Form F of the Schedule.

The existence of the claim of the creditor the records available in an IU, if any, or other relevant documents sufficient to establish the claim, including any or all of the following: documentary evidence demanding satisfaction of the claim; (ii) bank statements of the creditor showing non-satisfaction of claim; an order of court or tribunal that has adjudicated upon non-satisfaction of claim, if any.

(Regulation 9A, CIRP Regulations, 2016 Amended Up To 28.11.2019)

Substantiation of Claims

The IRP or the RP, as the case may be, may call for such other evidence or clarification as he deems fit from a creditor for substantiating the whole or part of its claim.

(Regulation 10, CIRP Regulations, 2016 Amended Up To 25.07.2019)

Cost of Proof

A creditor shall bear the cost of proving the debt due to such creditor.

(Regulation 11, CIRP Regulations, 2016 Amended Up To 25.07.2019)

Rights and Obligations of Persons submitting Financial Information

A person who intends to update or modify or rectify errors in the financial information submitted under Section 215 of IBC, may make an application to the IU for such purpose stating reasons therefor, in such manner and within such time, as may be specified.

A person who submits financial information to an IU shall not provide such information to any other person, except to such extent, under such circumstances, and in such manner, as may be specified.

(Sec 216, IBC Amended Up To 12-08-2021)

"Information" means financial information as defined in section 3(13)

(Regulation 2 (h), IBBI (Information Utilities) Regulations, 2017, Amended Up To 25.07.2019)

"Financial information", in relation to a person, means one or more of the following categories of information, namely: (a) records of the debt of the person; (b) records of liabilities when the person is solvent; (c) records of assets of person over which security interest has been created; (d) records, if any, of instances of default by the person against any debt; (e) records of the balance sheet and cash-flow statements of the person; and (f) such other information as may be specified.

(Sec 3 (13), IBC Amended Up To 23-09-2020)

IBC, A TRANSFORMATIONAL CHANGE

IBC has brought about a transformational change in India's financial sector. As many as 18,629 applications, seeking resolution of more than Rs 5,29,000 crore of debts, have been resolved even before getting admitted.

"(In the World Bank Report) India's rank, in terms of 'resolving insolvency' which reflects ease of exit from business, has improved by 56 places to 52 from 108 the previous year. The overall recovery rate for creditors jumped from 26.5 cents on the dollar to 71.6 cents, and the time taken for resolving insolvency reduced significantly from 4.3 years to 1.6 years. India is now, by far, the best performer in South Asia on resolving insolvency and does better than the average for OECD high-income economies in terms of the recovery rate, time taken and cost of proceedings."

("Moving Up in 'Ease of Resolving Insolvency'" post on IBBI website, by Mr. M. S. Sahoo, Chairperson, Insolvency and Bankruptcy Board of India (IBBI))

With promoters facing the risk of losing control of their company in case of a default, IBC has brought a significant improvement in resolving bad loans cases. As mentioned earlier, recent statistics on the number of applications made and the amount realized even before the cases were admitted under IBC proceedings are truly astonishing.

Some of the important details furnished in the Government of India's Economic Survey report, 2020-21 are:

The Code has rescued 308 CDs (Corporate Debtors) as on December 2020 through resolution plans. They owed Rs 4.99 lakh crore to creditors. However, the realizable value of the assets available with them, when they entered the CIRP (Corporate Insolvency Resolution Process), was only Rs 1.03 lakh crore.

Under the Code, the creditors recovered Rs 1.99 lakh crore, which recovery of NPAs by banks. RBI data indicates that as a percentage of claims, scheduled commercial banks (SCBs) have been able to recover 45.5 per cent of the amount involved through IBC for the financial year 2019-20, which is the highest as compared to recovery under other modes and legislations (Figure 23). Further, the amount recovered by SCBs under IBC was Rs 1.73 lakh crores which is more than all the amount recovered by all other alternative mechanisms combined for 2019-20.

Status of Twelve Large Accounts

ince a few cases accounted for a large proportion of money involved in the resolution process, the resolution process of 12 large accounts was initiated by banks, as directed by RBI in June 2017. Together they had an outstanding claim of Rs 3.45 lakh crore as against liquidation value of Rs 73,220 crores. Of these, resolution plan in respect of eight CDs have been approved and orders for liquidation have been passed in respect of two CDs. Thus, CIRPs for two firms and liquidation in respect of two firms are ongoing and are at different stages of the process. The status of the 12 large accounts is presented in Table A below:

TABLE A: STATUS OF 12 LARGE ACCOUNTS

NAME OF CD	CLAIMS OF FINANCIAL CREDITORs UNDER RESOLUTION			REALIZATION BY ALL CLAIMENTS AS % OF LIQUIDATION VALUE	SUCCESSFUL REOLUTION APPLICANT
	AMOUNT ADMTTED	AMOUNT REALIZED	REALIZATION AS % OF CLAIMS		
Electrosteel Steels Ltd.	13,175	5,320	40.38	183.45	Vedanta Ltd.
Bhushan Steel Ltd.	56,022	35,571	63.50	252.88	Bamnipal Steel Ltd.
Monnet Ispat & Energy Ltd.	11,015	2,892	26.26	123.35	Consortium of JSW & AION Investments
Essar Steel India Ltd.	49,473	41,018	82.91	266.65	Arcelor Mittal India Pvt. Ltd.
Alok Industries Ltd.	29,523	5,052	17.11	115.39	Reliance Industries Ltd, J M Financial ARC – March 2018 Trust
Jyoti Structures Ltd.	7,365	3,691	50.12	387.44	Group of HNIs led by Mr. SharadSanghi
Bhushan Power & Steel Limited	47,158	19,350	41.03	209.12	JSW Limited
Jaypee Infratech Ltd.	23,176	23,223	100.20	130.82	NBCC (India) Ltd.
Amtek Auto Limited	12,641	2,615	20.68	169.65	Deccan Value Investors L.P. and DVI PE (Mauritius) Ltd.

UNDER PROCESS	
Era Infra Engineering Limited	Under CIRP
Lanco Infratech Limited	Under Liquidation
ABG Shipyard Limited	Under Liquidation

(Source: IBBI)

Two important figures in this table are: one, Realization Amount as a Percentage of Claims; and two, Realization Amount as a Percentage of Liquidation Value. Both these figures for the 12 large accounts (whose claim amounts are in the range of Rs 7,365 crore to Rs 56,022 crore) work out as: Electrosteel Steels Limited: 40.38 % & 183.45 %; Bhushan Steel Limited:

63.50 % & 252.88 %; Monnet Ispat & Energy Limited: 26.26 % & 123.35 %; Essar Steel India Limited: 82.91 % & 266.65 %; Alok Industries Limited:

17.11 % & 115.39 %; Jyoti Structures Limited: 50.12 % & 387.44 %; Bhushan Power & Steel Limited: 41.03 % & 209.12 %; Jaypee Infratech Limited: 100.20 % & 130.82 %; Amtek Auto Limited: 20.68 % & 169.65 %.

While the realization amount as a percentage of claims is much lower, that as a percentage of liquidation value is robust. This happens because when a non- performing loan keeps rotting for years, the unpaid interest keeps getting added to the claim amount every month or every three months, whereas the realization amount of the assets (plant & machinery, factory building, etc.) keeps declining. As against that, the liquidation value, if assessed well, is the right way to figure out the realization value.

Pre-Packaged Insolvency Resolution Process (PPIRP)

As mentioned earlier, in the field of insolvency, IBC has been leading from the front. Another quantum leap for it is the new window of Pre-Packaged Insolvency Resolution Process (PPIRP).

PPIRP was introduced by way of an amendment in the Insolvency and Bankruptcy Code (IBC) for resolving the severe stress that the Micro, Small, and Medium Enterprises (MSMEs) had – in the backdrop of the COVID 2019 pandemic – got engulfed in. Resolution of their stress required a different treatment due to the unique nature of their businesses and simpler corporate structures. Therefore, for corporate MSMEs, it was considered expedient to provide an efficient alternative insolvency resolution process under the Code that ensured quicker, cost-effective and value-maximising outcomes for all the stakeholders, in a manner least disruptive to the continuity of their businesses. The Insolvency and Bankruptcy Code (Amendment) Ordinance, 2021, promulgated on 4th April, 2021, introduced PPIRP under the Code for this purpose. PPIRP is built on trust and honours the honest MSME owners by enabling resolution when the company remains with them.

There are two broad processes for resolving corporate stress: (a) Corporate Insolvency Resolution Process (CIRP) that resolves stress either through a resolution plan rehabilitating the Corporate Debtor or through liquidation of the CD; and (b) Pre-Packaged Insolvency Resolution Process (PPIRP) that resolves stress either through a resolution plan or closes without resolution.

PPIRP is available for resolution of stress of corporate MSMEs as an alternate option, should the stakeholders like to use it. It is available for resolving stress where default is at least Rs 1 crore for which CIRP (Corporate Insolvency Resolution Process) is available under the Insolvency and

Bankruptcy Code (IBC). It is also available in cases where the default is at least Rs 10 lakh, and the defaults arose between 25th March, 2020 to 24th March, 2021.

A corporate debtor that falls in the MSME category under sub-section (1) of section 7 of the Micro, Small and Medium Enterprises Develop-ment Act, 2006, is eligible to apply for initiation of PPIRP, if it-

i.   has committed a default of at least 10 lakh;

ii. is eligible to submit a resolution plan under section 29A of the Code;

iii. has not undergone a PPIRP during the three years preceding the initiation date;

iv. has not completed a CIRP during the three years preceding the initiation date;

v.   is not undergoing a CIRP; and

vi. is not required to be liquidated by an order under section 33 of the Code.

PPIRP blends debtor-in-possession with creditor-in-control. It allows the company, if eligible under section 29A of IBC, to submit the base resolution plan (BRP) aimed at value maximisation. It safeguards the rights of stakeholders as much as in CIRP and has adequate checks and balances to prevent any potential misuse. It entails a limited role for courts and IPs.

Unlike CIRP, it does not yield if there is no resolution plan. Though PPIRP and CIRP are alternate options, some stakeholders may prefer one over the other in certain circumstances.

The following activities need to be undertaken in pre-initiation stage:

i.   For seeking approval of creditors under section 54A(2)(e) and (3), the applicant (corporate applicant filing an application for initiation of PPIRP) shall convene meetings of the unrelated financial creditors (UFCs), that is, financial creditors who are not related parties of the CD. Where the CD has no financial debt or where all financial creditors are related parties, the applicant shall convene meetings of unrelated operational creditors (UOCs) and the UOCs shall perform the same duties and functions as the UFCs. ....

v.   The UFCs representing not less than 66% in value of debt due to such creditors shall approve the appointment as RP ....

viii. The CD shall prepare a BRP (Base Resolution Plan) in conformity with the requirements under section 54K.

ix. Along with the notice for convening the meeting(s) seeking approval for filing of an application for initiating PPIRP, the applicant shall enclose (a) a list of creditors and the amount due to each of them

Application for Initiation

i.   Only a corporate applicant can file an application for initiation of PPIRP.

     ....

iii. The application shall be accompanied by the following documents:

K. Latest and updated Udyam Registration Certificate, or proof that the CD is an MSME;

L. Affidavit stating that the CD is eligible under section 29A of the Code to submit resolution plan in the PPIRP of the CD;

....

iv. The applicant shall serve a copy of the application (for initiating PPIRP) to the IBBI before filing it with the AA.

v. Within 14 days of the receipt of the application, the AA shall admit the application, ...

Post-initiation Phase

i.   The process is required to be completed within a time frame of 120 days from the PPIRP commencement date. ....

ii. During the PPIRP, the management of the affairs of the CD shall continue to vest in the Board of Directors / the partners of the CD, (who) shall make every endeavour to protect and preserve the value of the property of the CD and manage its operations as a going concern .... and discharge their contractual or statutory rights and obligations in relation to the CD.

iii. The CD shall, within two days of the PPIRP commencement date, submit to the RP, updated as on that date, (a) a list of claims, along with details of the respective creditors, their security interests and guarantees, and (b) a preliminary information memorandum (PIM) containing information relevant for formulating a resolution plan. If any person sustains any loss or damage as a consequence of the omission of any material information or inclusion of any misleading information in the list of claims or the PIM, every person who

a. is a promoter or director or partner of the CD at the time of submission of the list of claims or the PIM, or

b. has authorised the submission of the list of claims or the PIM, shall be liable to pay compensation.

iv. The CD shall submit the BRP to the RP within two days of the PPIRP commencement date. It may revise the BRP if permitted by the CoC.

v.   The RP shall make a public announcement, in Form P9, within two days of the commencement of the process in the manner specified in regulation 19.

vi. The RP shall exercise powers and carry out duties as required under section 54F.

Approval of Resolution Plan

i.   If BRP does not impair claims owed to operational creditors (OCs), the CoC may approve it for submission to the AA.

ii. If the CoC does not approve the BRP or the BRP impairs the claims of OCs, the RP shall invite prospective resolution applicants to submit resolution plans to compete with the BRP. He shall publish brief particulars of the invitation for resolution plans in Form P11, not later than 21 days from the PPIRP commencement date, in accordance with regulation 43.

iii. The invitation for resolution plans shall detail each step in the process, and the manner and purposes of interaction between the RP and the resolution applicant, along with corresponding timelines. It shall include (a) the basis for evaluation; (b) the basis for considering a resolution plan significantly better than another resolution plan; (c) the tick size; and (d) the manner of improving a resolution plan. It shall not require any non-refundable deposit for submission of or along with resolution plan.

iv. The resolution plans received in response to invitation and complying with the requirements of the Code and the Regulations shall be evaluated on the basis for evaluation. The resolution plan which gets the highest score shall be selected as Best Alternate Plan (BAP) for competition with the BRP.

v. The CoC may consider BRP for approval if no resolution plan is received.

vi. The CoC may consider the BAP for approval if it is significantly better than the BRP. If it does not approve a significantly better BAP, the process terminates. If the BAP is not significantly better than the BRP, the RP shall disclose the scores of the BAP and BRP to submitters of these plans and invite them to improve their plans in accordance with Regulation 48.

vii. The process of improvement shall continue till either of the submitters fails to use the option within the specified time. The resolution plan having a higher score on completion of process of improvement shall be considered by the CoC for approval. If the CoC does not approve it, the process terminates.

Closure of PPIRP

The PPIRP closes in the following circumstances:

i.   On approval of either the BRP or the BAP by the AA.

ii. On expiry of 90 days if no resolution plan is submitted to the AA for approval.

iii. On rejection of resolution plan by the AA.

iv. On approval by the AA of application filed by the RP for termination of PPIRP, where the CoC approves termination with 66% of voting share.

v.   On conversion into CIRP based on an application filed by the RP, where the CoC approves so with 66% of voting share, and the CD is eligible for CIRP. The RP of the PPIRP is appointed as the IRP of the CIRP.

vi. On an order of termination in case either no resolution plan is approved by CoC or the resolution plan approved by the CoC does not result in change in management, where the AA has vested the management of the CD with the RP under section 54J.

(Excerpts from "Pre-Packaged Insolvency Resolution Process: Information Brochure", IBBI)

IBC was launched with the prime objective of resolving the stress of Corporate Debtors (CDs). It has rescued a good number of CDs and distressed assets through resolution plans.

The provision under IBC that a promoter may lose control of its company (in case of liquidation proceedings or bankruptcy proceedings, or even otherwise) has transformed the process of tackling distressed assets, whose value gradually declines with time. Thousands of debtors are resolving distress in the early stages of distress because of this. Further, a total of 527 CIRPs have been withdrawn under section 12A of the Code until September 2021. Almost three fourth of these CIRPs had claims of less than Rs 10 crores and 701 CIRP cases have been closed on appeal/ review/settled.

IBC and PPIRP for Corporate MSMEs

The provision of multiple competing options for the resolution of stress makes an economy a great place to do business. In line with this thought, the Insolvency and Bankruptcy Code, 2016 was amended through an Ordinance on April 4, 2021, to provide for a Pre-Packaged Insolvency Resolution Process (PPIRP) for corporate Micro, Small and Medium Enterprises as an alternative insolvency resolution process to ensure quicker outcomes.

PPIRP has the rigour and discipline of the CIRP. It is informal up to a point and formal thereafter. It is neither a fully private nor a fully public process - it allows the company, if eligible under section 29A, to submit the Base

The informality at the pre-initiation stage offers flexibility for the CD and its creditors to swiftly explore and negotiate the best way to resolve stress in the business, while the post-initiation stage drives value maximisation and bestows the resolution plan with statutory protection. The process is required to be completed within a time frame of 120 days from the commencement date. During the PPIRP, the management of the affairs of the CD shall continue to vest in the Board of Directors / partners of the CD and the resolution professional conducts the process under the guidance and oversight of the creditors.

Within two days of the PPIRP commencement date, the CD shall submit to the RP, a list of claims, along with details of the respective

creditors, their security interests and guarantees, a Preliminary Information Memorandum (PIM) containing information relevant for formulating a resolution plan, as well as a Base Resolution Plan (BRP).

If BRP does not impair claims owed to operational creditors (OCs), the CoC may approve it for submission to the AA. If it impairs the claims of OCs, the RP shall invite prospective resolution applicants to submit resolution plans to compete with the BRP.

The resolution plans received in response to invitation shall be evaluated on the basis for evaluation and the resolution plan which gets the highest score shall be selected as Best Alternate Plan (BAP) for competition with the BRP. If the BAP is not significantly better than the BRP, the RP shall disclose the scores of the BAP and BRP to submitters of these plans and invite them to improve their plans in accordance with regulation 48.

The resolution plan having higher score on completion of process of improvement shall be considered by the CoC for approval. If the CoC does not approve it, the process terminates.

The PPIRP closes in the following circumstances:

i.   On approval of either the BRP or the BAP by the AA;

ii. On expiry of 90 days if no resolution plan is submitted to the AA for approval;

iii. On rejection of resolution plan by the AA;

iv. On approval by the AA of application filed by the RP for termination of PPIRP, where the CoC approves termination with 66% of voting share;

v.   On conversion into CIRP based on an application filed by the RP, where the CoC approves so with 66% of voting share, and the CD is eligible for CIRP. The RP of the PPIRP is appointed as the IRP of the CIRP;

vi. On an order of termination in case either no resolution plan is approved by CoC or the resolution plan approved by the CoC does not result in change in management, where the AA has vested the management of the CD with the RP under section 54J.

("Pre-Packaged Insolvency Resolution Process: Information Brochure", IBBI)

Voluntary Liquidation

Liquidation can be involuntary as in the case of insolvency or bankruptcy; or voluntary which could be due to personal reasons, subsidiaries being merged etc. A company may decide to voluntarily close its operation even when it is viable.

In India, two options are available for voluntary liquidation – one under section 248 of the Companies Act, 2013 through the Registrar of Companies (RoC), and the other under the IBC. Although former is still the more popular route, the Insolvency and Bankruptcy Code (IBC), 2016 has been a metamorphosis in the process of winding-up of companies.

Section 59 of IBC and IBBI (Voluntary Liquidation Process) Regulations, 2017 are the fulcrums for voluntary liquidation of a corporate person. Under Section 59 of IBC, a corporate person who intends to liquidate itself voluntarily and has not committed any default may initiate voluntary liquidation proceedings.

As on September 2021, 1042 cases had been filed under this scheme, final reports had been received for 483 cases, and the final order of dissolution had been passed in 257 cases. Out of the ongoing cases, nearly 32 per cent of the cases were pending for over 2 years and 19 per cent for between 1 and 2 years. The procedure of voluntary exit of business still needs to be simplified significantly.

The step-by-step procedure of the voluntary liquidation process under IBC is as follows:

Step 1: In a board meeting, majority of the directors of the company shall pass

a. a declaration, verified by an affidavit, stating that: (i) they have made a full inquiry into the affairs of the company and have formed an opinion that either the company has no debt or that it will be able to pay its debts in full from the proceeds of assets to be sold in the voluntary liquidation; and (ii) the company is not being liquidated to defraud any person;

b. the declaration under sub-clause (a) shall be accompanied with the following documents, namely: -

   i. audited financial statements and record of business operations of the company for the previous two years or for the period since its incorporation, whichever is later;

   ii. a report of the valuation of the assets of the company, if any prepared by a registered valuer;

(IBC Sec 59 (3) (a) & (b))

Step 2: Within four weeks of the declaration, a special resolution shall be passed by the members of the company in a general meeting requiring the company to be liquidated voluntarily and appointing an insolvency professional to act as the liquidator. Creditors representing two-thirds in value of the debt of the company shall approve the said resolution within seven days of such resolution.

(IBC Sec 59 (3) (c) (i) & (ii))

Step 3: Liquidator shall file the resolution to Insolvency and Bankruptcy Board of India (IBBI) and RoC within seven days of such resolution or the subsequent approval by the creditors as per section 59 (4) of the Code and regulation 3 (2) of the Voluntary Liquidation Process Regulations. Under regulation 14 of the Voluntary Liquidation Process Regulations, the liquidator is required to make a public announcement (in English and Regional Newspapers) within five days from his appointment calling upon stakeholders to submit their claims as on the liquidation commencement date within 30 days from the liquidation commencement date. (Section 38 (1) of the Code).

(IBC, Sec 59 (4) & Regulation 14 of Voluntary Liquidation Regulation)

Step 4: Liquidator shall open a bank account in the name of the corporate person followed by the words 'in voluntary liquidation', in a scheduled bank, for the receipt of all moneys due to the corporate person. The money in the credit of the bank account shall not be used except in accordance with section 53(1). (Regulation 34 of Voluntary Liquidation Regulation)

Step 5: Apply for No Objection Certificate (NOC) in Central Board of Direct Taxes, Central Board of Indirect Taxes and Custom, Employee Provident Fund Organisation and sectoral regulators *(These NOCs are not explicitly mentioned in IBC but are implied to be taken).*

Step 6: Liquidator gives final remittance to shareholders. Also, the liquidator deposits applicable withholding taxes and then closes the bank account opened for liquidation.

Step 7: Liquidator then submits a final report to shareholders, RoC, IBBI and National Company Law Tribunal (NCLT).

Step 8: Order is passed by NCLT.

Step 9: File copy of the order for dissolution of corporate debtor with RoC vide Form INC 28 and RoC to strike-off the name of Corporate Debtor from RoC.

The first key issue in the process is delays in obtaining No Objection Certificates (NOCs) from departments including Central Board of Direct Taxes, Central Board of Indirect Taxes and Custom, Employee Provident Fund Organisation and other sectoral regulators. The NOCs are implied to be taken although not specifically mentioned in the Code. This leads to confusion regarding the procedure to be followed among the departments, liquidators etc. with regard to the exact procedure to be followed. Another issue in the process is that there are no well-defined Standard Operating Procedures (SoPs) in the departments for granting NOC. As per the current practice, the liquidators write a letter to the head of the departments asking for any claims that the department has on the company and to grant NOC. The department then assesses the application and responds. Since there are no SoPs, the claims raised by the departments come with a lag and are not within the stipulated period. Further, another problem leading to delays in certain cases is that there are no standard guidelines on requirements by NCLT bench, creating lags in the processes as the company has to contact various departments to take the specified clearances as required by NCLT.

Another issue is the hesitancy in the banks for closure of existing bank accounts and also for the opening of the new liquidation bank account by the liquidator, which is a mandatory step in the liquidation proceedings.

To sum up, there is a case for simplifying the problems in the Voluntary Liquidation process, to improve ease of exit for business. Apart from simplifying the issues in the various steps in the processes, there is a need for the creation of a single window for the entire process. A portal that combines all the steps of the liquidation process altogether, starting from application by companies to processing by all departments will prove to be very useful.

Cross-Border Insolvency

Here are some important excerpts from the Government of India *Economic Survey 2021-22* on this new topic:

Cross-border insolvency signifies circumstances in which an insolvent debtor has assets and/or creditors in more than one country. Typically, domestic laws prescribe procedures for identifying and locating the debtors' assets; calling in the assets and converting them into a monetary form; making distributions to creditors in accordance with the appropriate priority etc. for domestic creditors/debtors. However, there are various insolvency cases in which corporations owe assets and liabilities in more than one country.

At present, Insolvency and Bankruptcy Code, 2016 (IBC) provides for the domestic laws for the handling of an insolvent enterprise. IBC at present has no standard instrument to restructure the firms involving cross border jurisdictions. The problem of not having a cross border framework problem was also expressed by the National Company Law Tribunal (NCLT) in Mumbai in a cross-border insolvency case involving an Indian entity[9]. NCLT stated that while insolvency proceedings against the corporate debtor have already been initiated before a District Court in Netherlands, "there is no provision and mechanism in the IBC, at this moment, to recognize the judgment of an insolvency court of any Foreign Nation. Thus, even if the judgment of Foreign Court is verified and found to be true, still, sans the relevant provision in the IBC, we cannot take this order on record." The absence of standardized cross border insolvency framework creates complexities and raises various issues such as:

- *The extent to which an insolvency administrator may obtain access to assets held in a foreign country.*
- *Priority of payments- Whether local creditors may have access to local assets before funds go to the foreign administration or not.*
- *Recognition of the claims of local creditors in a foreign administration.*
- *Recognition and enforcement of local securities, taxation system over local assets where a foreign administrator is appointed etc.*

Presently, while foreign creditors can make claims against a domestic company, the IBC currently does not allow for automatic recognition of any insolvency proceedings in other countries. Cross border insolvency is regulated by Section 234 and 235 of IBC. Section 234 empowers the Central Government to enter into bilateral agreements with other countries to resolve situations about cross-border insolvency. Further, the Adjudicating Authority can issue a letter of request to a court or an authority (under Section 235) competent to deal with a request for evidence or action in connection with insolvency proceedings under the Code in countries with the agreement (under Section 234).

As can be seen, the current provisions under IBC are ad-hoc in nature and are susceptible to delay. Entering into mutual (reciprocal) agreements require individual long-drawn-out negotiations with each country. This leads to uncertainty of outcomes of claims for creditors, debtors and other stakeholders as well.

Therefore, there is a need for a standardized framework for Cross-Border insolvency. This issue is not new and in fact, the proposal to frame a robust cross border insolvency framework has already been highlighted in the report of the Insolvency Law Committee (ILC)[10] (October 2018). The Committee had recommended the adoption of the United Nations Commission on International Trade Law (UNCITRAL) with certain modifications to make it suitable to the Indian context. In fact, UNCITRAL on Cross-Border Insolvency, 1997 has emerged as the most widely accepted legal framework to deal with cross- border insolvency issues. It provides a legislative framework that can be adopted by countries with modifications to suit the domestic context of the enacting jurisdiction. It has been adopted by 49 countries until now, such as Singapore, UK,

---

[9]   *State Bank of India v. Jet Airways (India) Ltd., CP 2205 (IB)/MB/2019, CP 1968 (IB)/MB/ 2019, CP 1938(IB)/MB/2019, Order dated 20 June 2019*

[10]   *Government had invited suggestions/comments on the ILC report (Draft Z) from stakeholders*

US, South Africa, Korea, etc. This law addresses the core issues of cross border insolvency cases with the help of four main principles:

- *Access: It allows foreign professionals and creditors direct access to domestic courts and enables them to participate in and commence domestic insolvency proceedings against a debtor.*

- *Recognition: It allows recognition of foreign proceedings and enables courts to determine relief accordingly.*

- *Cooperation: It provides a framework for cooperation between insolvency professionals and courts of countries.*

- *Coordination: It allows for coordination in the conduct of concurrent proceedings in different jurisdictions.*

TURNAROUND MANAGEMENT

A business turnaround management process starts with an in-depth analysis of the company's past and present operations in order to figure out the reasons behind its current situation. A Techno-Economic Viability (TEV) Study for the company – conducted by someone who is an expert in this field – is a prerequisite for this.

The TEV Study contains an in-depth analysis of the company's performance over the last 5 to 7 years. Professionals involved in preparing the Study Report visit the manufacturing plant to take a close look at its plant & machinery and production system, interact with key members of the company's management team so as to get an insight into the specific issues the company is facing and collect all important information from the company.

The TEV Study Report gives full details of the Company's products, production capacity and actual production levels and provides insights into its financial performance based on an analysis of the profit & loss account, balance sheet and funds flow statement. For instance, the reason for a deficit in the long-term sources of funds may point to diversion of short-term funds to cover cash losses, purchase of fixed assets, repayment of long-term loans, etc. The most common reasons for incurring losses are: fall in sales turnover, increase in raw material cost, increase in debts, etc.

It analyzes the marketing parameters for the company's products and evaluates its strategy in marketing and sales. It also examines whether the company has an adequate quality control system at the factory, whether it needs to make any capital investment in order to meet the production targets, whether it has a good organization structure and adequate manpower strength, and whether it needs to improve its sales and marketing plans, etc.

An in-depth SWOT (Strengths, Weaknesses, Opportunities and Threats) analysis of the company and its business sector leads to the conclusion whether it has the potential to get revived or not; and, if it has, then what reforms will be needed to rejuvenate it.

Based on this, the TEV Study Report finalizes a Rehabilitation Scheme which may include: (a) restructuring of loans by converting irregular portion of working capital loans into term loans; (b) waiver of penal interest; (c) sanction of need-based working capital loans; (d) sanction of new term loans to meet capital expenditure requirements; (e) one-time settlement (OTS) for some term loans; (f) promoters making more funds available by investing in the company's equity share capital; and (g) projected figures of production, sales and company's financials over the next five years.

Implementing Turnaround Management Plan

The Study Report also covers the marketing organization structure of the company, and the names and numbers of people deployed in each role.

It then formulates an implementation strategy, identifying monitorable targets for each stage and for the key persons and implements the Plan.

The key elements in preparing and implementing a Rehabilitation or Turnaround Management Plan will be:

1. Gather the objective – as well as anecdotal – data to review the grim situation the company is facing and, then, determine the causes for it and the impact it will have on its business.

2. Figure out the best strategy and prepare a robust plan after assessing all the steps that need to be taken for making the business turnaround proposition successful.

3. The business turnaround plan has to be a workable proposition that everyone must respect and support – the fulcrum for evaluating how good or bad the results will be in the future.

4. Arrange a get-together with managers and key personnel and explain to them the grim situation that the company is facing and the corrective actions that need to be taken urgently. Also, give them a sense of what actions they would need to take under the plan and request them for their comments, if any, on the same. It should be a positive address that attracts them to the turnaround management process so that they start playing their role with enthusiasm. This would be one of the important critical success factors for business turnaround of the company.

5. Meet with all the employees, as well as their union representatives, and explain to them why some of the steps – which may have a negative impact on them (such as job losses, etc.) – need to be taken.

6. Reassure the key customers of the company that the turn-around plan would help in improving customer service, quality of products, etc. and, once the business situation improves, benefits will start accruing to them.

7. Once support for the turnaround plan gains traction with the lenders, hold meetings with the suppliers to inform them about the company's plan and how and when their unpaid bills will get paid.

8. Revamp the credit management procedures, including extended payment terms to suppliers.

9. Conduct a thorough examination of all the assets of the company and sell off the unused ones, rent out spare office space, make excess employees redundant and eliminate all unnecessary overhead costs.

10. When vendors, whose dues have remained unpaid, get a murmur of the business turnaround activity from others, they may impose severe payment terms which may have a drastic impact on the business turnaround recovery plan. To avoid that, hold meetings with the vendors,

outline the company's plans, inform them, in advance, about how and when their debt will be discharged, and seek their continued support.

Key to Unlocking Value

Identifying the right cases for turnaround management first, and then conducting a detailed TEV study would be the right mechanism for speedy corporate resolution in such cases. In fact, it would be the need of the hour because the law mandates that the resolution professional (RP) – working with an IP agency – has to take responsibility for protecting and preserving the value of the company.

The RP has to make every endeavour to achieve that and "manage the operations of the Corporate Debtor as a going concern", with full authority to appoint professionals, enter into contracts on behalf of the Corporate Debtor, raise fresh funds, etc.

Reorganization professionals, i.e. people with experience – and expertise – in rehabilitation/turnaround management, would be a key player in this game. They have to work in tandem with accounting and law professionals and IP agencies. The respective registering authorities (ICAI for accountants, ICSI for company secretaries, BCI for lawyers, IEI for engineers and IIBF for banking professionals) need to evolve standards for their professionals so as to ensure that they do not function as an extended arm of the company promoters, or as a tool for extracting concessions from the creditors.

With turnaround management as the weapon to unlock maximum value from stressed assets, the bankruptcy code, in its new *avatar,* may well catapult India a long way up in the ease of doing business ranking.

PILLARS OF A REORGANIZATION LAW

A miniscule provision for reorganization had been inserted under section 9

(a) in the SARFAESI Act, stipulating that "proper management of the business of the borrower by change in, or take-over of, the business of the borrower" will be a measure of asset reconstruction, but it failed miserably because it was just a section in another law, not the full law itself. The number of cases where reorganization of business has been attempted under this section – forget about successfully implemented –are very few and far between.

Under the Companies Act – one of the most important laws for businesses operating in India – the criterion for determining sickness is failure to pay debt within 30 days of a demand notice served by the secured creditors, whereas the standard definition in finance is erosion of *half or more* of the Company's *net worth*. More importantly, under the Companies Act, the petition has to be filed by the secured creditors in a civil court, where it keeps lingering for many, many years.

As against that, in the US a petition can be filed under Chapter 11 (Reorganization) of the Bankruptcy Code – either by the debtor or the creditors – in a Bankruptcy Court.

Once the petition is filed, the debtor becomes a *debtor in possession* and has a 120-day period during which it has an exclusive right to file a plan. A committee consisting of the *seven largest unsecured creditors* having claims against the debtor is then appointed by the U.S. Trustee under the United States Trustee Program.

The Trustee has the responsibility to take legal action to: enforce the requirements of the Bankruptcy Code and prevent fraud and abuse; consult with the debtor in possession to ensure that bankruptcy estates are administered; and convene the meetings of creditors' committees; investigate the debtor's conduct and operation of the business; and participate in formulating a plan. The U.S. Trustee, the committee, or another party in interest acts to ensure a timely resolution of the case. The creditors' right to file a competing plan provides incentive for the debtor to file a plan within the exclusivity period and acts as a check on excessive delay in the case.

ROAD-MAP FOR TURNAROUND IN INDIA

In India, under the Insolvency & Bankruptcy Code (IBC) framework, it is the Resolution Professional, or RP, who has to take the responsibility for doing all this, including managing the operations of the Corporate Debtor as a going concern, with full authority to appoint professionals, enter into contracts on behalf of the Corporate Debtor, raise fresh funds, etc.

RBI Notification on the framework for "Early Recognition of Financial Distress", January 30, 2014, outlines the following road-map for unlocking value from turnaround cases: one, allow PE firms and other institutions, with proven expertise in turnaround management, to participate in NPA auctions; two, use their expertise for restructuring troubled company accounts; and three, permit banks to extend finance to duly approved 'specialized' entities engaged in such operations.

In order to attract such investment, we need to do two things: one, set up duly approved 'specialized' entities for undertaking turnaround management; and two, allow both – such entities as well as the PE funds/foreign investors – to invest in turnaround companies and acquire the same, if required.

The pre-requisites for undertaking this would be making investments in troubled companies, by way of both debt and equity, a feasible and attractive proposition for foreign investors. In order to do this, banks have to be nudged to showcase potentially revivable cases to investors before the debts turn non- performing. In case the debts have already been sold to an ARC/ ARCs, the ARCs would need to attract such investment in the security receipts (SRs) held in the ARC trust.

Twin Balance Sheet Problem

As per the Economic Survey 2016-17, *"around 40 percent of the corporate debt monitored by Credit Suisse was owed by companies which had an interest coverage ratio less than 1, meaning they did not earn enough to pay the interest obligations on their loans."* It then concludes that the reason behind this was the *"twin balance sheet problem"* – with both the banking as well as the corporate sectors being under *"one of the highest degrees of stress in the world.* At 9.1%, India's NPA ratio was *"higher than any other major emerging market (with the exception of Russia), higher even than the peak levels seen in Korea during the East Asian crisis"*.

While the TBS (Twin Balance Sheet) problem and high NPA levels had triggered banking crises in other countries, this did not happen in India because the bulk of the NPAs were in the books of public sector banks – entities in which the government, with adequate resources to deal with the NPA problem, has a majority shareholding. No wonder that, since the emergence of the TBS problem in 2010, there had neither been any bank runs, nor any stress in the inter-bank market.

Initially, India's public sector banks had conjectured that TBS was a minor problem, which would get resolved by economic recovery over the next few years. Later, they realized that economic growth itself cannot resolve this problem and what India needed was a new PARA (Public Sector Asset Rehabilitation) Agency charged with the responsibility of resolving the large bad debts cases – the same solution which the East Asian countries had applied when they were hit by severe Twin Balance Sheet problems in the 1990s.

Forming a PARA Agency was the need of the hour because: *(1) "It's not just about banks, it's a lot about companies"*: The TBS problem can be resolved only through expertise – by employing the right structure and methodology; *(2) "It is an economic problem, not a morality play"*: While it is true that, in many cases, mis-demeanors such as diversion of funds by borrower companies may have been the root cause of the debt repayment problem, in most cases, the problem emanates from un-expected changes in the economic environment, growth rate assumptions going wrong, etc.; *(3) "The stressed debt is heavily concentrated in large companies"*: Given a relatively small number of such cases, this may look like an opportunity but actually it is a bigger challenge because large cases are inherently difficult to resolve; *(4) "Many of these companies are unviable at current levels of debt requiring debt write-downs in many cases"*: In large stressed companies, cash flows keep deteriorating over the years, to the point where debt reductions of more than 50 percent may often be needed to restore viability. The only other alternative would be to convert debt into equity, take over the companies, and then sell them at a loss; *(5)"Banks are finding it difficult to resolve these cases, despite a proliferation of schemes to help them"*: The two most important issues that public sector banks in India face are: one, coordination problems among lenders as large debtors have many creditors, with different interests; and two, if a public sector bank allows large write-offs in payment of debt by the borrowers, this could attract the attention of the investigative agencies. It may also be politically difficult for banks to take over large companies; *(6) "Delay is costly"*: Since banks cannot easily resolve big cases, they simply refinance the debtors, effectively kicking the can down the road. As the bad debts keep rising, so does the recapitalization bill for the government; *(7) "Progress may require a PARA"*: Private Asset Reconstruction Companies (ARCs) haven't been more successful than banks in resolving bad debts. But international experience shows that a professionally run central agency, PARA (Public Sector Asset Rehabilitation), can overcome the difficulties that have impeded progress.

NARCL, BAD BANK

On 7^(th) July 2021, the National Asset Reconstruction Company Limited (NARCL) was incorporated as a 'bad bank' for handling the stressed assets of Indian banks, and its associate IDRCL (India Debt Resolution Company Limited) given the responsibility to aggregate and resolve the Non- Performing Assets (NPAs) of the banking Industry.

Once NARCL acquires the assets from a bank, IDRCL shall prepare and suggest the proposed restructuring / resolution plan, strategies, etc. for each Underlying Trust Assets. Post the approval of resolution from NARCL, IDRCL shall also assist in implementing it within the RBI framework for ARCs.

Resolution mechanisms of this nature typically require a backstop from Government as it imparts credibility and provides for contingency buffers. Bad banks were set up with Government participation in the form of equity in Malaysia and UK, as Danaharta Nasional Berhad (Danaharta) and UK Asset Resolution Ltd (UKAR) respectively. On the same lines, the Indian government has provided a guarantee of up to Rs 30,600 crore to back the Security Receipts (SRs) issued by NARCL.

The guarantee will remain valid only for a period of 5 years, during which it can be invoked – upon completion of the resolution or liquidation process – to cover the shortfall between actual realization and the face value of the assets held. The amount for which the guarantee is issued will be based on actual assets acquired by NARCL. This arrangement will not only safeguard the face value of Security Receipts but it will also take away the need for 100 per cent upfront capitalization of NARCL. The government will charge a guarantee fee on the amount which it guarantees, which will increase annually to incentivize the early and timely resolution.

NARCL is a strategic initiative to clean up the legacy stressed assets, with an exposure of Rs 500 crore and above each. Public Sector Banks hold a majority stake in NARCL and private banks hold the balance.

Canara bank is the Sponsor, with a shareholding of 12 per cent. In the course of its finite life of five years, NARCL would be capitalized through a combination of equity and debt from various banks. It may acquire stressed assets of about Rs 2 lakh crore in two phases, within the extant regulations of RBI, implying that the consideration for acquisition will be 15 per cent in cash and 85 per cent in Security Receipts.

In phase I, fully provisioned assets of about Rs. 90,000 crore are expected to be transferred to NARCL, while the remaining assets with lower provisions would be transferred in phase II.

The strategy focuses on aggregating the stressed assets under one roof so as to ensure efficient resolution of such assets. Since the security receipts issued by NARCL to an investor, who wants to acquire a part or whole of a company's stressed loan assets held by NARCL, will be backed by a Government of India guarantee, it will be another unique strategic advantage for preserving their value and driving the resolution process.

IDRCL has to provide end-to-end assistance to NARCL in resolving the acquired assets – from figuring out the most appropriate resolution strategy to adopt under the RBI framework, to initiating the Corporate Insolvency Resolution Process, to executing enforcement of security and liquidation proceedings under the Insolvency and Bankruptcy Code, to taking a decisionon sale of assets / slump sale, sale to Stressed Funds, Alternate Investment Funds, Strategic Investors, etc.

The NARCL-IDRCL structure is the initiative for tackling the large stock of legacy corporate NPAs that banks in India have been grappling with. Under it, cases which have the potential for insolvency resolution under IBC can get resolved quickly and more effectively. *As the holders of these stressed assets and SRs, banks will receive the gains.* This will bring about improvement in banks' valuation and enhance their ability to raise market capital.

The Insolvency and Bankruptcy Code (IBC), SARFAESI (Securitization and Reconstruction of Financial Assets and Enforcement of Securities Interest) Act, Debt Recovery Tribunals and setting up of dedicated Stressed Asset Management Verticals (SAMVs) in banks for large-value NPA accounts have brought sharper focus on recovery. In spite of these efforts, substantial amount of NPAs continue to remain on the balance sheets of banks primarily because the stock of bad loans is not only large but fragmented across various lenders. High levels of provisioning by banks against legacy NPAs has presented a unique opportunity for faster resolution. To disincentivize delay in resolution, NARCL will pay a Guarantee Fee which will increase with passage of time.

NARCL has been capitalized through equity from banks but it may also raise debt in future, if required.

SUGGESTED BEST PRACTICES

As per the February 2004 ADB Report on ARCs in India (TA No. 3943- IND), among the AMCs (Asset Management Companies) set up in different countries for handing the bad loans problem, Danaharta in Malaysia, KAMCO in Korea, Securum in Sweden and RTC in USA were recognised as successful AMCs. The factors that contributed to their success were: Government strategy, role of AMCs in the overall financial reforms/ restructuring programme, legal environment prevailing in the country, regulations and incentives instituted to facilitate asset transfer, special legal powers conferred on AMCs with regard to resolution, extent of funding support from the Government and NPA investors and tax benefits accorded to the AMCs.

With enactment of the Insolvency & Bankruptcy Code, the structure for handling bad loans has been created in India. The road map for corporates saddled with bad loans in India, now, would be either Corporate Insolvency Resolution Process (CIRP), or Liquidation, both out-of-court processes handled by a Resolution Professional (RP) working under the supervision of the Adjudicating Authority (AA), the National Company Law Tribunal. With the legal framework already in place, what Indian ARCs would need to have is the acumen to facilitate asset recovery and reconstruction.

The out-of-court process for financial and corporate restructuring, conducted by the Resolution Professional (RP), may be backed up by credible procedures for insolvency resolution, seizure, foreclosure, liquidation, receivership and reorganization.

Here is a list of the suggested best practices for corporate restructuring that we need, now:

1. A Bankruptcy Regime under which unsecured creditors are able to force liquidation and secured creditors can enforce seizure and sale; court-supervised reorganization; legal presumption that equity interests of all shareholders, including minority shareholders, would get wiped out in case of corporate insolvency; institutional capacity in terms of experienced judges, receivers and professionals;

2. Agreed standards among financial institutions and banks for out-of- court work-outs, including appointment of lead creditors and a Steering Committee; development and sharing of information; priority of new lending; apportionment of losses among creditor classes; thresholds for creditor's approval of proposed workouts; reliance on market participants to structure and negotiate out-of-court workouts; a strong regulator that can force banks to take immediate losses on corporate restructuring;

3. Market for impaired assets, and a well-developed secondary market for corporate debt including distressed debts; ARCs working on the basis of best commercial and market

principles; no legal barriers to debt-equity conversion or swift redeployment of corporate shares, real estate and other productive assets; no immediate taxation of non- cash corporate reorganization such as mergers, share swaps, etc.;

4. Realistic valuation and pricing of assets through either mark-to- market or against recovery value estimated at the time of transfer so that stakeholders of ARC are able to evaluate its performance.

(The Thai Asset Management Company (TAMC), Mallory Dreyer,
Yale School of Management Yale Program on Financial Stability
Case Study June 23, 2021)

5. Small **NPA**s should remain with banks;

6. Banks should restructure their non-performing corporate debts through debt-equity swap, and ARCs should play an important role by sponsoring corporate restructuring, infusing fresh funds and managing the corporate restructuring tasks on behalf of the banks;

7. Profit sharing should become the new norm in sale of bad loans by a bank to an ARC, on the lines of Thai AMC that shares, equally, first 20% of the gain with selling banks, with the remaining 80% going to the investee banks;

8. An effective strategy of NPA resolution must involve financial and operational restructuring of unviable industrial borrowers. Its success depends not only on an efficient and effective corporate insolvency regime but also on labour laws, competition policies, trade policies and other structural factors;

9. Raise funding from independent investors instead of sourcing it from government (like what KAMCO does), or from Head Office (on the lines of Taiwan AMC);

10. Use ARCs as advisors for carrying out loan workouts – from conducting TEV Study, to preparing debt re-structuring plans, to monitoring performance and ensuring compliance with repayment schedules by employing debt collection agents.

IBC Conundrum Resolved

An IIM, Ahmedabad *Study Report on Effectiveness of the Resolution Process: Firm Outcomes in the Post-IBC Period*, released in *August 2023*, has finally resolved the IBC Code conundrum by concluding that the Code has *remarkably altered how distressed and defaulting businesses are handled by their stakeholders*, with its 'resolution' provision *allowing a firm to continue as a going concern, despite the default. By focusing on the revival and continuity of financially distressed entities, the IBC seeks to preserve jobs, protect investments, and maintain the operational viability of such businesses.*

The conclusion is based on an empirical analysis that involves a univariate trend analysis and a multivariate regression analysis covering the entire population of resolved firms with publicly available financial information.

Following are some of the *key findings* of this *Study Report*:

- *Creditors have, on average, realised 32% of the admitted claims and 168% of the liquidation value in cases resolved under IBC;*

- *Average sales have shown an increase of 76% in three years since resolution;*

- *While the net margins continue to remain negative, the resolved firms have operationally broken even in the post-resolution period, which is a significant improvement from the pre-resolution period;*

- *There is around 50% increase in the average employee expenses in the three years post-resolution – indicating higher employment intensity in the resolved firms (listed) in the post-resolution period;*

- *The trends indicate a significant increase of around 50% in the average total assets of resolved firms post resolution, coupled with a 130% increase in CAPEX, which indicate a build-up of tangible assets of these firms in the post-resolution period;*

- *Trends in the market capitalization of listed resolved firms indicate a significant revival in the average market valuations in the post- resolution period;*

- *The aggregate market valuation of all the resolved firms has increased from around INR 2 lakh crore to INR 6 lakh crore in the post- resolution phase. The results suggest that the market has priced and acknowledged the potential of these firms in the post-resolution period;*

- *Liquidity has improved in the post-resolution period by about 80%;*

- *The profitability and margins of the resolved firms saw a sharp uptick post the conclusion of the statutory process under IBC;*

- *Their average capex saw an increase of approximately 130% in the three years post-resolution;*

- *Findings of the survey and interviews showed that approxim-ately 75% of those surveyed were happy with the post-resolution productivity levels; Those interviewed indicated satisfaction with the working of the National Companies Law Tribunal;*

- *Post-resolution disputes with the Income tax, Customs and the RBI were flagged as being onerous, and a source of delay in obtaining clearances;*

- *Those interviewed felt that the Resolution Professionals needed skills for business and management.*

Overall, based on the empirical analysis and the surveys conducted, we observe that:

- *The resolved firms have significantly improved their performance across all important financial metrics in the post-resolution period. Several financial metrics of the resolved firms indicate a recovery to levels that is comparable to other healthy firms during the same period. Overall, the post-resolution activity and performance suggests an increase in the value addition by the resolved firms to the economy.*

- *Survey participants are largely satisfied with the resolution process and exuded confidence in their ability to meet the projected plans.*

- *Focus interviews validated the survey findings; however, it also revealed some room for improvements in the resolution process, especially with respect to the understanding of the resolution process across various stakeholders.*

The outcome of IBC can be gauged from the following latest figures: the number of cases closed before admission in NCLT benches (25,565) is 3.7 times higher than the number of cases admitted (6,811); and the Gross NPAs of Scheduled Commercial Banks has come down from 11.18 % in 2017-18, to 3.9% in 2022-23. (*"Promoters clear dues to avoid insolvency", The Times of India, 24 August, 2023*)

EPILOGUE

This book is the epitome of my life's professional experience in banking and asset reconstruction – from conducting Techno-Economic Viability (TEV) studies for industrial units, to managing large-value corporate stressed assets, to effecting turnaround through rehabilitation/ restructuring, to recovering the dues through settlements or legal recourse, to leading from the front in raising issues plaguing the asset reconstruction industry.

In one of my articles, *"Don't Let Stressed Assets Rot"*, published in *The Economic Times* on 7th January, 2013, I had identified three pillars of the 'system trap' (banks' heedlessness to sell their NPAs to ARCs) that the public sector banks were caught in: one, 'going concern valuation' (which is totally inappropriate for sick unit cases); two, 'fear of vigilance'; and three, 'no accountability for not doing'.

For solving the issue, I had proposed that RBI exhort banks to follow a time- bound, step-by-step procedure for tackling NPAs.

The first step would be to categorise all corporate NPAs above Rs 1 crore into one of the following three categories: revivable cases, recalcitrant borrower/ one-time settlement (OTS) cases and seizure and sale cases.

Thereafter, monitor resolution of NPAs under each category at quarterly intervals; enforce a system of maximum age of NPA in each category; stipulate a market price-based system for taking all three measures of resolution, etc. And, finally, if an NPA remains unresolved even after exhausting all the measures, then, at the end of five years, compulsorily sell the same to an ARC at the highest bid price offered.

My gently prodding FSLRC (Financial Sector Legislative Reforms Commission) on this issue may have led to their taking up the matter with the Government of India and, thereafter, the Ministry of Finance setting up a Key Advisory Group on ARCs.

REFERENCES

RBI Report on Trend and Progretss of Banking in India 2020-21 SBI Annual Report 2020-21

SBI Annual Report 2021-22

Business India, April 26 to May 9, 1982 SBI Monthly Reviews

"Banking Policy in India: An Evaluation" by D. N. Ghosh, ex-Chairman, State Bank of India (Published:1979)

"Public Sector Banks in India's Economy: A Case Study of the State Bank" by O. P. Mathur (Published: 1978)

"State Bank Group: A Statistical Profile of the SIB Segment as on December 31, 1981", SI & SB Banking Department, State Bank of India, Central Office, Bombay

IDBI Bank Annual Report 2010-2011

Asian Development Bank Report on Developing the Enabling Environment for and Structuring Asset Reconstruction Companies in India, Volume I

("Recommendations for Changes in the Existing ARC Framework February 2004")

Master Circular - Asset Reconstruction Companies, April 21, 2022

RBI Report on Trend & Progress of Banking in India, 2020-21": Report of the Committee to Review the Working of Asset Reconstruction Companies (ARCs)

RBI Guidelines on Early Recognition of Financial Distress, Prompt Steps for Resolution and Fair Recovery for Lenders: Framework for Revitalising Distressed Assets in the Economy", effective since April 1, 2014

The SARFAESI (Securitisation and Reconstruction of Financial Assets and Enforcement of Security Interest) Act, 2002

The Insolvency & Bankruptcy Code, 2016